THE
LAST
SALUTE

THE TRUE STORY OF
A WEST POINT CADET'S DREAM
TO HONOR HIS DYING FATHER

ROBERT PALEY

WEST POINT CLASS OF 1989

FOREWORD BY MARK BEAL

Published by Paley Publishing, LLC

ISBN: 978-0-578-47348-2

First Printing: 2019
Printed in the United States of America

This book is dedicated to my lovely wife Alison.

You accepted me when I was "broken," and helped to heal me with your love. I couldn't have done this without you, and I thank God that He brought us together. I love you.

And to my Mother, Atsuko.

You have the courage of a samurai and the heart of Mother Teresa, and I love you with all of my heart. Thank you for planting within me the seed of a dream that would take me on the adventure of a lifetime.

IN HONOR OF

THOSE WHO HAVE SERVED,

AND

THOSE WHO HAVE FALLEN.

ACKNOWLEDGEMENTS
& GRATITUDE

There are many people who shared this amazing journey with me and made it possible, and I simply cannot overlook any of them.

BEA BARNETT DORMAN

When I returned to Columbus, Ohio in 1999 after a long absence of fifteen years (spanning my time in uniform and in the corporate world), I received a phone call from the principal of Groveport Madison High School, Bea Barnett-Dorman. Bea was one of my most important mentors when I was in high school, and when she heard I was back in town she asked me to meet her for lunch. We met at a Bob Evans Restaurant in Canal Winchester, Ohio, and Bea came straight to the point. "Everyone who knows you knew that you wanted to go to West Point ever since you were a kid," she said. "But no one knows *why* it was so important for you to go there?" I sipped my coffee and smiled, then asked her, "How much time do you have?" When I finished telling her an abbreviated version of my story, she said, "You *have* to write a book about this." And thus, in 1999, the seed was planted to write this book. It would take me twenty years to complete it, due to the difficulty of the subject matter...but thanks to Bea for planting the seed that would eventually take root.

SOUTHEAST MESSENGER NEWSPAPER STAFF

I would like to thank former staff writer of the *Southeast Messenger* newspaper, Chiree Spencer McCain, for her early enthusiasm and support for this project; and for the countless hours she put into helping me write my earliest drafts. I would also like to thank the editor of the Southeast *Messenger*, Rick Palsgrove, for his support and encouragement over the years.

WRITER'S GUILD INITIATIVE (WGI)

I made several attempts to write this book, and in 2008 I was on the verge of giving up, unsure of how to proceed. That's when I received a fateful email that would change the course of my life. I was working in the Ohio National Guard headquarters when an email popped up on my screen in early 2008. The subject: *Veteran's Writing Workshop*. The host: The Writer's Guild of America East (WGAE), which was on strike at the time. Sensing the hand of fate, I immediately signed up, and in April 2008, I attended the first *Veteran's Writing Workshop* in Columbus, Ohio, under the auspices of the WGAE's Writer's Guild Initiative (WGI), which was under the visionary leadership of its president, Michael Weller (*Ragtime, Hair, Moonchildren*). Michael and David Tucker (Seattle-based playwright, photographer) became the first of my personal mentors, and they set me on a ten-year course of self-discovery which would progressively bring me to this book. Along the way, I was supported and/or inspired by several other selfless mentors of the WGI, to include: screenwriter Christopher Kyle, writer/producer and current WGI president Richard Dresser, Discovery senior VP of digital content, Fred Graver, Comedian/Actress Carla Briscoe, WGI Executive Director Jenna Jackson, writer Lulie Haddad, Director Susanna Styron, Emmy-award winning writer Delaney Yeager, writer/producer Jenny Lumet, and screenwriters/

producers Richard Lagravenese and J.V. Hart, and all of the Board Members and mentors who make the workshops possible. Okay, enough name-dropping, but I would be remiss not to acknowledge these loving, caring and generous masters-of-their-craft for voluntarily sharing their time and their talent with Veterans and Caregivers who, otherwise, would not have had a voice. They are not just mentors, they have become true friends. I've seen them change lives through writing. I know they've changed mine.

SAVE A WARRIOR (SAW), JAKE CLARK

I was scheduled to complete my Master's thesis (for an MA in Military History) in May 2018. However, I ran into a wall called writer's block (on steroids!) and I had to take extensions for six months in a row, just to complete a 50 page requirement. Fancying myself a writer thanks to the WGI, I knew that something was amiss. I was recommended to Save A Warrior (SAW), which is an experiential based Warriors-helping-Warriors organization for Combat Veterans and First Responders. This organization, founded by Jake Clark, has won numerous awards for helping those Veterans and First Responders who have suffered trauma to learn to reintegrate into society when they run into a proverbial wall of their own. The results have been astounding! I was scheduled to attend Cohort 062 in Malibu, California, on Veteran's Day 2018, but the Woolsey/Malibu fires burned down Camp Hess Kramer and the Cohort had to be rescheduled. Thanks to the efforts of Brian Haggerty (Director of Programming, Malibu, California) and Adam Carr (Executive Director, Warrior Village in Newark, Ohio), the Cohort was brought together again on 2 December 2018, which ironically was the anniversary of my father's death twenty-seven years earlier. I leaned-in to the program, and five and one half days later, on December 7th, I emerged a renewed man, and *six weeks later, this book was completed.* I owe a special debt of gratitude to Jake Clark for having the guts to step-out on faith to create this program which has saved hundreds of lives, as well as the Shepherds who volunteer their time to run each Cohort. Recently, Jake Clark was invited to share the tenets of this program with the Behavioral Sciences Department at the United States Military Academy at West Point, New York. I would also like to thank and acknowledge my Cohort 062 SAW brothers for their support and encouragement in pursuing my dream to complete this book: Mike Crothers, Mark DelTosto, Jacob Edgell, Trey McBane, Guy Riley, Jake Sawyer, John Schmoll, and Troy Treit. Additionally, I would like to thank the Shepherds who volunteered their time to hold space for us during the momentous week: Jake Bame, Adam Carr, Wes Hanlon, Carlos Holstein, Mark Long and Billy Otter. Also, a special thanks to Doctor Steven Johnson for referring me to the program.

UNITED STATES MILITARY ACADEMY PREPARATORY SCHOOL (USMAPS)

A special thanks to the Commandant of USMAPS, the late Colonel Melville Drisko, as well as my tactical officer, then-Captain Craig Schwegman, my tactical NCO retired 1SG Frank Withers, my advisors then-Captain Bohichik, Mr. Kaplan and Rabbi Dana.

In March 2018, I attended my United States Military Academy Prep School (USMAPS Class of '85) reunion at West Point, New York, where I ran into my former classmate Mark Beal. Mark called me over to his table and asked me about the book I was writing, and he showed great support and interest in my project. Mark and his wife Michele have since become valued friends, and I thank them for their early encouragement. Mark has published three books of his own: *101 Lessons They Never Taught You In High School About Going to College*, *101 Lessons They Never Taught You in College*, and *Decoding Gen Z*. Mark's books are fantastic, and when I purchased them and saw their quality, I inquired about them, and Mark led me to...

EVAN CARROLL

Evan Carroll, author and speaker, whom I emailed in December 2018 with a request that he help me to produce a "miracle." I asked for his support and guidance to take my book from project to completion in time for my retirement ceremony from the Ohio Army National Guard in February 2019, and he was a gamer who accepted the challenge. I would like to thank Evan first and foremost for his patience, his expertise, and his invaluable guidance in helping me to navigate the waters of self-publication through Amazon and for producing such a beautiful book.

KATHY MANOS PENN

I simply could not have published this book with the sense of pride that I have in it were it not for the efforts of my good friend from Georgia, Kathy Manos Penn. My wife Alison and I met Kathy and her Vietnam Veteran husband, Hugh, while we were on vacation at Amelia Island, Florida, four years ago. We hit it off and became fast friends, and in the course of getting to know each other, Kathy mentioned that she was a writer and editor in her corporate job and a newspaper columnist on the side. I jokingly said, "I'm an aspiring writer, perhaps we can collaborate someday." Four years later, and with one and a half weeks until the final copy was due to Evan, Kathy masterfully edited all of the chapters of this book. If any mistakes are found, they are surely mine for adding sentences without Kathy knowing about them! I simply cannot thank Kathy enough for getting on board with this project and helping to make it into one I can truly be proud of. Thank you, *Madam Editor!* Kathy and her dog, Lord Banjo, are the proud authors of several books as well. Kathy has penned, *The Ink Penn: Celebrating the Magic in the Everyday*, and Lord Banjo has pawed *Lord Banjo the Royal Pooch*, and *Coloring with Lord Banjo the Royal Pooch*, and there are more Lord Banjo books on the way!

U.S. MILITARY ACADEMY STAFF, 1984-1989

To then-Captain Belton of the Admissions Office, this dream would not have been possible without your support, and I hope that somehow this message finds you so that I can finally say, "Thank you!" on behalf of the entire Paley family.

To Brigadier General Retired Jack Grubbs, the "angel in disguise" who made this story possible—you showed me the meaning of compassionate leadership.

To former Superintendent of the United States Military Academy, Lieutenant General (Retired) David R. Palmer for your courageous support at a crucial time in my cadet career. You and the entire chain-of-command stood by me at one of the most difficult junctures of my life, and I saw the meaning of true character first hand. And to the late Brigadier General Roy K. Flint, Dean of Academics, and the entire Academic Board for demonstrating to me the meaning of compassion, commitment and loyalty.

And to all the soldiers and families of the 25th Infantry Division—past and present—you will always have a special place in my heart.

FRIENDS & FAMILY

I have had several friends, family members and classmates who have volunteered to be early readers of my draft or were my confidants, and I would like to thank all of them now, as well. Your support and feedback has been invaluable, and I hope the final product makes all of you proud to have helped in some way. Thanks go to: Kathy Manos Penn, Nancy Paley Rosch, Karen Paley Zimmerman, Matt Paley, Steven Paley, Ella Buckley, Michael Weller, David Tucker, Rick Dresser, Mark Beal, Jake Clark, Bea Barnett Dorman and Keith Notter. Fellow West Point/USMAPS classmates and friends: Mark Beal, COL (Ret.) Scott Morrison, COL John Hurley, Donna Crouch Ward, Guy Moore, Paul Sariego, Wally Roy, Patrice Boemio Sutherland, Stephen Miller, and 1SG (Ret.) Frank Withers.

Lifelong friends who supported me on this journey over the years: Lori Rockwell, Glen Gardner, Jozefa Mentrak Hernon, Patty Meadows Schmidgell, Kimm Vance Arnold, Leslie Brungarth, Diane Caswell Shirk, Shelley Volpe Doke, Jill Schaffner Whaley, Mark Steele, Kim Spaulding, and Tom Lascola.   And to my neighbors, Jordan and Jess Burke for your timely and unexpected random act of kindness of shoveling our drive when I was on a tight deadline.

MOTT'S MILITARY MUSEUM

A special thanks goes to Warren, Daisy and Lori Motts of Motts' Military Museum in Groveport, Ohio, for the honor of having my West Point uniform displayed in your incredible museum.

MENTORS

I would like to acknowledge my personal and professional mentors who I owe so much to for impacting my life in a such a positive way over the years: Major General John Harris, Major General Mark Bartman, Major General (Retired) Deborah Ashenhurst, Major General (Retired) Michael McHenry, Brigadier General (Retired) Maria Kelly, Colonel (Retired) Chip Tansill, Colonel (Retired) Homer Rogers, Colonel (Retired) Craig Baker, Colonel Mark Raaker, Lieutenant Colonel Michael Draper, LTC (Retired) Terry St. Peter, LTC (Retired) William Hauschild, Colonel Joel Smith, the late Colonel (Retired) Moore, Dr. Gerald West, the late Sensei Bernie Ele, Marvie Ele Wilson, Marissa Ele Ward Dement, James Pendergast, Ms. Bea Barnett Dorman, the late Mr. Robert Peters, Mr. Bob Garvin, Kathy Benson Moling, Susan White and the late, great Mrs. Ellen Miller.

TEACHERS

To all of my teachers and mentors at Groveport Madison Local Schools, thank you for helping me grow up to be the man I am today!

FAMILY

And finally—last but certainly not least—my family members—this story is yours just as much as it is mine. Thanks go to my mother, Atsuko "Betty" Paley for continually nudging me to get this book done, but most of all for planting the seed which led to the dream that changed my life. I love you and admire you so much for your strength, your loyalty, and most of all, for your kind and generous heart. Thanks to my brother Phil, who has been our family's rock since Daddy went down with his illness. You never wavered or blinked in the face of adversity, always helping each and every one of us when we needed your help the most. You and Dad are my heroes. And to my lovely sisters, Nancy and Karen. Nancy, head bump. Karen, stroller. Instant golden memories that I will always cherish. I couldn't have asked for better, more supportive sisters. I love you both so much.

Karen, you are and always have been my loyal sidekick, and I couldn't have made this journey without you. Thanks for always having my six!

To my nieces and nephews: Stacy, Steven, Matt, Jack, Joe, Sara, Kira, Samantha, Hannah, Katrina, and Midori. Also, my great nieces and nephews: Tori, Aubrie, Brianna, Laila, Krista, Gavin, Dylan, Kobe, Jacob and Ryan. May you always be proud of your heritage and the great people "from which you came." And I certainly can't forget my lovely British niece, Ella Buckley, for continually asking me, "How's your book coming?" whenever we spoke on the phone. Ella, it's finally finished and I hope you enjoy reading it. I love you all very much and want nothing but the best that life has to offer for each of you. Set huge dreams and then go after them—it makes life worth living!

Matt, Steven, Jack and Kira, the grandfather you never had a chance to get to know would have been proud of you for donning the uniform of our Armed Forces. And Kira, as the first registered female Ohioan to earn the Purple Heart for your courage in combat, I salute *you.*

Cousin Jon Paley, you were my wingman when I was at West Point, and you made my four years there "fun"—as fun as West Point can be, that is. I couldn't have made it through without your help and support. Thank you, cuz!

Cousin Glen Feinsilver, aka "Ozzstar" on YouTube. You are truly one of the Good Guys and I'm so glad to call you my cousin and my friend. I appreciate you and your lovely wife Tracy for your support and encouragement on this project. The same goes to my cousins Larry and Becky Lapp, Jeffrey Lapp, and Marilyn Ojeda. Thank you all for always supporting and encouraging me.

And to my in-laws across the pond, Sheila and Derek Haines, Pete Haines, Sid and Alex Haines and your beautiful children Ella, Ophelia and Laurence, I love you all very much and I'm honored to be part of your family.

And yes, the West family must also be included here. You "adopted" me like I was one of your own and in doing so, you enriched not only my life but the lives of my family members as well. We love you all!

And finally, to my wife Alison. Your kindness, understanding and compassion have restored me. You saw through the troubled man that I once was to the person that I aspired to be. And now, thanks to your love and devotion, I am one step closer to being that man. I absolutely love sharing my life with you. Thank you for patiently waiting for me to come out of the darkness and back into the light. You are the love of my life, and I will live the rest of my life trying to deserve you.

PRAISE FOR THE LAST SALUTE

"What a story. Rob Paley recalls both minute and gigantic events in a man's life as he tells of his quest for *The Last Salute*. His love for his father overtakes the reader in a bit-by-bit manner while concurrently presenting an autobiography of his growth from a timid child to a man of great strength. There are stories to make one smile or laugh and others taking Rob and the reader to dark places of humanity. Remember this - although the vehicle for the story is the military, the real story is one of love and loyalty. It was a great read."

JOHN H. GRUBBS, PH.D., P.E.
BRIGADIER GENERAL (RET.), U.S. ARMY
WEST POINT CLASS OF 1964

"Major Paley arrived at a *Writer's Guild Initiative* weekend workshop with a few rough pages of prose and an enormous question: Am I a writer? *The Last Salute* is the resounding answer. Not only can Paley write; he can bring us straight to the heart of every obstacle he overcame, every setback, family tragedy, personal demon and childhood secret that might have left a lesser person in the dust. And he is funny! Read *The Last Salute* and celebrate Paley's lively engaging spirit and his vivid prose."

MICHAEL WELLER
PLAYWRIGHT/SCREENWRITER
RAGTIME, HAIR, MOONCHILDREN

"Robert Paley has survived his own personal storm and has written a stunning memoir. At the heart of his journey from a Midwestern childhood shadowed by trauma to a West Point graduate is a deeply moving father and son story and a promise Robert made to his father when he was twelve years old. What Robert does to keep that promise is truly inspiring. Paley faces the truth of his life head-on, writes straight from the heart, and every page radiates his courage and compassion. *The Last Salute* is one American story that has to be told."

RICHARD DRESSER
PLAYWRIGHT
PRESIDENT, WRITERS GUILD INITIATIVE

"*The Last Salute* is not only a compelling and powerful piece of writing and storytelling from new author Robert Paley, but it should be required reading for anyone who has proudly served in the military or anyone who has had a family member serve. After reading *The Last Salute*, readers will be convinced that anything is possible no matter the obstacles or the sacrifices. This book brings to life the realization of what was once considered an impossible dream. If Hollywood is listening, they should bring *The Last Salute* to the big screen!"

MARK BEAL
USMAPS CLASS OF 1985
AUTHOR, DECODING GEN Z

"Rob Paley brings you into his world with an easy-going humor and keeps you there with his honesty and humility. His book, *The Last Salute*, takes you on his personal journey of determination, tribulation and self-discovery. Most importantly, it is a heart-warming tribute to his father and his family. Rob Paley has reason to not only be proud of the Soldier he became, but the writer he's become. I truly enjoyed reading Paley's break-out book and look forward to reading his next."

DAVID TUCKER II
PLAYWRIGHT/NOVELIST/PHOTOGRAPHER
U.S. ARMY, MAJ (RETIRED)

"Robert Paley is an author who will hold your interest from start to finish as he shares with you his obstacles, tragedies, and personal self-reflections. Robert is a survivor who, by pure determination, went on to fulfill an incredible dream. *The Last Salute* is a road map to achieving one's dreams and believing that real life can be whatever you want to make of it. I would like to see this book in every school library so students will be encouraged to pursue their dreams and to make what seems impossible, possible."

BEA BARNETT-DORMAN
GROVEPORT MADISON HIGH SCHOOL
1979-2000

"*The Last Salute* is a touching account of family, service and perseverance through numerous personal challenges within the Paley family. It is a heartwarming and moving story of a son's unconditional love for and dedication to his father during his final years."

LIEUTENANT COLONEL JOSEPH SCHWADE
SR. LEGAL ADVISER TO THE ADJUTANT GENERAL
OHIO NATIONAL GUARD

CONTENTS

FOREWORD

BY MARK BEAL

On May 12, 1962, General Douglas MacArthur, in a speech to the Corps of Cadets at the United States Military Academy in West Point, New York, boldly stated, "Duty, Honor, Country — those three hallowed words reverently dictate what you ought to be, what you can be, what you will be. They are your rallying points to build courage when courage seems to fail, to regain faith when there seems to be little cause for faith, to create hope when hope becomes forlorn."

Robert Paley would not even be born for four more years, but the message that MacArthur delivered in 1962 would be brought to life when Paley achieved the impossible dream of honoring his dying father by graduating from West Point 27 years later in 1989 despite rejection, failure and a series of endless obstacles, challenges and roadblocks.

Rob and I both arrived at Fort Dix, New Jersey in the summer of 1984 just a few weeks after high school graduation. We had been accepted into the United States Military Academy Preparatory School (USMAPS) and we were quickly immersing ourselves into life in the United States Army. A few weeks later, we would make the 45-mile trek to Fort Monmouth, New Jersey where we would be stationed for the next 11 months.

Ironically, despite being two of only 300 Cadet Candidates who comprised the USMAPS Class of 1985, Rob and I did not really get to know each other until a USMAPS class reunion in 2018, 33 years after leaving Fort Monmouth and going our separate ways. I went on to study journalism at Rutgers University in New Brunswick, New Jersey and Rob, like the majority of USMAPS graduates, traveled 100 miles north to West Point and entered the United States Military Academy in July 1985 as a member of the Class of 1989.

I actually moved to West Point as a four-year-old in 1971 as my dad, Colonel Harold Beal Jr., was appointed the associate director of admissions at the academy and would hold that position for the next seven years. During this same period, Rob visited West Point as a child with his family, and family photos show him walking along Trophy Point and sitting on the canons which would one day become so familiar to him.

In 1978, at the young age of twelve years old, the sudden hospitalization and near-death of Rob's disabled Veteran father, Sergeant Major Jerome Paley, would spark in Rob a burning desire to fulfill his father's unfulfilled dream of attending and graduating from West Point.

Coincidentally, the path of my dad—who finished his duties at West Point the same year and would eventually become the academic dean at USMAPS where he was well known as Dean Beal—would intersect with Rob's path six years later, as depicted in *The Last Salute*.

The Last Salute is a story of love, family, sacrifice and forgiveness that will inspire all those who read it. For those who don't believe that dreams can come true and that achieving the impossible is possible, this book will transform your mindset and make you a believer.

While Rob and I have reconnected after first meeting 35 years ago as teen-agers at USMAPS, we learned that we share a passion for storytelling that inspires. As authors, we love writing about the human spirit, plain and simple. It has taken Rob more than 20 years to complete his first book, *The Last Salute*. Great things come to those who wait, and *The Last Salute* is the greatest book and gift Rob could give to anyone who has served in the military or anyone who has had a family member serve in the military – Duty, Honor, Country.

INTRODUCTION

Stories have been an important part of my life since I was a child—whether in books, in movies or in my own mind. Early on, my inability to speak forced me to turn inwards towards my imagination—where I had no limitations or inadequacies to overcome and where I could create dreams which were more powerful than my nightmares. It was a defense mechanism I was forced to develop at a young age to try to make sense of the world and to try to find the good in the bad.

Of all my early childhood challenges—and we've *all* had childhood challenges, right?—it was my imagination that informed my current, grown-up version of "reality" more than any other factor. As an adult, this translated into a romanticized, idealistic view of the world that often lead others to characterize me as a "dreamer," though not necessarily in a complimentary way.

Today, I own it. In fact, I embrace that characterization wholeheartedly because at my core, that's what I am. A dreamer.

There were times when I lost the ability to dream, to hope, to want, and to desire—and it was during these times, the "Dark Night(s) of The Soul", if you will— when I found "reality" to be too darned depressing and mundane. What is life if you don't have something to dream about, to hope for or to aspire to—even if you don't get it?

But it was also during these dark, sometimes depressing periods of my life that my mind would wander back to a time and place where the dreams in my imagination manifested themselves in real life and drove me—with all my faults and foibles—against an "impossible dream" to honor my dying father by first getting into, and then graduating from West Point.

I now know that thirty years after living the story I'm about to share—a story of love, sacrifice, honor and forgiveness—that my version of reality is still heavily influenced by my childhood perceptions, hopes, and even fears, and that those parts of me cannot be stayed. I present them to you—faults and all—on the following pages.

Every scene and every conversation that I recall in the forthcoming pages is true to the best of my knowledge and recollection, and for anything I get wrong, I take full responsibility. In very rare cases, when my young mind couldn't fully understand an adult conversation, I wrote the exchange according to what I understood it to be for purposes of clarity.

That said, I invite you to take a journey with me—if you will—into a land of granite castles, Dragons, and Black Knights, and miracles large and small.

ROBERT PALEY
COLUMBUS, OHIO
10 FEBRUARY 2019

PART 1:

—

CRAWL

I only knew my father for twelve years before I lost him
—and I've spent the rest of my life trying to find him again.
I now realize that in that search, I was also trying to find myself.

—Robert Paley, Author

CHAPTER 1:

ARMY BRAT

1966

Schofield Barracks, Hawaii

There isn't a time in my memory that the Army wasn't a part of my life. I was born at Tripler Army Hospital in Honolulu, Hawaii in February 1966. My father, Jerome Paley, 31, was a Master Sergeant at the time, assigned to Headquarters Company of the 65th Engineer Battalion (Combat), 25th Infantry Division. He deployed to Vietnam in January 1966, leaving my mother, Atsuko, 29, to fend for herself with two children—Phil, 10, and Nancy, 3—and one on the way. That was me.

My older brother Phil was painfully aware of what was happening in Vietnam. He witnessed his friends being taken out of class to be informed their fathers were killed in action. Vietnam was not just something on the news to him.

On the day my father was saying his goodbyes to our family prior to deploying to Vietnam, Phil refused to say goodbye. Instead, he turned and ran upstairs and locked himself in his room. A few minutes later, Phil watched our father walk across the grassy field towards his unit. Suddenly, my father stopped, turned around, and saluted my brother. My brother waved as tears streamed down his cheeks.

Cherished postcards and letters from my father from this period represent the last letters he would write as a healthy young man in the prime of his career and of his life. I would never know that version of my father.

The following month, my mother was watching a William Holden movie when I decided to make my debut. She quickly arranged for Phil and Nancy to stay with a babysitter while she drove herself down a winding, two-lane road flanked by pineapple fields, towards Tripler Army Hospital—which was famous then, and still is, for being Pepto Bismol Pink.

When the doctors proclaimed, "It's a boy," I presume she was overwhelmed with joy and thought I was the cutest baby she'd ever seen, though early photos tell a different story. I was a fat baby, and in one family photo, I look like a miniature Buddha statue sitting on my brother's lap. In other photos, my mother put a grass skirt on me, possibly to hold my diapers up.

When it came time to name me, my mother told the nurse to name me "Robert." When they asked her for a middle name, she thought about it for a moment, and decided that she liked the name "Holden." Thus, I was named after an actor my mother apparently had a crush on and had last seen on television when she went into labor with me. I'm just glad she wasn't watching *Bugs Bunny*.

When it came time for my mother to sign my birth certificate, however, she was very unhappy. The nurse misspelled my first name. The birth certificate read "Lobert" when it clearly should have read "Robert."

Assuming it was just a typo, my mother pointed out the error and asked them to fix it immediately. When the nurse asked her to repeat what my first name should be, my mother did so, loud and clear: *Lobert!*

The nurse pointed to the birth certificate and said, "That's what it says."

My mother replied, "Not 'Lobert.' *Lobert!*" Much slower this time, as if that would make a difference.

Blank stares all around.

Frustrated, my mother said, "Like *Lobert Ledford!*"

Apparently, my parents had not taken my mother's cute Japanese accent into account when they chose a name for me. To this day, she calls me "Bobby."

Phil, 10, holds me in his arms as we soak up the rays.

My mother wasn't the only one who had trouble pronouncing names, however. When she arrived in the States after marrying my father, his family had trouble pronouncing her Japanese name, Atsuko. To help them out, she decided to take an American name. One day, while watching TV, my mother saw the cartoon "Betty

Boop". She thought she resembled Betty Boop, and from that time on she's been known as Betty.

Meanwhile, at Cu Chi, Vietnam, my father received a Red Cross message announcing my birth. The next day, my father received a second message from the Red Cross, announcing my birth again. Thus, for several days, my father thought he had twin sons...*Robert and Lobert*, perhaps? It remains a mystery. Thus, began my inauspicious life as an Army Brat.

CHAPTER 2

—

AMONGST GIANTS

1970

Fort Hamilton, New York

I inherited my love for the movies from my father. Some of my fondest childhood memories revolve around going to the movies at the Post Theater. We would stand in a long line with other military families to pay for our tickets at the outside ticket window, then file inside to the concession stand in the lobby which was alive with the sound of screaming kids and the scent of popping popcorn.

When we got to the concession stand, my father would ask what I wanted and I'd point to the popcorn and then to the soda machine. I don't recall why I didn't speak back then, nor do I recall not speaking, but according to my family I didn't speak until I was six years old. I guess I just didn't have anything to say at the time.

My older sister Nancy recalls acting as my interpreter and translator of my sounds and gestures back then, and because of her I have no residual memories of wanting for anything.

I ate my popcorn and sipped my soda in silence as the theater filled up around me and my family. When the lights dimmed and the curtains closed, heralding the start of the movie, a rush of adrenalin flowed through my body and I sat up in my seat. I loved where movies could take me.

When the curtains opened again, a beam of light and the sound of film rolling on the projector signaled the start of the National Anthem, and everyone in the theater rose in unison.

As images of the armed forces in action flashed across the screen, I felt as if I were surrounded by giants. All around me, soldiers stood at attention while the National Anthem played, and I felt safe in their presence. I didn't know how to put it into words, even if I could, but I sensed the pride that each soldier felt when the National Anthem played, and deep down I knew I wanted to be a part of that someday.

Atsuko "Betty" Paley

SFC Jerome "Jerry" Paley

My mother shared a story with me about my father's love for the movies. She said that when they were dating in Japan, my father would take her to an American movie on post and not seem concerned that she couldn't understand a word of it. Then, after the movie was over, he would insist on going to another movie at a different theater at a nearby post. At first, she indulged him, but one night she finally put her foot down and said that if he wanted to go to yet another movie, he'd have to go by himself.

He did.

That's when she learned that nothing came between my father and a John Wayne war movie. I took that as a lesson in what *not* to do.

Later that year, in September, my mother gave birth to the fourth and final child of the Paley family.

Though I badly wanted a monkey, I got a sister, instead. Her name is Karen, and she was born with rosy red cheeks and had our mother's jet-black hair.

I don't recall being jealous of her, exactly, but I do remember all the attention heaped upon her whenever people saw her. They mentioned how cute she was with her little dimples and her hair pulled up in a short ponytail on top of her head. They said she looked like a Kewpie Doll. *Oh, brother!*

One day, a photographer arrived in our apartment with a complete portable studio setup in honor of the cutest baby of the Paley family. I don't recall seeing formal portraits of me, Nancy or Phil when we were babies. But I wasn't bothered.

Karen was in her usual happy mood and smiled readily for the photographer, holding every cutesy pose he put her in as he flashed away with his camera.

"She's a natural," exclaimed the photographer

I stood behind him wondering what the big deal was. *I wanted a monkey!*

One day, while we were going for a walk, my mother forgot something in the apartment and asked me to watch Karen, who was in her big navy blue stroller with oversized wheels. I rolled Karen back and forth in the stroller as she giggled and became fascinated by her own hands. She was cute, I had to admit to myself. *Too cute.*

That's when I noticed the hill.

I released Karen's stroller to see if it would roll down the hill on its own, and *boy did it!*

Me and Karen at Fort Hamilton, New York, 1970.
Karen would set a downhill speed record in this stroller.

Before I could catch it, the stroller zoomed out of my reach and continued to pick up speed as it headed towards the street and the parking lot below.

I chased the stroller down the hill and watched as it swerved first a little to the left and then a little to the right as it seemed on the verge of flipping over. It was at that moment I realized I didn't want that to happen, that I actually *liked* my cute little sister after all. She was growing on me.

But the stroller continued to pick up speed, and try as I might, I couldn't catch it. I couldn't believe how fast it was going! I held my breath as it reached the bottom of the hill and rolled out into the middle of the road. Fortunately, no cars were coming, and when I finally managed to catch up with Karen, she was laughing. That made me laugh too … relieved. I felt like a horrible brother, and after that, I would never knowingly put her in danger again. I could always get a monkey some other time.

CHAPTER 3

———

FALSE IMPRESSIONS

1971

Fort Hamilton, New York

My mother was in the Post Exchange, or "PX," writing something in her checkbook when I saw my father enter through the main doors. Karen, who was seated in a stroller, giggled and held out her arms when she saw him. I ducked under the wall-mounted table my mother was writing on and looked up at my father from below. I was excited to see him too, but I couldn't verbalize it.

My father leaned down to give my mother a kiss, and she turned her cheek to him at the last minute. "Not in public," she said.

"Okay," my father replied, amused.

"Did you get them?" my mother asked, turning to face my father now.

My father looked around self-consciously, then smiled, showing off his "new" teeth. My mother said they looked great, but I didn't know what they were talking about.

My father must have seen my confusion, so he popped his dentures out right then and there, scaring the bejeezus out of me and Karen. She screamed for both of us, and then we both started to cry in horror. "Jerry!" exclaimed my mother as he popped his teeth back in his mouth, laughing.

It took me a long time to wrap my head around the concept of false teeth, and I'm sure I had a few nightmares about it afterwards. You think you know someone, and then they pop their teeth out right in the PX.

One day, my Mom parked the car at the edge of the parade field where it seemed like every soldier on Fort Hamilton had assembled. They were wearing their helmets with their summer Khaki uniforms, a green belt around their waists, and their pant legs tucked into their combat boots. I believe they were there for Retreat, or the lowering of the flag at the end of the workday.

I scanned the entire parade ground looking for my father in the ranks, but I couldn't see him. Nonetheless, I was completely enthralled at the sight of what seemed like thousands of soldiers standing in formation on the parade field, unit guidons blowing gently in the wind.

Retreat sounded and Mom told me and Nancy to "stand straight," while she held Karen in her arms. On the parade field, sergeants barked orders to bring their companies to attention.

Then they shouted, "Present, arms!" and hundreds of arms came up in unison, saluting the flag.

When the cannon went off, I placed my right hand on my heart as I was taught to do, and I watched in awe as the flag came down. Afterwards, my mother pointed my father out to me. He was standing alone at the front of a company, a First Sergeant. He looked stern and confident, and I felt a twinge of pride knowing that he was my father. When the parade ended, he came over to where we were standing, and I was surprised that the stern, serious soldier I saw on the parade field had such a ready smile when he saw my mother.

It was clear to me by the way his face lit up whenever he saw her how much he loved my mother, and I never once heard him raise his voice to her. Through his example, I saw what a man was, both at his sternest and at his most gentle, and I wanted to be just like him someday.

CHAPTER 4

——

DENNIS

1972

One of the earliest memories I have of not speaking is the number of times I had to see a doctor or a therapist. It amused me when the doctors would talk to my parents as if my near-muteness meant I was also incapable of hearing. I would further this impression by deliberately not looking at them when they consulted about my "condition."

"He seems to understand everything we're saying," one doctor would whisper as I looked disinterestedly away at some random part of the exam room, eavesdropping.

A different doctor would examine my pupils and my ears, and that too amused me.

"Open your mouth and say, 'Ah.'" *Now you're getting closer, doctor!*

The most amusing exam I had was when an older lady with cat eye glasses came to our house for a private consultation. She rambled on to my mother about things I don't recall, but she gave me the impression that she thought she had the answer to my silence. She also thought that speaking slowly to me was necessary, since I couldn't speak.

"Now, I would like for you to take this sheet of newspaper and crumble it up in your right hand, using *only* your right hand. Do you understand me?"

Blank stare. *I don't talk, remember?*

She handed me the paper and I proceeded to crumble it up with my right hand. With *only* my right hand. When I closed my fist around the ball of crumbled up paper, she seemed perplexed.

"Very good," she said, barely hiding her disappointment. She handed me another piece of paper, this time in my left hand. Same speech, different hand.

I stared at her as I crumbled up the paper with my left hand. With *only* my left hand.

"Well," she said, seeming confused. "Let's try something else."

That's the first time I saw the "Square peg in a round hole," test. It's also the first time that all these doctor visits made me start to feel like there was something "wrong" with me. Like I was the square peg.

I proceeded to put each shaped peg in the correspondingly shaped hole on the board, wondering what this was supposed to prove. When I was done, the lady literally packed up her toys and left.

Though I don't recall exactly what was going through my mind during my six years of near silence, I can say that I became very adept at creating my own inner world, which seemed to keep me entertained just fine, thank you. I said "near silence" because I do have vivid memories of laughing and crying out loud on numerous occasions, especially when I didn't get my way. It seems that forming complete sentences was the "issue."

Though no specific memories of the inner world I created come to me now, not speaking for so long didn't have any long-term negative effects on me. At least, that's what my psychologist told me.

One doctor, however, saw past my facade, my apparent self-imposed vow of silence. I secretly admired him.

My mother asked, "Is he re—"

"There's nothing wrong with your son," the doctor stated confidently as he turned to my parents. "When he's ready to talk, he'll talk."

Queens, New York
August 26, 1972

That doctor was right.

The first time I spoke was at my cousin Linda's wedding. It was a black-tie affair with hundreds of people. Linda looked absolutely beautiful in her wedding gown, and her husband, Dennis Feinsilver, looked impressive in his tuxedo.

After the ceremony was over, Linda found me lying on a loveseat in the lobby of the synagogue.

"What are you doing out here all by yourself?" she asked.

I sat up and she took my hand and pulled me up to my feet. Then she knelt down and straightened up my jacket and placed the yarmulke back on my head.

"You look like a little man in that suit," she said, smiling. "Come on, let's go thank everyone for coming today, okay?"

I liked my cousin Linda a lot, so I nodded 'yes.'

Linda and I walked to the far end of the rows of tables. Everyone noticed Linda immediately, and they stopped talking.

"I would like to thank all of you for coming today," Linda said. "I'm so happy that you could be here."

"Who's the little one?" someone asked.

Linda smiled and looked down at me, but she knew I didn't speak, so she started to speak for me. "This is my cousin—"

"Hi, I'm Dennis, and I shrunk!" I announced   .

Linda's face lit up with shock, and everyone at the table started to laugh.

"He spoke," she said to no one in particular.

"You spoke," Linda said, looking at me with a big smile. Then she pointed her finger at me. "I knew you could talk, you little stinker!"

She threw her head back and laughed, her brown eyes sparkling. Then she grabbed my hand and dragged me over to my family's table where my mother, father, brother and sisters were sitting.

"Is he causing any trouble?" my father asked, smiling.

"None at all. But he does have a surprise for you."

Linda bent down and said, "Now, I want you to tell them what you just told the other people, okay?"

I liked the attention that I was suddenly getting, so I pulled my shoulders back and bellowed, *"Hi, I'm Dennis, and I shrunk!"*

Everyone started laughing, but no one seemed happier or more relieved than my parents.

CHAPTER 5

—

DUNCE

1973

In 1971, my father was transferred from Fort Hamilton, New York, to West Virginia, where he served as the senior Active Duty enlisted advisor to the West Virginia National Guard, headquartered at Coonskin Park. He was promoted to the highest enlisted rank in the Army, Sergeant Major, fulfilling his lifelong career goal. It was here, at my father's last military assignment of his career that my memories begin to become more vivid.

Big Chimney Elementary School
Big Chimney, West Virginia
Spring 1973

"Robert talks too much in class."

Those were the words my first-grade teacher Mrs. Minor wrote on the bottom of my latest report card. I couldn't believe it. *She was telling on me!*

Mrs. Minor was young and pretty, but I pushed her too far past her point of patience. She was strict about not talking while she was teaching.

"You have two ears and one mouth for a reason," she'd explain. "And you're not learning if you're talking." She usually directed these comments in my general direction.

It seems that once I'd started talking a year earlier, I began trying to make up for lost time. Earlier that day, I got in trouble for talking too much yet again.

"Robert, I warned you to quit talking. Now get down on the floor." This unusual punishment, it seems, was Mrs. Minor's own, personal invention.

"Again?" I asked, frustrated.

My goody-two-shoes classmates who never got in trouble with Mrs. Minor giggled as I lay face down on the floor in front of the desks for the second time that day.

"You too, Tommy," my teacher said.

Tommy grumbled under his breath as he moved to lie on the floor beside me. "But I wasn't talking," Tommy moaned.

"Don't talk back to me, Tommy, or you'll be down there for the rest of the day with Robert."

For the rest of the day?

I raised my head and said, "It's true, Tommy wasn't talking to me, Mrs. Minor. I was talking to him." Tommy Ramsey was my best friend, and I felt bad that he got punished, too. The teacher's face turned red, and she somehow spoke by only moving her lips and keeping her teeth tightly together.

"I don't want to hear it, Robert." She leaned her head back and glared at me as she pointed to the floor with her finger extended like a dagger—moving it up and down in a chopping motion as she spoke each word. "Now you put your face down and keep it down!"

She looked like she was going to explode, so I did as I was told and put my face back down, my forehead resting on the top of my hands. I had to lie face down on the floor so many times throughout the school year that I became an expert in floor tile patterns.

I also developed a system that would allow me to breathe easier and to keep my mouth from touching the ground.

I found that by joining the tips of my pointer fingers and the tips of my thumbs together, forming a triangle, my nose and mouth would fit perfectly inside of it. The only problem was that I couldn't see anything this way—except for the tip of my nose—so I would close my eyes and try not to fall asleep as my teacher continued to teach class.

Tommy lay down beside me and our elbows touched.

"Put your fingers like this," I whispered to Tommy as I raised my head up to show him the triangle shape I made with my fingers. This was Tommy's first time lying on the floor, and as the resident expert I was trying to be helpful. But Mrs. Minor must have been standing right beside me because she shouted, "Robert Paley!"

When she used my last name I knew she was really, really mad.

Daddy was strict about getting good grades, and he wouldn't be happy at all with this report card. Not only did it say I talked too much in class, but it also showed I'd failed math...again.

Earlier that day, Mrs. Minor placed my latest math test on my desk. It was bloodied by a red pen and had a big "0" written on the top of it. There was so much red I could barely see the one thing I did get right—my name.

I held up the paper to see what all the red marks and comments were, and someone behind me shouted, "Look at Robert's paper."

"He got a zero," pointed out another student.

I quickly laid the paper face-down on my desk and tried to hide it, but it was too late.

"He's a dunce," someone else hollered.

"He can't even add two plus two."

Everyone laughed, except Tommy. I felt stupid because I didn't even know what a "dunce" was, but I knew it wasn't good to be one.

I glanced over at Tommy's test, and it had a gold star stuck to the top of it—not one red mark. Tommy was smart. He even looked smart in those glasses he had to wear. *Smart people wear glasses,* I concluded. I made up my mind to get glasses as soon as possible.

The school bell saved me from further humiliation. I was out the door of the classroom before the bell finished ringing. Behind me, I heard Mrs. Minor shout, "Bring your signed report card back tomorrow."

I recall stepping out into the warm spring air, thankful to be out of the confining classroom.

I crumpled the report card and stuffed it into my pocket, but I wasn't ready to go home yet. I intended to enjoy my last hours of freedom before getting grounded, so I took the long way home.

I passed behind the small Boy Scout building, then cut across a field towards a small creek—or "crick" as we called it—which separated the schoolyard from the trailer park where I lived. The creek was clear and flowed into the Elk River below. I hopped across familiar rocks that quickly got me to the other side of the creek and entered the "Indian graveyard" on a well-worn trail. I loved the peacefulness of the woods.

My friends and I called it the "Indian graveyard" because we often found Indian arrowheads buried or lying on the ground near lots of old headstones. We would spend hours playing *Cowboys and Indians* in the woods.

I was always told to play an Indian for some reason, but I didn't mind. I was fascinated by the Indian culture. We played in the woods and let our imaginations guide us on one adventure after another, only suspending our break from reality when someone shouted, "I found one!"

We would then rally to whoever found the arrowhead, and marvel at the craftsmanship. The arrowheads were a dark gray or black slate and usually fit in the palms of our hands.

After admiring it, we would argue about whether it was bigger or smaller than the last one *so-and-so* found. Whenever I held an arrowhead in my hand, I wondered who the person was who'd made it and what had happened to them? I found the Indian culture fascinating and mysterious, and I wondered if the maker of the arrowhead had once stood where I was standing now.

The leaves and branches of the tall trees split the sun's rays into hundreds of shafts of light angling into the woods and lighting up parts of the graveyard. As I walked in, the air felt cooler on my skin and the scent of new spring flowers filled my nostrils. I listened to the singsong banter of birds that I couldn't see and noticed new plant growth coming back after a long, cold winter. My spirits rose as I took it all in, and soon I forgot all about the report card in my pocket.

The distant sounds of screaming kids being let out of school were soon silenced as the woods engulfed me. I walked slowly and looked at the old moss-covered grave markers randomly scattered on each side of the trail. The headstones were small, and some were so old you could no longer read the names or dates on them. Some headstones stood upright, while others seemed to be sinking into the ground or tipping over. Wildflowers and small brush grew between the stones, and some of them were completely hidden by vegetation. A tiny headstone, with faded letters barely visible, read "2 years old." That one made me sad.

I was comfortable in the woods, and I imagined myself as an Indian walking quietly to stalk prey or to sneak up on some unknown enemy, or as a young, fearless Brave, a great warrior, watching out over my tribe, the Great—I looked around for inspiration, and found it on my black high top tennis shoes—*Converse* Tribe.

To my right, a noise! Dozens of kids were crossing the creek or walking along the trail, oblivious to my presence in the woods. They were upperclassmen. *The enemy*, I thought to myself.

I knelt down and took cover behind the stump of a tree.

From my vantage point just inside the wood line, I saw the Huffmans, the Liveleys, the Vances and the Merrifields pass before me one-by-one and in small groups, all talking or laughing—completely oblivious to my presence—and that gave me a thrill. I liked being invisible.

A moment later I saw my older sister Nancy, who was in the fourth grade, walk by with her best friend Kim Mullins, a blond- haired, blue-eyed girl.

"I got all As and Bs," Nancy said to Kim.

"Traitor!" I yelled as I sprung out from behind the tree wielding a small stick like it was a hatchet. I grabbed Nancy's arm and said, "Come back to the reservation, Squaw!"

Both girls screamed, then started laughing.

"You idiot," Nancy laughed, shaking her head. Nancy had long brown hair pulled back on the sides with barrettes, and she had a single, black freckle in the middle of her forehead that made people think she was Indian for some reason. Only later would I learn that they meant people from a country called "India", and not American Indians.

"What were you doing in there?" Nancy asked.

"Nuttin, just walking around."

"Did you get your report card?"

"Yep, all A's."

"All A's?" asked Kim.

"You wish," Nancy replied, shaking her head at me. "I heard you got in trouble with your teacher again today?"

"Where'd you hear that?" I grimaced, really wanting to know how she'd already heard about it.

"It's a small school, Rob. Let me see your report card." She extended her hand, palm up.

"Can't—gotta' go. See you later, alligator."

Nancy yelled after me, "You better be home in time for dinner. Daddy will be home early today!"

I re-crossed the creek running as fast as I could. I headed upstream towards the main road, then went back down to the creek to cross to the trailer park. A thick, moss covered log lay across the deeper part of the creek, so I decided to cross there. I was lost in my thoughts about my bad report card and I didn't realize where I was until it was too late. I was halfway across the log, trying not to fall off when suddenly—

Splash!

A large rock landed in the creek right next to me and I got drenched from head to toe.

Looming above me on the bank of the creek was Bryce Reynolds, the trailer park bully.

Bryce stood laughing and pointing at me as water dripped down my forehead and blended with the tears that began to form in my eyes. Between my report card and Bryce, I'd had all the humiliation I could take for one day. The more Bryce laughed, the more I felt my lips quiver, and I was ashamed at myself for being such a scaredy-cat.

What I wanted to do was to go up there, grab him and throw him into the creek to see how he liked it.

Instead, I just stood in the middle of the log, drenched from head to toe, feeling helpless.

"You can't come this way," Bryce said, as he flipped his head back to get his long dishwater-blond bangs out of his eyes. Bryce was wearing a dirty T-shirt and oversized bell-bottomed jeans which flared out so wide at the calves that they nearly covered both of his worn-out tennis shoes. I doubted if he was even at school today.

I looked at the trailer behind Bryce and saw his mother looking out the window. I thought she was going to help me, but instead she just turned away.

Desperate, I looked down and saw the clear stream flowing below me. The rushing water made me dizzy, and I nearly lost my balance. Bryce laughed and taunted me more, but I couldn't turn back.

"I have to go home," I said plaintively. "My parents are waiting for me."

Bryce bent down and picked up another rock, the size of a small boulder.

"Then cross," he said, grinning and tossing the small boulder from hand to hand. "Who's stopping you?" I couldn't understand how Bryce could be so mean.

It wasn't cold out, but I began to shiver. "Puh—please, let me go."

I did my best to stop myself from quivering, but the harder I tried the more I shook. Moments before, I had imagined myself an Indian Brave, a warrior. But when confronted by the trailer park bully, my *real* enemy, my legs turned to Jell-o and there was nothing brave about me. I was reminded of how weak and scared I really was, and that completed my day's humiliation.

I must have looked pathetic, standing there on that log dripping and shaking. I was too scared to go forward but unable to go back.

Bryce shook his head in disgust. "You're nothing but a big sissy. Go run to your mommy and daddy."

He tossed the rock in my general direction and I flinched as it splashed into the creek beside me with a "ker-plunk."

Then, Bryce turned his back to me and walked away.

That was worse than getting punched in the face, and the anger at my own helplessness soon replaced my fear. I clenched my fists and stared at his back as water dripped down my face, blending with my tears. Deep down, as my teeth chattered and my body shook, I made a vow that I would get my revenge someday.

CHAPTER 6

GROUNDED

My family lived in a two-story apartment building at the end of the trailer park. We used to live in a trailer which backed up to the hill overlooking the Elk River below, but as soon as an apartment came open, my father and mother quickly took the opportunity to move our six-person family into it. To me, it felt like a mansion it was so big.

Our rooms were upstairs, but there were only three of them, so I shared a room with my brother Phil, who was seventeen. I got the top bunk, and he slept on the bottom bunk. He was always out with his girlfriend, Sheila, so I usually didn't see him much. That was okay with me because it made me feel like I had the room all to myself.

My older sister, Nancy, who was eleven, slept in the room next to mine with our baby sister, Karen, who was three.

"You failed math again?" said my father as he reviewed my report card at the dinner table. It was more of a statement than a question.

I nodded my head and looked down at my plate.

"Finish your peas," my mother said.

"I don't like peas," I muttered. Besides, I'd lost my appetite knowing what was coming.

"You're grounded until you get your math grade up," my father said. "Now finish your peas, then go to your room."

I knew better than to talk back to my father, so I forced myself to eat as many peas as I could. I was nearly finished eating them when all of a sudden, I felt sick.

"What's the matter?" my mother asked, seeing the expression on my face.

I tried to speak but instead, I threw up all the peas onto my dinner plate. *Pea soup.*

Nancy, sitting beside me, cried, "Gross," as she pushed back from the table and stood up.

My mother jumped up and said, "It's okay, go upstairs and brush your teeth."

I pushed back from the table and headed for the stairs. As I walked away, I heard my father laugh, "I guess he really doesn't like peas."

Later that night, I heard my mother and my father laughing hard, and I crept down the wooden stairs from my bedroom to see what was so funny.

Just as I got to the bottom step before the landing, I heard my father say, "Robert talks too much in class." He was holding my still-crumpled report card in his hand.

He laughed hard and Mom laughed right along with him. I was confused. I was sure I'd get in trouble for talking too much too, but my parents only punished me for failing math.

"First he doesn't talk for six years—" Mom said.

"And now he won't shut up!" Dad replied, and they laughed again. "Let's call Minn."

I heard them walk from the living room into the kitchen and pick up the phone. I crept down a few more steps, and I peeked around the corner in time to see my Dad push a button on a pop-up telephone directory. My mother dialed the number on the black rotary phone which sat on the desk as my father read her my grandmother's number in New York City.

"Hi, Minn," my mother said. "No, nothing's wrong, everybody's fine. Yes, Jerry's fine, too. He's standing right beside me."

My father handed my mother my crinkled, now-dried report card, and my mother held it up.

"Bobby got another report card today," she said.

"No, still having trouble with math. We called because we wanted to tell you what his teacher wrote on his report card. Right. His teacher said 'Robert talks too much in class.'" She smiled and looked at my father.

"That's right!" laughed my mother. "He talks *too* much."

I smiled as I saw the obvious joy this brought to my parents. If I'd known that talking would make my parents so happy, I would have done it much sooner.

One night, my father sat in his favorite chair reading a thick book while the rest of our family watched TV. Beside him, another stack of thick books was neatly arranged on the end table, waiting to be read. When no one was around, I'd open one of his books to try to figure out what was so interesting to him, but there were no pictures. *What kind of book doesn't have any pictures?* I wondered.

Perhaps my father liked to read so much because in the books he could "hear" everything that was being said. He was completely deaf in his left ear, and mostly deaf in his right ear. Mom told me it was because of a "bug" he caught when he was fighting in Vietnam.

I never knew him any other way. To talk to him, I'd have to tap him on his knee to get his attention, then speak clearly while looking directly at him so that he could read my lips in addition to hearing me with his good ear.

He always wore a hearing aid in his right ear, and mom kept a small pack of round hearing aid batteries on the refrigerator shelf. Sometimes, if we were too loud, Dad would reach up to his hearing aid and we'd hear it whistle, then click off. Peace and quiet for him.

I watched as my father read. He crossed one leg over the other and rested the book on his knee as he slid his pointer finger down the middle of the page. It amazed me how quickly he went from one page to the next. My older brother told me it was called "speed reading."

My father was a Sergeant Major in the Army, and I knew that he had fought in that placed called "Vietnam" that I was seeing on the news every night. No one would dare pick on him, I knew, and I wanted to be more like him.

I got up off the floor of the living room and stood next to him, then tapped his knee to get his attention. He jumped whenever I did that, but he didn't seem to mind. Dad stopped reading and clicked his hearing-aid back on so he could hear me.

"What's the matter?" he asked, folding his book closed but keeping his index finger on the page he was reading.

"Will you teach me how to fight?" I asked.

"To fight?" he said. I nodded my head and looked down at my feet. I didn't want to tell him that I was afraid of Bryce Reynolds, and he didn't ask.

He stood up and said, "Come over here," pointing to an open area at the back of the living room. My older sister Nancy and my younger sister Karen stopped watching TV and turned to watch the lesson.

"Show me your fighting stance," my father said.

I didn't have a fighting stance, so I just awkwardly held up my fists.

"Like this," my father explained as he got into a boxing stance. I mimicked him.

"Good. Your forward fist is for jabbing," he said as he jabbed at the air. "And your rear fist is for your strong punch."

For the next few minutes, Dad showed me how to throw punches and move around while maintaining a good boxer's stance. He watched me as I practiced.

"Planning on fighting someone?" he asked, eyebrows raised.

"No," I said, only half meaning it.

My sisters got bored and turned back to watch TV, and my father sat back down to read his book.

Later, in my room, I continued shadow-boxing my not-so-imaginary opponent until my arms hurt.

One day after school, I was playing with my friend Herbie under a big chestnut tree when we came across a wad of chewed tobacco which somebody had spit out. It was dried by the sun, so I picked it up and told him that we should make a cigarette out of it and smoke it. My father smoked filterless Camel cigarettes all the time, and I thought it looked cool.

"We need something to put it in," said Herbie, looking around. Herbie had big ears and a face full of freckles, and the kids in the trailer park made even more fun of him than they did me. I liked Herbie, though, and I never made fun of him.

"My Paw rolls his own cigarettes in wrappers," Herbie said.

We looked around but didn't find anything like a paper wrapper, but we did find a plastic straw.

"This could work," I said, as I studied the straw. Herbie shrugged, and then grabbed some of the chewed tobacco from my palm and began stuffing thin shreds of it in one side of the straw, while I did the same on the other. A few minutes later, we had a very long, plastic straw cigarette.

"We need matches," I said.

Herbie reached into his pocket and pulled out a small box of matches. "Like these?" he asked, revealing his missing front teeth. I wondered why he had matches in his pocket.

"Let's light it!" I said. Herbie agreed and removed a wooden match and struck it on the side of the box.

He held the flame under the tip of the cigarette and I inhaled.

Everything seemed to be working fine when suddenly the end of the straw erupted into a two-inch flame and molten plastic began dripping quickly onto the ground. Herbie jumped back so that the molten plastic wouldn't burn his feet, but I was mesmerized by the flame as it consumed the straw, fueled further by the dried tobacco inside of it. My eyes widened, then crossed as the straw gave off an acrid, black smoke and the flame continued moving rapidly towards me.

"Drop it!" shouted Herbie. "Drop it!"

I wanted too, but I couldn't. I was transfixed by the flame and amazed at how well our self-made cigarette was burning.

Finally, as the heat neared my fingers, I snapped out of my trance and threw the straw onto the ground. We watched it curl up from the heat and melt into a black, melted heap of plastic and tobacco. The smell was pungent, and it hurt my nose to breath in the fumes.

We watched it until a final puff of black smoke told us that the fire had consumed all that it could, and then we looked at each other and started laughing.

Herbie and I headed home for the trailer park, but we came to a dead-halt when we saw Bryce the Bully sitting on his bike and blocking the trail we needed to get home. Bryce was looking the other way and didn't see us, so I motioned to Herbie to follow me. I angled to the right for the Indian Graveyard, but just before we got to the wood line, Bryce saw us.

"Hey!" he shouted as he stood up on his pedal and kicked gravel up with his back tire as he turned his bike towards us.

"Run!" I shouted to Herbie as we ran into the woods. Bryce was coming fast, but I led Herbie to a trail that led down to a spillway too steep for Bryce to follow us on with his bike. As we got to the edge of the drop-off, I stopped, and Herbie bumped into me, nearly sending me flying. He was even more afraid of Bryce than I was.

"Follow me," I said, as I sat on the edge of the drop-off and slid on my butt down the near-vertical drop off to the ground below. The clay was moist, and tree roots snagged my jeans as I descended. Herbie slid down right behind me, and none the worse for wear, we looked up and saw Bryce, contemplating the drop-off, his front tire sticking out over the edge.

"Wussies!" he shouted, as he backed away and left.

I held out my hand, and Herbie gave me five as we victoriously walked down to the river and followed it home towards the trailer park. But no sooner did we get into the clear, when we saw Bryce careening down the hill towards us on his bike. We had nowhere to run with the river to our rear, and the wood line offered no protection from this level. We were trapped.

Bryce was yelling obscenities at us when he skidded his bike in the grass and jumped off. Herbie and I were frozen with fear, not knowing what to expect.

Bryce raised his hands in the air with his fists half closed and challenged, "Which one of you wussies wanna fight me?"

Herbie and I looked at each other, hoping that the other would volunteer. Neither of us did.

"I will," spoke a deep voice from behind me.

Bryce's confident angry face turned pale, and he lowered his fists to his side. Walking up from the river bank, pole and tackle box in hand, was my older brother, Phil.

I was so relieved. Phil scared the kids in the trailer park with his serious demeanor and piercing scowl, but to me, he was always my supportive big brother whom I looked up to and admired.

Phil stopped directly behind me and Herbie and put his pole and tackle box down. I smiled at him and enjoyed seeing Bryce squirm for once. "Get him, Phil!" I said.

"Yeah, get him," Herbie repeated.

My brother looked at Bryce and said, "One...two..."

Bryce's eyes got wide and he turned and picked up his bike and pedaled away, making it back up the hill with surprising speed.

"Three!" I shouted as Herbie and I laughed and thanked my brother for saving us.

"Why do you guys let him push you around like that?" my brother asked as he shook his head.

I looked up to my brother, and his words stung. I knew he was disappointed in me, just as I was disappointed in myself.

This wasn't the first time my brother had gotten me out of a jam, and something told me it wouldn't be the last time, either.

CHAPTER 7

———

KICKBALL

It seemed like every kid in the trailer park had turned up in the small, grassy field next to our apartment to play kick-ball on one of our last night's in West Virginia. My father was retiring from the Army and we were moving to Ohio. I was looking forward to the new adventure, and to making new friends. Anywhere was better than this old trailer park with Bryce the Bully picking on me every day.

Elementary school kids like me found themselves on the same team as the high school kids, who usually didn't want us little kids around.

We formed two teams and were having a blast when Bryce the Bully came riding up on his bike. He had cousins on the opposing team, and they told Bryce he could join them in the outfield.

"I don't want to play outfield," Bryce said. "I'll play short-stop." Herbie was at short-stop, and he frowned as he walked off the field so Bryce could take his spot.

Bryce's presence on the field immediately dampened everyone's spirits, but we continued to play.

My sister Nancy was next up to kick, but the pitcher hesitated to roll the red, rubber ball while Bryce had his back turned to home plate. He was busy yelling at a girl in the left field about something.

"Just roll the ball!" I shouted.

"You stink!" Bryce said, as the little girl in the outfield hung her head. He continued to taunt her as the pitcher rolled the red ball towards home plate, where my sister, Nancy—an athletic Tom-boy with her dark brown hair pulled back in two braids—was waiting.

As the rubber ball bounced and rolled in the grass towards home plate, Bryce continued his harangue of the helpless little girl in the outfield. His back was still turned when Nancy charged the ball and kicked it with all her might.

The sound of the rubber ball smacking off her foot was enough to get Bryce's attention, and he turned around just in time for the red ball to hit him smack in the face and knock him on his butt.

No one moved, not even Nancy, who should have been running towards first base. The teenagers were laughing as Bryce— his bangs now sticking straight up in the air and his forehead reddened from the impact of the ball—got on his feet and saw everyone laughing at him. That did it.

"Who kicked that ball?" he shrieked as he ran towards home plate. I started to back up so he wouldn't think I'd done it, but then I saw the scared look on my sister's face.

Bryce had never hit a girl as far as I knew, but it seemed certain that he was about to make an exception as he neared home plate.

Despite my own fears, I couldn't let him hit my sister. To my utter shock, I heard myself say, "I kicked it," as I stepped forward and placed myself between Bryce and my sister. I glanced at Nancy, and I saw a look of respect on her face that I'd never seen before. I gently pushed her back and nodded.

The years of being bullied by Bryce had built up inside of me, and knowing he'd hit my sister was the final straw.

"Then I'm going to kick your ass!" he screamed as he approached me with his hands down by his side.

I got into the boxer's stance my father had shown me, and when he charged me, I jabbed him in the nose.

As his head snapped back and blood formed under his nose, I saw something in his eyes I'd never seen before. Fear.

Then came the rage.

Bryce sneered and lunged at me again, and we tumbled to the ground in a heap, vying for advantage and rolling in the grass and dirt.

To my surprise, Bryce was not as good a fighter as I expected him to be, and his usual yelling and cussing which had served him so well in the past, no longer affected me.

What had started off as a friendly kickball game had degenerated into a fight which was a few years in the making, and I unleashed my frustration and humiliation on him while the crowd formed a rough circle around us, screaming at the top of their lungs.

"Get him, Robert!" shouted anonymous voices from the crowd. All the kids who had lived in fear of Bryce were now cheering me on, and I gained strength and confidence with each tumble we took.

The fight seemed to go on endlessly, but I was getting the better of Bryce the entire time. I knew it, and so did he.

Bryce disengaged from the headlock I was trying to place him in and struggled to his feet, tears visible in his eyes. He had the wild, desperate look of a trapped animal, and for a brief moment, I thought he was going to run away, but the crowd closed in tighter and blocked any route of escape.

I stood up to meet Bryce's gaze but was surprised when he bent down and picked up a stick that appeared out of nowhere. Bryce had cousins in the crowd, and I could only guess that one of them had tossed it his way out of loyalty.

"No sticks!" Nancy shouted in my defense.

Bryce turned toward her and held up the stick, and she wisely backed away.

The rest of the crowd told Bryce to throw the stick down, too, but it was no use. Bryce turned towards me and swung the stick at my head. I backed up to avoid being hit and fell to the ground. I couldn't regain my feet and held my left hand up to protect my head. Pain shot through my right hand as I placed it in the dirt and gravel to try to get up.

Dirt...and gravel?

My right hand closed in a fist as I clenched as much dirt and gravel as I could.

Bryce, emboldened now, closed in on me determined to finish me off.

Just when he was about to strike, I threw the handful of dirt and gravel as hard as I could at his face, and his eyes and opened-mouth filled with both. Bryce dropped the stick and grabbed at his eyes as he tried to spit the dirt from his mouth.

Tears, snot, and blood running down his face formed wet streaks against the dust that covered his face, and I almost felt sorry for him.

I got to my feet and closed in to finish the fight, but the sound of car tires crunching on the gravel drive silenced everyone.

"Dad's home!" shouted Nancy.

Bryce, seeing his chance to get out of the losing battle, shouted pathetically, "I'm telling your Dad!" as he turned and ran towards our apartment.

The crowd closed in on me and I felt people patting me on my back saying things like, "Way to go, Robert!" and "You kicked his ass, man!" as I tried to push through them to chase after Bryce.

Nancy appeared out of nowhere, grabbed my hand and said, "C'mon!"

We ran as fast as we could to catch Bryce, but it was too late. By the time Nancy and I rounded the corner of the garage, Bryce had already intercepted our father at the door to the apartment and was telling his lies about the fight.

My father, standing nearly six feet tall and wearing his Army summer Khakis, seemed confused by Bryce's animated explanation.

As Nancy and I ran up behind Bryce, my father looked at me, took note of my disheveled appearance, and then looked back at Bryce.

"Who started the fight?" my father said.

Bryce glanced over his shoulder at me and Nancy, then shouted, "He did!" as he pointed his finger accusingly at me.

"Did not!" I shouted back, amazed that he would lie to my Dad.

"He's lying!" shouted Nancy, and I joined her in trying to talk over Bryce, so we wouldn't get in trouble.

Finally, my father raised his hand and his voice and said, "Enough!" We all fell silent and stared up at my father's imposing figure.

"Nancy," said my Dad. "Who started the fight?"

Nancy pointed at Bryce, and Bryce started to argue again, mentioning something about a ball to the face, but my father quieted Bryce with a look.

To my surprise, Nancy said, "Robert was protecting me from Bryce."

The thought of Bryce hitting his daughter was enough to warrant a sharp look from my Dad. Bryce bowed his head in shame as he wiped the blood from his nose.

Just then, my Mom appeared at the screen door, took one look at Bryce and took him inside to clean him up.

Nancy and I stood in front of Dad and waited for the punishment we felt was inevitable.

Dad reached his hand out, cupped my chin with his hand, and studied my dirty face. I thought I saw him holding back a smile as he said, "Go play."

The next morning, a ray of sunlight broke through the crack in my bedroom curtains and woke me up. I sat up, stretched, and then winced as my sore muscles reminded me of the fight I'd had the previous day. I looked at my right arm and hand and saw some minor scratches, and that's when I realized that finally getting my revenge on the trailer park bully wasn't just a dream. I had actually done it.

I swung my legs out over the top bunk and let them dangle for a minute as I reveled in the strange feeling I was experiencing. I felt a lightness of spirit I had never known before, but I understood it to be the absence of fear.

For the first time since moving to West Virginia, I no longer feared Bryce the Bully.

I heard my brother Phil stir on the bunkbed below me. I didn't want to wake him up, so I turned onto my belly and quietly lowered myself to the floor. I walked to the bedroom window which overlooked the entire trailer park below, and I smiled.

"I heard you got into a fight with Bryce," Phil said, breaking my reverie.

I turned to Phil and nodded my head.

"Dad said he looked pretty beat up," Phil said, as he raised himself up on his elbows and squinted at me through the sunlight.

I couldn't understand the feelings I was experiencing. I hated Bryce Reynolds. I hated how he controlled me and every other kid in the trailer park. I hated how many times he had humiliated me in front of others. I hated how he pulled the corners of his eyes back to make himself look Asian and then called me a "Jap." I hated how he told me where I could and couldn't play in the creek. But most of all, I hated how he made me feel about myself.

But now, instead of feeling hatred towards Bryce, I found myself feeling sorry for him.

"Good job," my brother said as he laid back on his pillow.

Like our father, my brother wasn't the kind to give easy compliments, and it made me feel good.

CHAPTER 8

———

THE JANITOR

"Bobby, I need to go to my office to pick up the last of my things," my father said. "Do you want to come with me?"

I loved going places with my father, and I immediately said, "Yes."

I quickly scooped the last few spoonfuls of *Peanut Butter Crunch* cereal into my mouth and, with the back of my arm, wiped away some milk that had dripped down my chin.

"Put your bowl in the sink," my mother said as I was walking out of the kitchen to join my dad.

"But I'm going to work with Daddy," I said, holding my arms up in frustration.

"Do what your mother told you," my father said canting his Army Service Cap to the right as he looked in the mirror.

How come he always seems to hear what Mom says? I wondered as I spun around on one foot and did as I was told.

A few minutes later we were on our way. Knowing that we would be leaving for Ohio in a few days, I found myself taking in all the sights, sounds and smells of Big Chimney as my father drove our blue, four-door Dodge towards Coonskin Park, where the West Virginia Army National Guard Headquarters was located.

As much as I was looking forward to the new adventure moving to Ohio would bring, I realized that I would miss Big Chimney too.

As we neared Smith's Hardware & Grocery, my father pulled into the parking lot which was on a slight downward slope. Everything sloped one way or another in West Virginia, it seemed.

"I need to get a box," my father said as he put the car in park. I walked beside him and tried to match his stride and his footsteps.

His leather Low-quarter shoes reflected the sunlight with each step he took. He would spend hours, it seemed, polishing his shoes with a white cloth and a can of Kiwi, and the result was a glass-like finish on the toes of his shoes.

A bell jingled as we walked into the hardware store and my father was greeted by the store manager.

"Good morning, Sergeant Major," he said.

"Good morning," my father replied. "I'm heading to my office to pack the last of my things, and I was wondering if you had a spare box I could have?"

The kind, elderly gentlemen behind the counter said, "I think I may be able to find something for you," as he walked around the counter towards the back of the store.

I was hanging by my arms and gently swinging back and forth on a long, metal rail in front of the counter with my feet raised up behind me as the man walked by and smiled at me.

"Stand up straight," my father said.

A minute later, the man returned with a small box and handed it to my father. "I threw some tape in there for you as well," he said. "Good luck in Ohio."

"What do I owe you?" my father asked, opening his wallet.

The man held up his hand and said, "Don't worry about it."

"Thank you," my father said.

A short drive later, I recognized the sign welcoming us to Coonskin Park, and I saw couples riding paddle boats in the small lake.

Soon, we pulled into the Armory where my father worked, and I saw the block-letter sign in front of it that said, "U.S. Army."

When we walked into the armory, a soldier sitting at the front desk shouted, "At ease!" as my father walked into his office. The Soldier stood up and placed his hands in the small of his back, his feet shoulder-width apart.

"As you were, Corporal," my father said. "This is my son, Bobby."

"Robert," I said, as the Corporal reached his hand out to shake mine.

"Nice to meet you, Robert" said the corporal. "How old are you?"

"Seven and a half," I said.

The corporal smiled and rubbed my head, messing up my hair. My father walked to his desk and began placing some items in the box. He seemed lost in his thoughts.

"Come here, Robert," the Corporal said. "I want to show you something really neat."

He walked over to some kind of machine and handed me a funny looking sheet of paper that smelled good and felt cool to the touch.

"Write something on it," the Corporal said.

"I don't know how to write yet," I replied.

"Okay, then draw a picture on it. Of anything."

He handed me a pen and said, "Go on, draw something."

I thought about it for a minute, then I drew a house with a tree and some stick figures.

"Okay, I'll take that now," said the corporal. He did some things with the paper and the machine and said, "Watch this."

I stepped closer to the machine and watched a large roller turn and pull the paper through it. On the other side of the roller the corporal picked up a second sheet of paper and held it up for me. Then he held up my original drawing beside it. It was an exact copy of what I had drawn, but it was purple instead of black.

"Neat!" I said.

"See that, it made an exact copy of your picture," my father said. "It's called a duplicate."

"That's neat!" I said again, as I carried the two drawings to my father's desk and laid them side-by-side to compare them. I'd never seen such a thing before. The paper had a nice scent to it, sort of like black licorice, and I held it up to my nose and inhaled deeply. My father and the corporal laughed.

"Are my papers ready?" asked my Dad.

"Yes, Sergeant Major, I'll go and get them," replied the Corporal.

The Corporal left the office just as a janitor walked in.

"I was hoping I'd catch you before you left, Sergeant Major," said the janitor as he walked up to my father and shook his hand.

The janitor's work clothes were dirty as were his hands.

"I'm glad you did, John," my father said.

"Bobby, this is John. He runs this place."

"Well, I don't know about all that," John said as he bent down and extended his hand to me. "Nice to meet you, young man."

I shook his hand, and when he turned to talk to my father again, I wiped my hand on my shorts.

"How's your car situation?" my father asked.

"Not good," said John. "It's totaled."

My father shook his head and said, "Insurance?"

"Nah. The deer I hit was uninsured!" John smiled then laughed hard, and I was surprised when my father laughed right along with him.

I didn't understand what they were talking about, so I turned back to my papers and started drawing on them.

"It'll be fine, Sergeant Major" said John as he rubbed the back of his neck. "My wife can drive me to work from now on. It's no big deal, really."

The corporal walked back into the office with my Dad's papers in hand.

"Well, I best get back to work, Sergeant Major. You sure will be missed around here."

"Thanks, John," my father said, shaking his hand again.

John smiled at me as he left, but he looked sad at the same time.

"Here you go, Sergeant Major," the Corporal said as he handed a manila file to my father. "You should drop off the medical records with your local VA when you get to Columbus."

My father nodded as he quickly glanced at the contents of the folder.

"I guess that about does it then," my father said. "Thank you, Corporal."

They shook hands, my father picked up the box, and we left.

As we walked out, I looked up at my father and he seemed sad too, for some reason. I'd never seen that look on him before.

It was the last time that I would ever see him in his uniform.

A few days later, my father pulled into the gravel drive leading to our apartment in a brand-new Oldsmobile Cutlass Cruiser station wagon with wood-panels on the side of it. It was huge!

Our whole family gathered around it to admire it. It was the first brand-new car my parents had ever owned, and you could see the pride on my father's face.

"You two will sit in the back," my father said, pointing to me and my older sister Nancy.

He swung the back door open and revealed a rumble seat facing backwards, towards the rear bumper.

"Cool!" I said.

"That's neat," said Nancy as we climbed in and tested out our new seat.

"You sure you won't come to Ohio with us?" my mother asked my brother Phil, while she held Karen in her arms.

Phil flipped his Beatles' style bangs back with a shake of his head and said, "I'm sure, Mom."

"You ready?" my father asked my brother.

My brother held up keys to the old Dodge.

"Alright, out of the car," my father said to me and Nancy.

"But I want to go with you," I said.

My father laughed and said, "You don't even know where we're going."

I shrugged my shoulders and he smiled. "Ok, you can ride with Phil."

My father pulled out onto the main road and my brother and I followed in the Dodge.

"Where *are* we going?" I asked my brother.

Phil smiled and said, "You'll see."

Fifteen minutes later, we pulled into the National Guard Armory where my father used to work.

We got out of the car and my brother handed the Dodge keys to my father.

"I'll be right back," my father said as he went into the Armory.

A minute later, we saw our father walk out with the Janitor John, whom I'd met several days before.

John looked at the Dodge and said, "I don't know how to thank you, Sergeant Major."

"No need," said my Dad. "Just don't hit any more deer."

John smiled and said, "I'll do my best not to."

John looked at me and Phil and nodded, then turned and walked back to the Armory, Dodge keys in hand. I thought I saw tears in his eyes.

"How much did you sell it to him for?" my brother asked as we walked towards the station wagon.

"Fifty dollars," my father said.

My brother smiled and nodded his head.

CHAPTER 9

———

OHIO

SUMMER, 1973

Columbus, Ohio

As we crossed a bridge over the Ohio River, a sign welcomed us to Ohio. It wasn't long before the Paley family tradition of singing Army cadences on road trips began. My father's booming voice filled the car as the whole family joined in.

"Ain't no sense in lookin' down!" he barked.

"Ain't no sense in lookin' down!" we repeated.

"Ain't no discharge on the ground!

Ain't no discharge on the ground!"

"Sound off!"

"One-Two!"

"Once more!"

"Three Four!"

"Break it on down!"

"One, two, three, four, one two (pause) three four!"

Laughter filled the car as we drove mile after mile singing Army songs and cadences. I never tired of them, and I always asked for one more.

"Okay," my father said, "last one."

Cheers all around.

"I know a girl from O-hi-o!" he barked.

"I know a girl from O-hi-o!"

"Boy that girl can really sew!"

"Boy that girl can really sew!"

"I know a girl from ol' Kentuck—"

"Jerry!" my mother shouted, interrupting him as he laughed and leaned away from her raised hand.

"What? Kentucky girls can sew, too."

I never got to learn the rest of *that* one.

The roar of jets screaming by overhead told me we were outside of Columbus, Ohio near Lockbourne Air Force Base, which would serve as our home for the next week until our household goods arrived. We couldn't wait to move into our first permanent home in the neighboring town.

We stayed in a run-down, single-story brick motel just outside the base, called the *Skyhawk Motel.*

Our room had a sliding glass door which led to a courtyard out back, and one day we heard a "thud" against the door. My mother walked over to investigate and saw a small bird lying on the deck, unconscious.

"Is it dead?" I asked.

"I don't know," my mother murmured as she slid the door open and kneeled down to study it.

My father walked over and said, "Betty, leave it alone. There's nothing you can do for it."

My mother looked up at him, then looked at me and said, "Go get me a hand towel from the bathroom."

I did as I was told and handed it to her. She bent down and gently picked the bird up in the towel as Nancy, Karen and I followed her back into the living room. My mother placed the bird on the back of the couch and formed the towel into the shape of a nest.

"It flew into the reflection in the glass," Mom said.

"Why?" I asked. Mom was too focused on the bird to answer me.

"Open the door all the way," she said. "In case it wakes up." I slid the door open and returned to observe the unconscious bird. It was very small with brown and tan feathers and a tiny beak. Mom stroked the bird gently and let us all take a closer look at it.

"It's breathing!" I said, relieved.

A few minutes later, the bird roused from its unconscious state and shook its head and fluffed its feathers. Suddenly, the startled little bird flew right towards the double glass doors again. Luckily, it chose the opened side and made a clean getaway.

We cheered as it flew away.

My mother looked at my father, and he just shook his head and smiled.

Later that week, we went to the NCO Club pool on base to swim.

I was sitting at the edge of the pool, kicking my feet back and forth in the water, when my father came up behind me and asked me why I wasn't getting in the pool?

"Because I can't swim."

"Do you want to learn?" he asked.

"Yes!" I said, and I stood up.

Before I realized what was happening, my father picked me up and threw me into the deep end of the pool.

Even as I floated through the air, I felt a stark sense of betrayal mixed with terror and confusion. Only one thing seemed certain in that split second before I hit the water—I was going to drown.

Splash!

I felt myself go underwater in a swirl of bubbles as I twisted and turned in a panic, trying to figure out which way was up. I was suspended in a no man's land between the top and bottom of the pool, with nothing to grasp onto. I instinctively followed the bubbles as they rose to the surface of the pool, and when I finally broke the surface, I was choking on water and gasping for air.

When I opened my eyes, my father seemed miles away standing at the pool's edge with his hands on his hips. I wanted to scream for help, but I couldn't speak as wave after wave threatened to drown me.

"Swim!" he shouted.

I had never been more scared in my life. Surely, any second now, he would jump in to save me, but he just stood there. The situation was getting dire.

The Paley family shortly after moving into our new house. Circa 1973.

By this time, Nancy had joined my father at the pool's edge and was watching me with a concerned look on her face. She stepped towards me, but my father seemed to say something to her and hold her back.

It was now quite clear to me that I was on my own. *Fine!*

Before I knew it, I managed to lean forward and to pull myself through the water with just my head and shoulders sticking out, and to my surprise, I began to make progress.

By the time I got to the edge of the pool, I was still coughing up pool water and gasping for air, and my father and sister finally reached down to pull me out.

I was *so* mad at my father, and for the first time in my life I wanted to yell at him and tell him what I thought of his 'lesson' I looked up at him with angry, betrayed eyes, my chest heaving for air.

"You did it," he said, as his eyes met mine.

That's when it hit me. I swam. It wasn't pretty, but I did it. The anger lessened within me and I nodded my head.

Tough love.

CHAPTER 10

NOT THE TRIUMPH...

SPRING 1974

Lockbourne Air Force Base Youth Center
Skyhawk Judo Team

My mother thought that taking up the ancient Japanese sport of Judo would be "good for me," so she signed me up for classes at the Air Force Base. The instructor was a black-belt of Filipino descent named Mr. Bernard "Bernie" Ele (pronounced, *Eal-ey*), who was a retired Air Force Master Sergeant. He had an uncanny likeness to Mr. Miyagi of future *Karate Kid* fame.

At my first class, I was handed a uniform and white belt and pointed towards the locker room where I could change. I recall unrolling the white belt and being amazed at how long it was. Stretched out, it was taller than me by nearly double. Surely, my mother must have bought me the wrong-sized uniform? I thought to myself.

I heard Mr. Ele call the class to attention to begin practice, so I quickly put the uniform on and tied the belt around my waste. Then I walked out to join the team for the first time.

As soon as I stepped out the door and turned towards the mat, several kids pointed at me and laughed. Then, the whole team looked at me and laughed.

What was so funny? I wondered, as I felt the blood rush to my head.

Even the Judo instructor stopped talking mid-sentence when he saw me, and I thought I saw him fighting back a smile, too.

Instead of wrapping the belt around my waist twice and tying it in a nice, clean square knot, I had tied it into two big bows which were so long that they reached down to my knees, like *Dumbo* ears.

When I noticed how the other kid's belts were tied, I was humiliated. I wanted to turn around and quit right then and there, and I would have if not for Mr. Ele's pretty teenaged daughters, Marvie and Marissa, who came to my rescue.

Marvie and Marissa were both black belts, and they wore their long, black hair pulled back in tight ponytails. They looked pretty yet tough, like the girls I saw in Bruce Lee movies.

"Let me fix that for you," Marvie said as she untied my belt and showed me the right way to put it on.

"I had trouble the first time I tried to tie my belt too," Marissa lied, giving me a warm smile before she turned back to join the others.

That was the beginning of my record-setting Judo career with Ele's Judo Team. For the next four years, from the age of eight to twelve years old, I would hold the record for the most *losses* in a row in both practice and in tournaments. Despite my being half-Japanese, I proved that pedigree does not always equate to natural athletic ability. Apparently, what I lacked was *fighting spirit.*

It must have been so frustrating for my mother to watch me fight and lose in so many tournaments over the course of four years. My father got so tired of watching me lose that he stopped going to my practices and tournaments altogether, and that made me sad.

I tried hard, but I just couldn't seem to get onto the winner's stand, and sadly, losing—like winning—is a habit that I didn't know how to break.

Despite my embarrassing record, my little sister, Karen was my greatest fan and supporter. Neither she nor my mother ever acted like they were embarrassed when I lost. Each time, they would tell me that I would "do better next time." Though I appreciated their unwavering support and unconditional love, I didn't even want there to be a next time.

Despite all my losses, I did get a "Certificate of Participation" at every tournament I entered, and soon my bedroom wall was covered with them. It was a virtual shrine to mediocrity.

I didn't fare any better in other sports, either. My parents thought that baseball might be my sport (since Judo clearly wasn't) so they signed me up for the Little League baseball team. I was on the *Astros* briefly before the season started.

One day, I was standing in left field with my right hand in my pocket during practice, rocking from left to right in great discomfort, when Coach Darling yelled at me all the way from home plate.

"Paley, get your hand out of your pocket!"

I wanted to tell him that I *couldn't* take my hand out of my pocket, but he was too far away. I saw my mother standing behind the dugout, with a concerned look on her face.

"I said get your hand out of your pocket!" he yelled again.

I did as I was told, and I immediately peed my pants. *There was a reason I had my hand in my pocket!*

I was so ashamed when Coach Darling showed up later that evening to pick up my baseball uniform. I stood in the foyer between my parents as my mother handed him my unused uniform.

"You sure you won't change your mind?" Coach Darling asked me.

I shook my head and tried to hide behind my father. It was clear to me and to my parents that their son was not going to grow up to be an Olympic athlete.

CHAPTER 11

—

MRS. MILLER

1975

Asbury Elementary School
Groveport Madison Local Schools

My third-grade teacher, Mrs. Ellen Miller, was beautiful. Not just because she was pretty, but because she had a kind, generous spirit and a strong belief in God. So deep was her faith in God that she risked her job every morning in defiance of public school regulations to recite the *Lord's Prayer.*

Although my parents raised us with strong morals and values, I had never been to church nor had I ever heard my parents discuss God in the house. Other than what I saw during Christmas time and Easter, I knew nothing about religion.

When Mrs. Miller asked the class to sit in a circle on the rug, close our eyes and bow our heads to recite the *Lord's Prayer,* I snuck one eye open to see how many other kids knew it. They *all* did. I felt embarrassed and humiliated, again. It was quickly becoming a common theme in my young life.

How could my parents have forgotten to teach me this secret chant that all the other kids knew? I wondered.

One day, Mrs. Miller said to the class, "I want to thank Robert for being so patient with us while we recited the Lord's Prayer this past week."

My heart rate increased at being singled out. She must have noticed that I didn't know all the words to it.

"Robert's family's religion is different than ours," she said. "And they don't recite the Lord's Prayer like we do."

The truth was, my immediate family didn't recite any prayers at all, and I couldn't have named the religion she was referring to if my life had depended on it—as it one day would.

Nonetheless, I wasn't surprised when I received backlash for Mrs. Miller's comment about my family being different. A skinny red-head kid named Jeff, who had lots of freckles and sat directly across from me at our assigned table, took the opportunity to make fun of me for being different. Just like Bryce the Bully in West Virginia, Jeff would pull the skin of his eyes back and make fun of me for being half Japanese.

Jeff's harassment and taunts continued day after day until I couldn't take it anymore. In the middle of class, I stood up and walked out, mentioning something about the bathroom, but Mrs. Miller saw right through it.

"Robert," she called as I walked down the hall towards the bathrooms, "Where are you going?"

I didn't want her to see the tears in my eyes, so I only turned halfway toward her and said, "I have to go to the bathroom."

Mrs. Miller walked over to me and kneeled down so that she could talk to me face to face. "Do you want to tell me what's really going on?" she asked.

"I don't want to be different anymore," I said, sobbing.

Mrs. Miller's face showed such compassion as she said, "Different in what way?"

"I don't want to be half-Japanese anymore." Then the waterworks began.

Mrs. Miller smiled and kind of laughed, and said, "Well, there's nothing wrong with being half-Japanese."

"Yes, there is!" I insisted, as I continued to cry. "People make fun of me."

"Aww," Mrs. Miller said as she touched my cheek. "You should be proud to be half-Japanese...*I am.*"

It took a minute for that to sink in, and then I looked at her and understood that she was telling the truth. The tears stopped.

"My father is Japanese," she said. "And I'm very proud of that."

Suddenly, my differentness became a badge of honor, because it gave me something in common with Mrs. Miller who I thought was one of the most amazing people I had ever met.

She stood up and put her hand out to me. "Come on," she said. "Let's go tell the class what we have in common." I smiled and took her hand.

At the end of the school year, Mrs. Miller announced a contest that would test our skills in math and in English. The prize: a weekend stay at Mrs. Miller's family farmhouse out in the country, where we would learn what it was like to live on an active ranch and learn about all the plants and animals on the farm. Two boys and two girls would be selected from each category, and naturally the winners would have to get written permission from their parents.

I couldn't believe it! The chance to spend a weekend on a real farm with Mrs. Miller and her husband, who was a doctor, marked the first time I recall getting motivated about anything in my life. Well, maybe the second.

There was the time when I won a coloring contest for a free foot-long hotdog (with coleslaw) and a Mr. Misty at the Dairy Queen at Big Chimney, but I'm not sure if that counts.

I knew that I didn't have much of a chance in math, but I was beginning to gain confidence in my ability to spell. For some reason, words made sense to me. I made up my mind to study as hard as necessary to try to win both the math and the English contests, just to be sure.

On the day of the contest, I got eliminated in math pretty early, so it came down to a spelling-bee. Tony Simpkins and Diane Caswell won the math contest, so the question was which boy and which girl would win the English contest.

It was a classic boys-against-girls showdown, where all the boys formed a single line and faced-off against all the girls who formed a single line facing them. Each boy and each girl at the front of the line would be given a word, and if they got it right, they would go to the back of the line and continue. If they got a word wrong, they would return to their desk.

I was the last boy standing against two girls, Tracy Joseph and Shelley Volpe, but in order to "win" my spot, I still had to spell my final word correctly. The word was given to Tracy Joseph, first. "Tracy," said Mrs. Miller. "Spell, Soldier."

Tracy cleared her throat, and said, "Soldier. S-o-l…g-e-r? Soldier."

"I'm sorry, but that is incorrect," said Mrs. Miller as Tracy returned to her seat, disappointed.

"Robert, for the win for the boys, spell 'Soldier.'"

I smiled at the irony, though I didn't know it was called irony at the time, and I proceeded to spell it correctly. It was the first time I'd ever won anything, and only later would I appreciate the symbolism of the moment that would eventually change the course of my life forever.

The Miller Farmhouse
Summer, 1975

"Robert, don't go in there!" Diane said. Diane Caswell was a pretty blond-haired, blue-eyed girl with a sensible disposition, and she was one of my better friends.

"She's right," Tony said, "Mrs. Miller specifically warned us not to go in there." Tony Simpkins was smart as a whip, and he even reminded me of a wise owl.

"Who's with me?" I asked again.

"I am," said Shelley with a mischievous glint in her eye as she stepped over the bottom rail of the picket fence to join me. Shelley Volpe was also a pretty blond-haired, blue-eyed girl, and I admired her adventurous spirit.

"Come on," I said to Shelley, as we slowly approached the huge, scary-looking bull that was standing broadside to us about twenty feet away.

"Guys, c'mon!" pleaded Diane. "It's dangerous."

Shhhh! I signaled to Diane and Tony with my finger to my mouth.

I continued creeping closer to the bull, and to my surprise I could feel Shelley's presence right there with me. The bull didn't seem so bad. Maybe we could pet him?

Just then, the bull turned directly towards me and Shelley and snorted; then it pawed at the ground with its forefeet.

"Run!" I shouted. But it was too late.

The bull charged us and was surprisingly fast. I felt it closing in on me, and I was sure that I was about to get gored by the ferocious beast.

Shelley scrambled over the fence, and I followed right behind her, falling to the other side. The bull pulled up just feet from the fence-line and snorted victoriously.

"Whoa!" I said as I realized how close we had come to getting gored by the bull. "Let's get outta' here!"

Our next adventure was on a broken-down, wooden wagon that looked like it came from the old West. From atop the wagon, we decided to play "time machine" as each of us took turns pulling a rusted-out lever that would launch us into each new adventure of our choosing.

Upon arrival at each imaginary destination, we'd get off the wagon to explore the new world, only to be chased by a dinosaur or an alien or an enemy soldier and have to run back to the wagon for safety and another leap in time.

We were completely lost in our imaginary worlds and could have gone on for hours when Mrs. Miller called for us.

"Dinner time!"

We briefly met Doctor Miller, but he wasn't home for long since he was busy doing doctor stuff.

After dinner, Mrs. Miller showed us all the fresh vegetables that were growing in her garden, and then she told us that we were going to go and pick strawberries the next day.

The smell of fresh strawberries filled my nose as I sought the largest, ripest strawberries I could find to put into my basket. Mrs. Miller squatted down beside me and commented on what a good job I was doing. She always said uplifting things to me.

As I reached into a shaded area to pluck a nice-looking strawberry, the strawberry hopped away from me, causing me to jump.

Then, a blackbird with a red and yellow spot on its wings came out of the shadow and looked at me and Mrs. Miller before it flew away.

"I thought it was a strawberry!" I said, laughing.

Mrs. Miller laughed right along with me, then told me it was a red-winged blackbird.

We chatted about lots of things that day, and I appreciated how Mrs. Miller made me feel like I was the most important person in the world. Though I don't recall the topics we discussed anymore, one thing stuck with me that would change the course of my life forever.

"Mrs. Miller," I said. "How do you pray?"

Mrs. Miller looked at me and smiled as she placed a strawberry into my basket.

"You've never prayed before?" she asked.

I shook my head.

"Well, I look at it like writing a letter. You start off with 'Lord', then you say whatever you want to say or to ask for, and then you end it with 'Amen.'"

"That's it?" I said, surprised at how simple it was.

She smiled her big beautiful smile and said, "That's it!"

Then she put her hand over her heart and said, "But it has to come from here."

I didn't know what she meant by that, but I nodded my head just the same.

When the weekend came to an end, none of us wanted to go home. We hadn't watched TV or listened to the radio once, yet we had the time of our young lives.

Life is funny that way, I've learned. In order to truly appreciate the good things, you also have to experience the bad—just to know the difference. That's how the best summer of my life also became the worst summer of my life, and how I knew the difference.

CHAPTER 12

———

THE HOUSE ON
THE CORNER

JULY 1975

Mr. Walter Hodge loved children. He and his family lived in the house on the corner of my street. He was a tall man with thinning hair combed to the side and he wore thick glasses. There wasn't anything that Mr. Hodge wouldn't do for kids.

He had children of his own, a son and two daughters, and he spoiled them with a treehouse and an above-ground pool placed where he could see the kids swimming from the kitchen window or a bedroom window anytime he wanted to. The more kids that came over to his house, the better.

Mr. Hodge claimed to have been wounded in Vietnam, and one of the things he liked to do was bring out a white sheet that had bloodstains on it and tell us it was his blood so that we would feel sorry for him. The more kids that felt sorry for him, the better.

But we shouldn't feel sorry for him, because he believed deeply in God and went to church every Sunday, and he made sure everyone knew it. He even welded a cross on top of his boxy van to show the world that he was a good guy who could be trusted, especially with other people's children.

Mr. Hodge loved children so much that he used his children to get other children to come over to play with them. And on the occasion that a child would go to his house to play with one of his kids, he was always kind enough to invite them in, even if his kids weren't home. And especially if his wife wasn't home.

"Is Alan or Gina home?" I asked as Mr. Hodge approached me on his beat-up, orange riding lawnmower. He obviously couldn't hear me over the din of the motor, but he smiled and cut the engine off as the mower rolled to a stop near me at the corner of his driveway.

"No one's here," he said. He wiped a bead of sweat from his forehead. His eyes seemed magnified as he looked at me through thick glasses.

"Ok," I said. I turned to walk home.

"Do you want to drive the lawnmower?"

I turned back to him, hesitant, but he scooted back on his seat and tapped it between his legs. "You can sit here."

I looked around, waiting for someone to tell me it was okay, but there were no other adults around.

"C'mon," he said. "I'll let you steer."

"Okay," I said. Driving a real riding lawnmower would be fun. I climbed on and Mr. Hodge turned the key and the lawnmower roared to life. He did something with a gear stick and the lawnmower lunged forward.

"Turn left," he said, pointing towards his house. I turned the steering wheel with both hands and we turned towards the house. "Good," Mr. Hodge said. "Straight ahead now."

We circled the small yard on the side of his house twice. I was driving for the first time in my life. I tried to push the gas pedal on the right side of the lawnmower, but my foot couldn't reach it. As we neared the back corner of the house, Mr. Hodge pointed not left, but right. "Turn right," he said. Right? There wasn't anything to cut on the right, he had already mowed the area by the above ground swimming pool. I hesitated. He had a strange look on his face and he leaned into me as he took the wheel and turned it to the right himself.

When we got behind the house near the door that led to the garage, Mr. Hodge shut the engine off and said, "I'm thirsty."

He started to get up, so I jumped down from the lawnmower and decided that I should probably go home. Our house was just across the street and about three houses down, and I wondered if my parents could see me driving the lawnmower. I planned to go home and ask them.

"Are you thirsty?"

I kind of was, so I nodded "yes."

He smiled and bent down to pick me up. "Okay, let's go inside and get something to drink," he said.

I didn't want him to pick me up. I was nine and a half, and no one picked me up anymore.

"I can walk by my—" but the breath was squeezed out of me as Mr. Hodge held me tightly against his chest. He was holding me so high that my hip was near his neck and I had to put my hands on his back to keep from falling over his shoulder like a bag of wheat. Mr. Hodge gently kicked the door to the garage open, stepped inside and then turned to close it. The pungent smell of gasoline filled my nostrils as I looked around to see if the garage was open, but it wasn't.

I heard the metallic "click" of the door locking, followed by the sound of a chain sliding across another lock. *Something wasn't right.*

I wanted to tell him that I had to go home, but I was too scared. The garage was dark and damp, and my mouth felt dry. I no longer wanted something to drink, I just wanted to go home.

Mr. Hodge was a big man, and when I tried to wriggle out of his arms, he held me tighter. He didn't say a word. He just rubbed his hand over the back of my thighs and onto my buttocks, then reached for another door that led to the kitchen. Mr. Hodge stepped quickly up the two steps, turned again, and locked the kitchen door.

Why was he locking all the doors?

I pushed against his back with my hands and arched to try to create space between us, but it was no use.

I thought he was going to put me down to get me a drink like he promised, but instead he carried me into the living room towards the front door.

Not another door, I thought to myself. I couldn't see it, but I could hear it, and it suddenly seemed important for me to listen to the number of locks on the front door.

Click.

CLICK.

Slide.

When Mr. Hodge turned around, I looked at the door to study the locks. A chain on top, a dead-bolt lock, and a push-button lock in the middle of the doorknob. These three locks would surely keep people out, but I didn't want them to keep me in.

I didn't have time to think about that. Mr. Hodge's breathing increased noticeably, and I figured it was because he was getting tired from carrying me.

He knelt down, and my feet touched the floor. I quickly stepped away from him, but the back of my legs hit the couch. Mr. Hodge's eyes were shiny, and he had a strange smile on his face.

"I want to go home," I said, feeling my lip quiver but trying to control it.

"Soon," he said. He pushed me onto the couch and turned me so that I was lying on my back. Mr. Hodge put a small pillow under my head and said, "It'll all be over soon."

As he pulled down my shorts, I concentrated and concentrated until my mind took me away, and soon I was no longer trapped in the living room with Mr. Hodge.

"Get up," he said.

I glanced down and saw that my shorts were back on. *Were they ever off?*

I sat up and swung my legs onto the floor and glanced at the clock. It was now "five minutes until five o'clock," just as Daddy had taught me to say it.

As I started to push myself up off the couch, Mr. Hodge lowered himself, and I recoiled towards the back of the sofa. Mr. Hodge had a strange grin on his face.

"You're not going to tell anybody about this, are you?"

"No," I said, knowing that's what he wanted to hear.

His grin left his face, and he got a serious look that scared me. He put his face really close to mine and said, *"If you tell anyone about this, I will kill your family."*

I ran home without looking back. I ran as fast as my nine- year-old legs could take me, knowing that the boy who ran out the front door was no longer the boy who was carried in the back door. The neighborhood looked the same, but my world had changed forever.

CHAPTER 13

BLOOD BROTHERS

AUGUST 1975

"Why don't you go out and play with your friends?" my mother asked me.

"I don't want to," I said.

For weeks, it seemed, my mother and father tried to get me to go out to play using every parent-trick in their arsenal of parent-tricks, but none of them worked.

I felt bad because I could see the worry and concern on their faces, but there was nothing I could say or do to help them understand what I was going through. I had to protect them, and to do that, I had to learn not to speak all over again.

I watched my friends play with Mr. Hodge's kids from the living room window. I watched them climb up the ladder to the treehouse or run back and forth from the pool behind the house. My friends were in danger, and there was nothing I could do about it.

"I'll kill your family" echoed in my mind day and night, and it scared me even to close my eyes to sleep.

It was no longer the monsters under the bed or in the closet that scared me, but the monster that lived in the house on the corner.

I fought sleep for as long as I could to hide from that monster, but inevitably, darkness would come and so would he.

I knew my parents didn't understand why I'd lost interest in riding my bike or playing with my friends in the neighborhood like I used to do, and I felt bad that I couldn't tell them.

Soon, even my friends stopped coming by to ask me to play with them. I retreated further and further into myself.

Even my older sister, Nancy, seemed worried about me. Nancy and I didn't exactly get along at this time, and we had some massive fights when our parents weren't home.

One day, we got into such a big fight that I tore her Donny Osmond poster in half, right through his teeth. She retaliated by tearing my Bruce Lee poster off my door. Then we went at it like heavyweight boxers.

But lately, she too had noticed the change in me and asked if I wanted to go and play with her and her friends.

"No, way!" I said. Why would I want to play with a bunch of girls?

I got used to the loneliness and isolation and found solace only in music. My bedroom was decked out in fluorescent fishnets and velvet posters which I illuminated with a black light. A portable disco light made my room spin around me as I lay on my bed, mesmerized. It was during this time that I first began to use music to imagine myself not as a weak victim of bullies and monsters, but as a mighty hero capable of protecting my loved ones.

I wanted so badly to be strong and unafraid, and in my mind I could be.

I watched my friends play at the house on the corner for so long that I began to notice something strange. Several of my friends would ride their bikes back and forth past the Hodge house, and even interact with some of the other kids who were playing in the yard, but they never went *into* the yard. Ever.

And now, they were sitting on their parked bikes at the corner opposite the Hodge house, where they always seemed to hang-out.

Curious, I opened our garage and took my bicycle out for the first time in weeks. I rode towards the Hodge house and felt my heart-rate increase with each passing second. I almost stopped and turned around when one of my friends saw me. It was Billy.

"So, you *are* alive," he said, smiling.

My other friends, Phil and Keith, saw me too and seemed sincerely happy to see me. I stopped my bike near their bikes and joined them in watching our friends play across the street. How care-free they all seemed. I was jealous of their ignorance and innocence.

"So, do you guys want to go over there?" I asked.

Each of them answered "no" in their own way, and that's when I knew.

"Can I ask you guys something?" I said.

They all looked at me, and I wondered if they already knew.

"Did Mr. Hodge ever do anything *weird* to you?"

Their reactions told me that they had never discussed it with each other before, but since I brought it up, all three of them nodded their heads. They seemed relieved that I brought it up.

With the sounds of happy, screaming kids in the background, we told each other our individual stories of how Mr. Hodge abducted, molested and raped us. One was molested in his van on the way back from church. One was molested in his van when they went to pick Walnuts. And the other was lured into his house just like I was.

We instantly bonded and acknowledged that Mr. Hodge threatened us and our families, and we made a pact never to tell *anyone* for our family's sake.

Someone had a sharp object of some sort, perhaps a pocket knife, and we decided right then and there to become "blood brothers." We pricked our fingers and squeezed a drop of blood to the surface of our skin, and then we joined our fingers together to mix our blood in a vow of silence for our families' sake.

Suddenly, I didn't feel so lonely anymore.

CHAPTER 14

THE WARRIOR

SEPTEMBER 1975

One night, while we were eating dinner promptly at 5:00 p.m. which was our family custom, the sounds of kids playing at the Hodge House kept drawing my attention away from my food.

"Quit playing with your food and eat, Bobby," my father said.

I nodded and forced myself to take a few bites of my dinner.

How many other kids besides me, Billy, Phil and Keith did the monster hurt? I wondered.

Despite learning that I was not the only one who'd fallen victim to the monster on the corner, I still refused to go out and play like I used to. I was content to stay in my room and lose myself in songs. Bruce Lee movies had caused a nationwide revival in the martial arts, and in every one of his movies he played the reluctant—but unbeatable—hero.

Meanwhile, the Certificates of Participation which lined my bedroom walls reminded me of who I really was. So, to escape from reality, I put on my 45 record of "Kung Fu Fighting" and imagined myself to be a great fighter, capable of defeating all-comers and protecting my friends and loved ones from the monsters of the world.

While I continued to think about the monster on the corner, Nancy finished eating and pushed back from the table. I glanced at her plate to confirm that she had eaten all her food, then turned back to my thoughts.

"Where you going?" my mother asked.

"Gina's house," Nancy said, as she put her plate in the sink and headed for the door.

Gina lived in the house on the corner!

Suddenly, I found myself shouting, "No!" as I ran after Nancy.

"Bobby, what's the matter?" my father asked, as I ran past him.

I ran down the stairs past Nancy and blocked the front door with my back pushed hard against it. I broke out in a cold sweat and felt my heart racing.

Nancy didn't understand and grabbed the doorknob. "Get out of my way," she said as she tried to pull the door open. "What's wrong with you?"

I pushed back harder against the door and it slammed shut.

"Don't go," I said, tears forming in my eyes. "I don't want you to go over...there."

Somehow, she seemed to understand, and she stepped away from the door.

"What's wrong?" she asked with compassion in her voice.

I'd never heard that voice from her before.

"Did something happen to you over there?" she asked.

I didn't know what to say, so I just nodded my head "Yes."

"Did someone hurt you?" she asked. Again, I nodded "Yes."

"Who?" she asked.

Suddenly, I saw his sick face pressed up near mine, his eyes glossy behind his thick glasses. "If you tell anyone what happened, I'll kill your family."

I pursed my lips and looked down at the floor, afraid to speak.

"Was it Mr. Hodge?" I was shocked that she had guessed it, and I looked up at her and nodded, "Yes."

"It's okay," she said. "You can tell me what happened."

I couldn't hold it in anymore. I wasn't sure how to explain it, so I simply said, "He locked me in his house. He pulled down my pants and, and..."

Nancy's eyes widened, then she pulled me to her and hugged me, and I didn't even mind.

"So that's why you...it's okay," she said. "It's okay, you didn't do anything wrong."

She walked back up the stairs with me and said, "You're not in trouble, but I want you to go to your room for a minute, okay?"

I saw my little sister finishing the last of her food, and my father finishing his meal while my mother cleaned up around the stove.

"I thought you were going to Gina's house?" my mother said to Nancy as she put a pan in the sink.

Nancy gently pushed me towards my room and nodded, and I understood. She then told Karen she could go play with her doll, and Karen left the kitchen.

"Mom, I need to talk to you." Nancy said.

I opened my door a crack and peeked out to see what was happening.

"Why are you still here?" my mother asked, pushing past Nancy to pick up a plate.

"Mom!" Nancy said more firmly this time.

This got my mother's attention, and she froze when she saw the look on my sister's face. "What's wrong?"

Nancy began talking in a whisper, and I couldn't hear what she was saying, but I was surprised at how quickly my mother understood.

"What? Who told you this?" my mother asked.

"Bobby did," said Nancy.

"Where is he?" she asked.

"In his room," Nancy said.

I saw my mother walk to the table and pull out her chair next to my father.

"What's wrong?" my father asked when my mother put her hand on his forearm.

Again, my mother spoke too low for me to hear what she said, but my father's reaction told me that now he knew, too.

"What? When? *I'll kill that son of a bitch!*"

My father's chair pushed back hard, and the legs squeaked as he got up and started walking towards his room. His footsteps were heavy and ominous. I thought I was in trouble, so I quickly shut my door as he walked by my room towards his.

"No, Daddy!" shouted Nancy as she ran by my room chasing after my Dad.

"Not like this, Jerry!" shouted my mother as she too ran past my room chasing my father.

I quickly opened the door and looked down the hallway into my parent's room. My father was removing a rifle from his closet and taking it out of its case.

"I'll kill that son of a bitch!" he said again.

Nancy was crying, and my mother continued pleading with my father, but it was no use.

I was terrified, but when I heard my father pull the bolt of the rifle back, load it with a bullet and slam the bolt forward, an inexplicable feeling of calm came over me. In that moment, my fear of Mr. Hodge left me. I never felt as safe in my life as I did in that moment, knowing that my father would risk his life to protect us, just like he did in the Korean and Vietnam Wars.

My mother and sister bravely stood in front of my father, blocking him so he couldn't exit through his bedroom door.

"Let me by," my father said. *"I'll kill him!"*

He had a look on his face that I had never seen before—and that's when I realized that the warrior had been awakened within my father.

For a moment everyone stood frozen, except for my little sister Karen, who stepped behind Nancy and my mother, crying and confused.

"Daddy," Karen said, and that was enough to stop my father in his tracks.

My father's pained face softened as he seemed to consider his options. Then he pulled the bolt of the rifle back, ejecting the bullet, and nodded his head.

He put the rifle back in its case and asked, "Where's Bobby?"

Relieved, both my sister and mother pointed towards my room. I quickly shut my door and sat on my bed, uncertain of what to expect.

My father knocked gently on the door and opened it. He stepped inside and then sat down beside me on my bed.

"Do you want to tell me what happened?"

I looked up at him and didn't know what to say. I didn't know how to explain what that monster did to me.

"It's okay, you're not in trouble," he said. *"You didn't do anything wrong."*

"But he said he would kill our family if I ever told anyone," I said, tears forming in my eyes.

My father turned towards me and put his hands on my shoulders. "I want you to listen to me. That bad man will never hurt you or anyone in our family ever again, I promise."

And with that, all the months of holding it in were released and I cried in my father's arms, I cried until there were no more tears left to cry.

CHAPTER 15

STORM CLOUDS

1978

Three years later.

In late January 1978, the Midwest and Great Lakes regions of the United States suffered an historical blizzard which shut down schools and commerce for weeks. For me and my friends, it was a godsend!

The snow was so deep that entire cars were covered from the snowdrifts, and chain linked fences that separated backyards from each other were easy to step over as me and my friends turned the winter wonderland into one giant battlefield for snowball fights. Unfortunately, our extended winter vacation was about to be cut short.

My father didn't like the fact that so many kids were missing school, so he called all the parents in our neighborhood and told them that come the next Monday morning, classes would be held in our living room for children of all grade levels, with him as the teacher. How embarrassing!

"Tell them to bring their books," he instructed.

I was surprised to see that most of the kids in the neighborhood showed up on time for the first day of "school." And they even brought their books!

It was obvious from the looks on their faces, however, that Nancy's friends—who were freshman—weren't too happy about being there.

Winter coats and children's boots of all shapes, sizes, and colors were stacked in the foyer by the door, and our living room was packed with kids sitting in a semi-circle on the floor around my father, who was seated on the couch with selected encyclopedias next to him.

"Who knows what the Ozone Layer is?" he asked. And then he proceeded to teach us all about it using the encyclopedia as a reference. Kid's hands shot up whenever my father asked a question, and each time, he picked someone other than me or Nancy to provide an answer.

School lasted from morning until lunchtime, and then we were released for the rest of the day. I don't recall any other classes he taught us that week, but I never forgot his lesson about the Ozone Layer.

Holding classes when school was canceled wasn't the only embarrassing thing our father did once we'd moved to Ohio.

Another instance occurred when we were in elementary school.

Nancy and I were running late one day, so my father drove us to school and dropped us off at the turn-around where the flagpole was. The patrols were just about to raise the American flag, and to our horror my father opened his car door, came to attention, and saluted as the flag rose.

Nancy and I waited impatiently for him to drop his salute while we stood at a loose position of attention on the other side of the car. Rather than honor the flag, we glanced around self-consciously. We weren't at an army post anymore, so why did he continue to do that?

Nothing was worse at that age than standing out, and as soon as our father dropped his salute, we took off for the school without even saying good-bye.

One day, I went to White's Pharmacy with my father to pick up a prescription.

"These should help you sleep," said Dr. White, as he handed my father a bottle of pills. *Why would anyone need pills to fall asleep? I wondered.*

While they were talking, I came across some plastic airplane models and picked up a Douglas X-3 jet I thought looked really cool. I carried it over to the register and asked my father if he would buy it for me.

"You want to build a model?" my father asked. I nodded.

"Then you'll need this," said Doctor White, placing an orange tube of plastic model glue on the counter.

I didn't know I had to actually assemble the model when I asked my father to buy it for me, but when I got home and opened it I embraced the challenge of taking something that was all in pieces and putting it back together. Soon, my room would be filled with model airplanes.

While my father was taking sleeping pills, I continued to try *not* to fall asleep. Though the nightmares had lessened considerably since I was nine, my imagination continued to get the best of me.

On several occasions, I was *sure* I heard the screen door which led to the backyard open and close. My room was in the middle of the hallway, just above the back door, and I did my best to remain awake as long as possible so I could hear anyone trying to come in. Unfortunately, sleep would overtake me eventually, and I would have to surrender to the night.

Every time I told my parents about hearing strange sounds during the night near the back door, they would brush it off and tell me "It's only the wind." *There sure was a lot of wind out back,* I thought to myself.

In my overactive imagination, I was sure it was Mr. Hodge trying to sneak in to fulfill his pledge to kill my family. But that was impossible, I knew, since Mr. Hodge was in jail. Despite the pact of my blood brothers, we did tell our stories to the court and were told we'd done a brave thing when it was all over.

The detectives who helped us during the trial came by afterwards and told our parents they'd overheard the Hodge family making threats towards the families of those who testified, and our parents told us that if we ever saw anyone from the Hodge family, we were to run to the nearest adult and ask them to call the police.

This admonition by my parents is probably what had scared me so much over the years and caused my imagination to run wild.

One day, when my brother was visiting from flight school in Vero Beach, Florida, I heard him talking to my father in the kitchen in a low tone. Phil's childhood dream was to be a fighter pilot, but he'd unfortunately dropped out of Air Force ROTC at Ohio University, and he was now pursuing his private pilot's license. I admired him for sticking to his goal to fly.

Curious—or nosy—I snuck out of my room and put my back to the wall adjacent to the kitchen, so I could hear what they were talking about.

"So, if I shoot him as soon as he steps foot in our yard—" my father said.

"You'll go to jail," said my brother. "He has to be in the house for you to legally shoot him in self-defense."

Shoot who? I wondered.

"Fine," my father said, "I'll shoot him as soon as he steps in the yard, and then I'll drag him into the house."

This caused them both to laugh hard, but I didn't get the joke.

CHAPTER 16

THE STORM

SPRING 1978

I was in my room listening to a record and building another airplane model when the phone rang in the kitchen.

"Bobby, telephone," my mother shouted.

I walked to the kitchen and took the phone from my mother.

"Hello?" I said.

"Hi, Robert, it's Diane." It was my childhood friend, Diane Caswell, who went to Mrs. Miller's farmhouse with me when we were in the third grade.

"Hi!" I said, happy to hear from her.

"Robert, are you sitting down?"

What a strange question. "No, why?"

"Mrs. Miller died," Diane said.

"What?" I sat down.

"When?" I asked as my heartrate increased.

"Yesterday," said Diane. I couldn't believe what I was hearing.

"But, didn't she just have a baby?" I said.

"Yes," said Diane, "last year. The baby's fine, but Mrs. Miller died due to some kind of sudden illness."

"I can't believe this," I said. I felt a numbness engulf me as I processed what Diane was saying.

"The viewing will be in Groveport. I'll call you later and let you know the details," Diane said. I could tell she was crying.

"Thank you," I said as I hung up the phone.

Myers Funeral Home
Groveport, Ohio

When Mom and I walked into the funeral home, I saw the familiar faces of teachers I knew from both elementary school and the middle school. Everyone's eyes were red, and everyone was speaking in hushed tones.

The funeral director pointed me and Mom towards a room in the back, where I saw Doctor Miller holding his infant son in his arms. That broke my heart.

To my surprise, Doctor Miller was smiling as he talked to some guests I didn't recognize. I knew the Millers were deeply religious people, and somehow this gave them a strength in times like this that I just didn't understand.

As Mom and I approached Mrs. Miller lying in her coffin, she somehow looked just as beautiful as ever. She looked like she was at peace and was just sleeping, and at any moment she would wake up and everything would be okay. *How I wanted her to be okay again.*

Mrs. Ellen Miller

I'd never seen a dead person before, and my mind was having trouble believing that this beautiful lady, who was only in her twenties, was gone. Mom touched Mrs. Miller's hand and seemed to say a silent prayer for her. Mom really liked Mrs. Miller, and I recall them speaking about their common Japanese heritage on several occasions.

"Come here," Mom said, "It's okay."

I stepped beside Mom and paid my respect to my teacher. I touched Mrs. Miller's hand and was shocked at how cold it was.

"Goodbye," I whispered, fighting back tears.

During the service, people spoke of Mrs. Miller's life and how active in and dedicated she was to her church. They spoke of Heaven having a new angel. They spoke of how happy Mrs. Miller must be to be with Jesus at last. I tried my best to understand what they were saying, but none of it made sense to me.

She was good. Why would God or Jesus or anyone take her when she'd just had a baby? It just didn't seem fair to me.

When the service was over and we were driving home, Mom said, "I thought you would cry more."

I stared out the window, numb, and said, "I only cry when I'm alone."

Years later, I would learn that Mrs. Miller knew that she had contracted cancer while she was pregnant, but she refused treatment in order to protect the life of her unborn child. Though it broke my heart, I would not have expected anything less from her. There is simply no love stronger than the love of a mother for her child.

CHAPTER 17

———

COACH RUSH

SUMMER 1978

At the end of my sixth-grade year, I decided I wanted to try baseball again to redeem myself from my earlier humiliation of peeing in my pants.

It was clear to me that Judo still wasn't my sport, and I just wanted to win at something, *anything*, so that my father would be proud of me.

Over the past few years, he'd stopped attending all of my sporting events for some reason, and I figured it was because he was ashamed of me.

I was placed on a team that had the worst record in the league--the Rangers. Our team was so bad the other kids in the league nicknamed us the "Bad News Rangers"—a reference to a movie called "The Bad News Bears" that had come out a few years earlier. My coach, Bobby Rush, didn't like the nickname, and neither did we. Coach Rush was a stocky, athletic man who carried himself with an air of authority. He was tough but compassionate, and he was determined to turn the team around.

Though I still lacked natural athletic ability, Coach Rush took an interest in me early on and spent extra time with me during batting practice. I whiffed a lot, but when I finally *did* make contact with the ball, it usually went deep into the outfield.

Taking a chance on me, Coach Rush placed me at the honored fourth spot in the line-up, the "clean-up" batter position, but unfortunately, I got too nervous during games, struck-out, and eventually lost that spot. In fact, I got benched. Perhaps I was trying *too* hard? I just couldn't seem to excel in sports...but that was about to change.

My first real girlfriend was a girl named Angie Swallow, and her little brother Jimmy was the biggest baseball fan I'd ever known. Every time I went over to Angie's house after school, Jimmy had his portable radio with him listening to a *Reds* game. It was his dream to grow up to play Major League baseball, but as luck would have it, he was flat-footed and couldn't even play on the little league teams.

I don't know what made Jimmy do it, but one day he gave me a copy of his favorite book. It was about a little boy who dreamed of playing baseball but lacked athletic ability. That got my attention!

The boy was so bad, in fact, that he couldn't even make it through team try-outs. Then one day, an old man nobody knew showed up while the boy was trying out for the team, and the boy's "luck" changed. He not only made the team, but he had a dream season, hitting the winning homerun against his team's rival during the last game of the season.

When the game was over, the little boy decided to give the game ball to that loyal old man who attended every game. When the boy turned to the bleachers, however, the old man was gone. The little boy tossed the ball up in the air, and when it came down, he dropped it. The old man was an angel, and he'd come to give the boy his dream for one season, and just one season.

The book moved me, though I can't recall its title, and I wondered if an old man/angel was in the cards for me. I was still wrestling with the whole God thing after Mrs. Miller's death, and I wasn't ready to accept that there was a Higher Power. If there was, how could someone as beautiful and devoted to God be taken away at such a young age?

Though I was no longer a major factor in the Rangers' game plan, I did get to play enough to develop some confidence in myself, and by the middle of the season, the Rangers finally won a game. Coach Rush masterfully developed each "underdog" on the team to believe in their abilities, and one day it seemed like everything just "clicked" for us. We were tired of being the underdogs and the laughing stocks of the league, and while no one was looking, we gelled as a team and came close to winning the final two or three games of the season.

The last game of the season proved to be a true *David and Goliath* story of the league. The Bad News Rangers team with one win was going up against the league champion Reds, who were undefeated.

The Reds team was stacked with some of the most talented athletes in Groveport Madison. They had a future high school All-State Quarterback, Chris Downing, and future Varsity Baseball star, Barry Cyrus, on their team, just to name a few.

No one thought the Rangers had a chance, but we had grown to care about each other as we fought our way out of some tough situations throughout the season, thanks to the inspired leadership of Coach Rush.

We got to the point as a team where we loved and respected each other, and we would not lie down for anyone—not even the Reds.

As I sat on the bench and watched the drama unfold in front of me, I was so proud of the guys on my team. They played their hearts out. Meanwhile, I continued to warm the bench.

The Reds weren't expecting us to play this way, and they became frustrated with each passing inning.

The assistant coach's son, John Feldmeier, pitched outside of himself that day as he "brought-it" to the Reds' line-up, inning after inning.

Word quickly spread to the teams that had just finished playing at the other diamond that the "Rangers were tied with Reds," and whole teams plus their fan base came over to watch the dramatic final innings. All of them stood behind our bench, hoping for an upset of epic proportions.

I'd never seen anything like it before, and I was just glad to be a small part of it. I sat at the end of the bench and watched it all play out. The dirty uniforms of both teams were testament to the battle this game had become, but my uniform was spotless. Coach Rush must have forgotten to put me in the game in all the excitement.

It was the top of the last inning, and the game was tied 2-2. That alone was already a victory for the Rangers, and everyone knew— expected in fact—that the Reds would find a way to beat us at their last at-bat at the bottom of the inning, just as they'd done so many times before.

The first Rangers' batter got up to bat and struck out. The tension was mounting as people in nearby houses hopped their fences to see what all the excitement was about.

The next Rangers' batter got up to bat, and he too, struck out.

The Reds' pitcher Barry Cyrus was throwing heat!

My buddy, Tommy Gunn, a stout African American kid with a big heart and a big smile, got up to bat. He bravely covered the base with his full size and didn't flinch when he got hit by the pitch. He literally took one for the team, and I admired his courage. He advanced to first base, representing our potential go-ahead run.

Finally, Norman Fry stepped into the batter's box. Norman was a fierce competitor but not the most athletic guy on our team, and his red face showed the pressure that he was under. We were at the bottom of our line-up.

The audience on both sides had worked themselves up to a fever pitch, and everyone from both teams was on their feet.

When I saw the pressure Norman was under, I recall thinking, *"I'd sure hate to be him right now."*

That's when I noticed that Coach Rush, who was standing at first base, was looking my way. I looked behind me to see who he was looking at, but no one else was there.

Finally, Coach Rush called time-out and jogged down the first base line to home plate. He put his arm around Norman and said something to him, and I assumed he was giving him a pep-talk. Good idea, ice the pitcher.

Suddenly, Norman's face turned even redder than it already was, and he walked out of the batter's box towards the bench.

"What's going on?" I asked as Norman walked past me and threw down his helmet and his bat.

"Paley! Get your helmet on," shouted Coach Rush.

What?!

"Come on, new batter," said the umpire.

I was not prepared at all to bat, and I felt a surge of adrenalin and fear run through me as I spastically tried to find a helmet that would fit me. The first one, way too tight. The next one, way too loose. The third one, just right. Almost.

The important thing, however, was to find my "lucky" Louisville Slugger bat, which was dark blue and had a fat handle—it was like swinging a tree. I looked at all the bats leaning against the backstop, and to my horror it wasn't there.

"Batter up!" shouted the umpire.

"Hurry up, Paley," shouted Coach Rush. "What's the matter?"

"I can't find my bat, Coach," I moaned. My lucky bat. It seems to have just disappeared.

"Just grab any bat, let's go," Coach said. And so I did.

As I walked out to home plate, I heard a few of my friends chant my name, "Paley! Paley!" and I admit that I liked the sound of that. But I had a big problem that they weren't aware of. This bat was too light and too thin at the grip.

How am I going to hit the ball with a bat like this?

I was defeated before I'd even stepped into the batters' box. I had already made excuses for my imminent failure, embarrassment, humiliation, and demise—all before the first pitch!

I wanted so badly to be the hero, and I would have been, if only I'd had my lucky bat! I could already hear my excuses, and I felt pathetic.

I stepped into the batters' box, completely aware of all the eyes that were on me and of all the screaming fans on both sides of the diamond.

Meanwhile, Barry Cyrus was the picture of calm and cool on the pitcher's mound. He nodded, checked Tommy at first base, squinted his eyes, and threw the first pitch.

Swing and a miss.

"*Striiiiike!*" shouted the Umpire.

Dang, was he good! I thought to myself. I had never faced a pitcher like Barry before. I didn't even see the ball go by me.

I shook my head and stepped out of the batter's box. I looked down the third base line to take the hand signals from Coach Feldmeier, and he gave me the "swing away" signal.

I stepped back into the batter's box and could feel my whole body shaking with nervous energy. Barry squinted again as he focused all his attention on his next pitch. His straight blond hair stuck out all around his cap, and his gaze was intimidating.

The wind-up, the pitch. Swing and a miss.

"*Striiiiike two!*" shouted the umpire.

I was determined that if I was going to go down, I'd go down swinging.

The crowd was really going wild, and I saw Coach Rush remove his baseball cap and push his hair back, wondering if he'd made the wrong decision. I was wondering the same thing. *I sure could use that old man from Jimmy's book right now.*

I stepped out of the batter's box again, took the "swing away" arm signal from Coach Feldmeier (combined with the sign of the cross, I believe) and then looked down the first base line to where my mother and little sister were sitting.

There, in the midst of the crowd that was going crazy all around her, sat my mother on her lawn chair—the calm in the storm. Our eyes met, and she smiled at me and nodded as she literally sat on the edge of her seat, her hands clasped together.

I thought I saw her mouth the words, "Come on, Bobby!" She always maintained her Japanese decorum.

Meanwhile, my little sister Karen was under no such cultural constraints, and she was on her feet screaming at the top of her lungs for me and the Rangers.

I then scanned the crowd, hoping against hope to see my father there, but he wasn't there.

Then I scanned my bench, and I saw all the guys who'd played their hearts out to get us to this point in the game, who'd given their all, and the magnitude of the moment hit me. *This isn't about me.*

I stepped out of the batter's box again and asked the ump to clean the plate. I turned towards Coach Feldmeier again as I heard the umpire complain that the plate was already clean.

Please, please, please...

"Batter up," said the Umpire.

I needed help. I couldn't do this alone.

As I looked down the third base line, the Reds' team and fans filled my view out of the corner of my eye. But beyond them, something else also caught my attention. It was the window to my third-grade classroom, Mrs. Miller's classroom.

Then came her image, at the strawberry patch, her hand on her heart. *"But it has to come from here."*

I bowed my head and looked down at my feet, as if I were checking my cleats, and I *felt* the words that came out of my mouth.

"Please be with me Lord, Amen."

It was a home run.

Tommy Gunn crossed home plate, and then I did, and our team embraced us. Coach Rush's face was beaming with pride, and his daughter Karen had tears in her eyes.

I ran into the arms of my Mom and little sister, and we jumped for joy together.

The Reds' were frazzled, and John Feldmeier secured our victory with clutch pitching. Coach Rush said, "Everyone, to the Dairy Queen!" I got a Peanut Buster Parfait, and it was the best one I ever had.

Later that evening, when I got home, I walked downstairs to the basement feeling light as air. I tossed my blue baseball cap onto the chair, then plopped down onto the couch to contemplate what had just happened. Then I looked up and said, "Thanks, God."

Little did I know then that my new-found faith would soon face the ultimate test.

CHAPTER 18

———

HOME

I don't recall how I spent the rest of the summer after that game-winning home run, but it was clear to me something special had happened on that baseball diamond after I whispered the first prayer of my life. As soon as I said, "*Amen*," a peaceful, warm energy washed over me from the top of my head down to my toes. I felt a tingling sensation and could feel the hairs on the back of my neck stand up—like a low electric current had charged my entire body.

I recall being aware that something special was happening, and as the energy passed through my torso, I felt all fear and nervousness leave me. When I turned back towards home plate, I couldn't hear the audience screaming anymore. All I could hear was the sound of my own breathing.

In that moment I had no past and no future. There was only the here and now—and it seemed to be happening in slow motion.

I hit home plate with my bat and felt the vibrations run through my body, adding to the energy within me.

I was aware of the movements of the players on the field and of the audience along the baseline as I brought my bat back, but there was still no sound except for my own breathing. I saw Barry go through his usual routine and I sunk down into my stance and felt myself relax as I waited for the pitch.

Everything came down to this moment.

The wind up, the pitch.

"Swing!" shouted Coach Rush as the pitch came flying towards me at full-speed.

I let loose like a coiled spring and felt the bat make contact with the ball. I watched as the ball rose and rose towards right field, where Chris Downing moved under it for what should have been an easy catch. Coach Rush was wind-milling his arm and shouting, "Go! Go!" as I approached first base. I got to first base just as the ball hit Chris' glove and I started to slow down, when suddenly it became clear that the ball somehow fell out of his glove.

Realizing what happened, I shouted, "Go Tommy!" I nearly caught up with him as he rounded second base.

As Tommy and I turned towards third, Downing's powerful arm threw what looked like a line-drive all the way from right field to the third baseman, who was waiting to tag Tommy out. Chris' accuracy was absolutely incredible as the ball passed by me and then Tommy and beat us both to third base.

I thought it was all over, but just as the ball hit the third baseman's glove it ricocheted off the tip and then went out of bounds. Coach Feldmeier wind milled his arm sending both me and Tommy home.

And getting home is what it's all about.

CHAPTER 19

———

BROKEN

It was sometime in the late summer or early fall of 1978 when the Vietnam War came home to my family.

My mother, sisters, and I had gone shopping for groceries, and when we got home, I ran to the front door to open it.

"Hey, take some bags with you," shouted Nancy. I just ignored her as usual. She was always telling me what to do.

I burst into the house expecting to see my father sitting in his usual armchair reading a novel while a Western or war movie played on the television, but instead—silence.

"Dad?" I said, too low at first. Then louder, "Dad!"

Karen bumped into me as she too entered the house. Our black and white Shitzu dog, Fi-fi, poked her head out from behind the couch, afraid to come out.

"Where's Daddy?" Karen asked instinctively.

"I don't know," I said, feeling my heart rate increase.

Nancy and Mom came in right behind us with a grocery bag in each arm. Nancy mumbled something about me and Karen blocking the door when she, too, noticed the silence.

We exchanged worried looks.

"Daddy!" I shouted again.

Nancy put the grocery bags on the bottom step and climbed the stairs calling for our father.

She stopped cold when she noticed a note on the floor at the top of the stairs. She picked it up to read it, then she looked down at my mother with a worried look on her face.

"They took him," she said.

"Who took him?" My mother asked as she dropped the grocery bags at her feet in the foyer and ascended the stairs.

"The police," Nancy said. Karen and I stood frozen, and I pulled her close to me. I had no idea what was going on, but I knew it wasn't good.

"It says that he called them," Nancy said as she re-read the letter out loud for our Mom. "He asked them to take him away because he wasn't thinking straight and he was afraid he'd hurt—" Nancy stopped herself and looked at me and Karen.

"Where'd they take him?" Mom asked.

"To a hospital, to a...mental hospital."

"Mental hospital?" my Mom asked as she took the note from Nancy.

My heart-rate increased as my mother dialed the rotary phone, then told whomever she was talking to that my father needed a medical hospital and not a mental hospital. She demanded that they transfer him to a medical hospital immediately and said she'd be there as soon as possible.

When she hung up the phone, Nancy asked, "Is it happening again?" and my mother nodded her head.

"Is what happening again?" I asked, but neither of them answered me.

"We have to go the hospital to see Daddy," Nancy said, "Come on."

My mother took Karen by the hand as she walked out the door, and Nancy followed closely behind them. I looked at the grocery bags sitting on the floor, confused, then turned to follow them. As I got to the screen door, I froze. *Mrs. Miller died in a hospital,* I thought to myself.

Nancy was halfway to the car when she noticed that I hadn't come out yet.

"Come on! Daddy needs us."

"I'm not going," I said.

Nancy stopped in her tracks. "What did you say?"

My heart felt heavy and tears formed in my eyes.

"I said, I'm not going."

Nancy was about to say something else when Mom said, "It's okay, he's old enough to stay home if he wants to."

Nancy shook her head in disgust and got in the car. As they drove away, I saw Karen's little hand waiving at me from the back window, and I held up my hand to wave back.

After the car drove out of sight, I shut the front door and looked up to my father's reading chair, where an unfinished book lay opened on the end table. That's when the tears began to flow.

The house was so quiet, and I'd never felt more alone.

"What's happening?" I yelled to no one particular. I walked to the basement and tried to comprehend what had just transpired.

"Please don't take my Daddy, too." I whispered, sensing that he was in trouble.

My father was my rock, and the leader of our family. I couldn't imagine life without him. I sat down on the couch and felt the tears stream down my cheeks. Sadness welled up from deep within me, followed by anger. I stood up and looked out the window towards the grey, gloomy sky and shouted, "Why are you doing this?"

I went from the ultimate high early in the summer to another low, and this time I felt like it would break me. I simply couldn't imagine life without my father.

I was desperate for answers, and that's when I saw the baseball in the china cabinet. I walked over to the China cabinet, removed the baseball and wondered if the prayer and the homerun that followed ever really happened at all?

Then I was struck by a horrible thought. What if God only gives each person one answer to their prayers, and I blew mine on a stupid baseball game? That thought threw me into a panic, and I began to negotiate with God.

"Lord, if you're there, please...give me a sign."

CHAPTER 20

———

THE BOX

I was seated at my desk drawing pictures of clouds with lightning bolts coming out of them when I heard my mother and sisters return from the hospital. Their eyes were bloodshot.

"How is he?" I asked.

"He has to have emergency brain surgery tomorrow morning," Nancy said, almost as if she wanted her words to hurt me. She still seemed angry at me for not going with them earlier.

"Surgery?" I said. It was worse than I had imagined.

Nancy's face softened, and she said, "Yes, he has water on the brain. They have to operate immediately to relieve the pressure."

I nodded, then went to my bedroom.

I was lying on my bed staring at the ceiling when my mother came into my room. She looked so tired.

"Did Nancy tell you what's happening?" she asked.

"Yeah," I said, as I sat up on the edge of my bed. "Surgery in the morning?"

My mother nodded and sat down on the bed beside me.

"What's wrong with him?" I asked.

"Vietnam disease," she said. "He caught a bug when he was in Vietnam. High temperature."

"Is that why he can't hear?" I asked.

My mother nodded. "Phil's coming home tomorrow," she said.

That's when I knew things were serious.

"Is Dad going to—" I chose my next word carefully. "Live?"

My mother looked at me, but she didn't answer. My heart sunk to my stomach.

"Why did he get sick again?" I asked.

"No reason," she said. "It just came back."

It was at that moment that I realized I might lose my father, and I didn't even really know much about him or his time in the Army. As if she read my mind, she said, "I'll be right back."

She went to her bedroom and I heard her open, then close her bedroom closet. A moment later, she returned with a tattered office-sized box.

"What's that?" I asked.

"Daddy's Army stuff," she said.

She opened the flaps of the box and I saw certificates, plaques and medals filled to the top.

"Take a look," she said. "I have to go call the hospital."

I nodded, then turned to sit on the middle of the bed with my legs crossed. I pulled the box closer and felt a sense of anticipation as remnants of my father's military career waited to tell me their story.

I reached into the box and picked up the first document that lay on the top. It was his retirement certificate from the Army. He served for 23 years on Active Duty, retiring in 1973.

I continued to study each and every item with great curiosity, and little by little each certificate, award, plaque and medal painted a picture of my father's military career. I sorted each item by type, creating neat, organized piles on my bed.

Somewhere in the middle of the box, I found a leather box filled with medals. The medals were all tangled together, and I spent several minutes untangling them and neatly laying them on my bed. The next leather box surprised me. It was a black, rectangular box with gold trim and the words, "Purple Heart" centered on the front of it. "Wow," I said to myself. I didn't know my father had earned a Purple Heart. I opened the box and marveled at the beauty of it. This one, I knew, was paid for in blood.

How did I not know any of this about my own father? I wondered.

When I got to the bottom of the box, I found a piece of black cloth smashed down flat. I picked it up, puffed it up and then studied it. It was some kind of skullcap, one-inch high all around with a circle on top. I'd have to ask my mother about this one.

Then I found my father's dog tags. There were two identical tags hanging on a small circular chain, and that one was attached to a longer chain that was worn around the neck.

I read the dog tags and saw my father's name, "Paley, Jerome" written across the top. Then I saw some kind of serial number, followed by another number, then blood type and religion.

When I read the religion part, I was shocked: JEWISH. *Jewish? My father's Jewish?*

No wonder we never get any Christmas cards!

I don't know how or why I didn't know this, but I didn't. I thought that wearing the "beanie" or yarmulke at family occasions was part of some sort of costume or something, and only now was it all starting to add up. It was very strange to learn about half of my genealogical and religious heritage from a worn-out box, and I wondered if it was the "Jewish God" that had answered my prayers.

I picked up the yarmulke and placed it on top of my head, but it slid off to the side. I put it on again, this time on the crown of my head, and it fit perfectly.

I'll have to look into this Jewish stuff more later, I thought, as I removed the yarmulke and placed it on the bed.

Finally, at the bottom of the box I found a leather case which felt much heavier than the others. The contents of this one perplexed me. There were about eighteen silver dollars in it, dating back to the 1950s.

I picked up one of the silver dollars and studied it.

My mother walked back into my room and saw what I was holding.

"Those mean more to Daddy than anything else," she said.

"They do?" I asked, incredulous. "Why?"

The thought of my father collecting coins seemed as contradictory to me as John Wayne collecting butterflies…what did coins have to do with the Army, anyway? I wondered.

"Silver dollars," my mother said, smiling. "Each one was given to Daddy by an officer."

"Wasn't Daddy an officer?" I asked.

"No, he was a Sergeant Major," she said. "Highest rank for sergeants."

"Wow," I said, impressed.

"He wanted to go to West Point and become an officer," she said, "But he gave it up to marry me."

"What's West Point?" I asked.

"The Military Academy," she said. "You know, where General MacArthur and Patton went."

"Oh, yeah!" I said. That sounded familiar to me.

She smiled and seemed to be lost in thought. "That's how I know how much he loves me," she said.

"Have you ever been there?" I asked.

"Of, course!" she said. "Many times. You have too, when you were little. Every time we go to New York City on leave, Daddy takes us to West Point to watch a parade." It was obvious by the way my mother smiled as she talked about West Point that it had special meaning for her, too. I was intrigued.

She picked up a silver dollar and told me the tradition.

"When an officer gets commissioned," she said, "he gives a silver dollar to the first sergeant who salutes him. It's a big honor for the sergeant to be asked," she said. "Only one first salute."

I thought that was the coolest military tradition I'd ever heard of, and then I looked at all the silver dollars in my father's box with new appreciation. Did the officers who gave them to him survive the Korean or Vietnam wars?

My mother got up to leave, and suddenly I had an inspiration. It was so clear and vivid in my mind and in my heart that it was impossible to consider it anything other than a vision, a glimpse into the future.

"Mom, do you have a silver dollar for this year?" I asked as she approached my bedroom door.

"I don't know," she said, curious. "I don't collect them as much anymore since they're not all silver," she said.

"That's not why I want it," I said.

"Okay, I'll check."

I heard her rummaging through her coin collection which she kept in her jewelry box, and a few minutes later she returned with a 1978 Eisenhower silver dollar.

"Found one," she said, handing it to me. "What do you want it for?"

"For Daddy," I said, without any hesitation or doubt. "Mom, not only is Daddy going to survive his surgery tomorrow, but someday he is going to give me my first salute when I become an Army officer."

"You want to be an officer?" my mother said.

"I *will* be an officer," I said, with more certainty than I've ever said anything in my life.

My mother seemed visibly moved by my declaration. She turned to leave my room and I said, "Mom, I'm going to West Point."

"Daddy will be very proud," she said, tears forming in her eyes.

CHAPTER 21

———

MINN

It was nice to have Phil home again, but Daddy's empty seat at the dinner table left a big hole in our family. Daddy survived his surgery and was recovering in the Intensive Care Unit. I still refused to go to the hospital to see him.

Grandma Minn was flying in from Florida, and soon we would be leaving for the airport to go and pick her up.

"One time we were visiting Grandma at her condo in Florida," Phil said, "and we asked her to take us down to the pool to go swimming." "I remember this," said Nancy, smiling.

"So, when we got down to the pool, there was this beach-bum look-ing dude with long hair standing at the entrance," Phil said, a smile forming on his lips.

"The kid pointed to a sign that said only three guests were allowed in the pool per resident, so Grandma put her hands on her hips, looked at each one of us, and said, 'Which one do you want me to kill?'"

That made us all laugh, and it was nice to laugh again.

"But then what happened?" I asked, concerned. I was a little slow on the uptake.

"Well, she didn't kill any of us," Phil said. "The pool boy thought it was funny, too, and he let us all go in." Grandma was a force to be reckoned with, and she usually got her way.

Columbus International Airport

"Grandma!" I shouted as soon as she came into view.

Grandma Minn was like a female version of Winston Churchill, without the cigar. She was short, strong, and formidable, and her slightly hunched back made her waddle left and right when she walked, like a battleship in rough seas.

Her eyes lit up behind her thick glasses when she saw us.

"My bubala," she said, as she grabbed my cheeks and planted a wet kiss on my forehead. She did the same to each of us children.

"When are you leaving, Grandma?" I asked as we walked towards baggage claim.

"Bobby!" my mother said.

"Leaving? I just got here!" my grandmother said, smiling.

"I mean, how long can you stay?"

"We'll see," said my grandmother as she took my arm in hers. "We'll see."

Mount Carmel East Hospital
Columbus, Ohio

When the elevator door opened, we turned left past a nurse's station and walked towards my father's hospital room. The hallways were brightly lit, and a strong smell of disinfectant permeated the air. Random beeping sounds could be heard all around, though I couldn't see their source.

My father's room was the first one to the right, and I hung back as my family walked in ahead of me. A nurse was standing beside my father writing on a clipboard.

"I just changed his bandages," she said, as she hung up the clipboard and left.

"Thank you," said my mother.

My mother and grandmother walked around to the left side of my father's bed, followed by Phil and Nancy. Karen was too young and wasn't allowed in.

As I passed the curtain which hung from the ceiling in the middle of his room, I was shocked at my father's appearance. His head was wrapped in a white bandage, and he was hooked up to all sorts of monitors.

"He's been through so much," said Grandma as she looked at her son.

My mother noticed me standing back and told me to come over to the side of the bed. "It's okay," she said.

I stepped in front of my mother and grandmother and looked at my father as he lay there unconscious. My heart was heavy.

"Go on," my mother said. "Wake him up, it's okay."

I looked at Nancy and she nodded, so I touched Daddy's hand, and he jumped, just like he used to do when I would touch his knee to get his attention. I was so pleased to see his eyes open.

He seemed to be in a daze as he squinted at the bright lights of his hospital room. Then he noticed me standing beside him, and he turned his head towards me.

I took the silver dollar out of my pocket, excited to tell him what I was going to do. "Hi, Daddy."

His eyebrows furrowed as he looked directly at me and said, *"Who are you?"*

I felt like I'd been stabbed in the heart.

"It's *me*, Daddy," I responded as tears streamed down my cheeks. I looked up at Mom and Grandma, confused, and they tried to say something to me, but I turned and ran out of the hospital room. I ran down the hall clutching the silver dollar in my hand, feeling like my father was already gone.

CHAPTER 22

———

ALONE

I was lying on my bed staring at the ceiling when my grandmother knocked on my door and opened it.

"Can I come in?" she asked.

I sat up on the edge of the bed and nodded.

She waddled over and sat beside me.

"You okay?" she asked.

I nodded again, but I felt hollow and empty inside. I wasn't okay.

"It's going to take time," she said. "Brain surgery is a tricky thing."

"Will he ever remember me again?" I asked.

"Of course, he will," she said, "It just takes time. This isn't the first time he's been through this, you know."

"It isn't?"

She shook her head. "This is his third surgery since Vietnam," she said.

"I didn't know that."

She went on to tell me that each time he had brain surgery, he eventually recovered, and hopefully this time would be no different. That gave me hope.

"What made him sick in Vietnam?" I asked.

"Some sort of cockamamie virus with a long name, but basically it was meningitis. The doctors said he may have contracted it from a mosquito bite."

I didn't know what meningitis was, but what shocked me the most was the idea that something as tiny as a mosquito could bring down someone as big and strong as my father.

"We just have to be patient," she said, as she got up to leave.

As she walked past my desk, she noticed the silver dollar lying on top of the pad where I had drawn the lightning bolts.

"Your mother told me you want to go to West Point?"

I nodded.

"Nothing would make him prouder," she said. "It's just too bad I won't be there to see it."

"Don't say that, Grandma," I said.

She smiled and left my room.

CHAPTER 23

MR. ELE

Skyhawk Judo Team
Youth Center
Lockbourne Air Force Base, Ohio

One month after my father's surgery, I finally returned to Judo practice. All my friends were happy to see me, and I was happy to see them. For the first time, my mother didn't have to force me to go to practice. I wanted to go.

At the end of class, as we stood in what I would later learn was a platoon formation, Mr. Ele made an announcement.

"Remember, the State Championships are in February at Wright Patterson Air Force Base. For those of you who have won there before, you know what to do to prepare yourselves. It's not what you do at practice that makes a champion," he said.

What did he mean by that? I wondered.

"*Kyutske!*" he commanded. We all came to attention. "*Rei.*" We all bowed, took one step backwards, and then walked off the mat.

"Sensei," I said.

Mr. Ele turned to me and smiled. "I'm glad you're back," he said. "How's your mother holding up?"

"Good."

"I'm sorry about your father. He's a good man."

"Thank you."

"If there's anything you or your mother needs, you let me know, okay?"

"Well, there is something," I said.

"What's that?"

"Will you train me to win the State Championships?"

Mr. Ele's face registered surprise at first, and then understanding.

"Does this have anything to do with your father?" he asked.

"Yes, Sensei. He's never seen me win anything before, and—"

"Because it's not what you do at practice that makes you a champion," he repeated. "It's what you do on your own to prepare between practices that makes a champion."

"Can we start now?" I asked, as I looked towards the mat. I knew that to even have a chance at medaling, let alone winning, the State Championships, I had no time to waste.

Mr. Ele smiled at my boldness, then held out his hand towards the mat, as if to say, "After you."

All eyes turned towards us as Mr. Ele and I walked onto the mat, faced each other, and then bowed.

On the way home, I held an icepack up to my bloodied lip, while Mom and Karen laughed at me.

What was I thinking?

"Mom," I said with some discomfort. "Can you buy me some weights? Mr. Ele said I need to run and lift weights every day."

"We'll see," my mother said.

That usually meant "No." Only later did she tell me that money was tight and that we couldn't afford weights right now. I'd have to find another way.

CHAPTER 24

———

THE VOW

The thought of my father permanently living in a VA hospital was unbearable to my mother, and not long after his surgery she tried to see if he could live with us at home, even with his memory loss. Unfortunately, that proved to be a bad idea. While at home, my father continuously worried about the bills and going to work, forgetting that he had retired five years earlier. The stress of being at home was simply too great on him, and my mother reluctantly agreed with the doctors that he should live in a VA hospital—at least until he recovered his short term memory.

One day, while we were walking to the car to go back to the hospital my father began to lose his balance. He started leaning towards the left with each unsteady step he took, and then he began to fall down, right towards the tree in our front yard.

I didn't know what was happening and I just froze.

My mother, who was walking in front of my father, looked back just in time to notice what was happening, and somehow she managed to step towards him, grab his right arm and lean back with such force that my father regained his upright posture just before his head hit the tree. I couldn't believe what I had just witnessed. My father must have been twice my mother's weight, yet somehow she managed to hold him up.

My father steadied himself for a moment, then told my mom that he was okay. With a tenderness I'll never forget, my mother wrapped my father's right arm over her shoulders and guided him to the car.

As I began to follow them, my mother looked over her shoulder at me and hissed, "Why didn't you help him?"

The disappointment in her eyes was also something I would never forget.

Looking back now, I realize that I was embarrassed about my father's weakened state. Even as my mother was saving him from a potentially devastating fall, I recall glancing at the neighbors windows, hoping they didn't see what had happened. It shames me to this day.

Chillicothe Veterans Hospital
Chillicothe, Ohio

A sign on the redbrick wall at the main entrance to the VA hospital read, "The price of freedom is evident here."

Grandma was heading back to Florida, and she came to say goodbye to my father. Phil had returned to flight school at Vero Beach, Florida a few weeks earlier, but he told us that he'd "met a girl" and would be moving back soon. That made me happy.

Mom turned off the radio as we entered the grounds of the VA hospital. The road to the entrance of the VA grounds was long and tree lined, with hints of the approach of fall in the changing leaves. A nicely kept golf course flanked the left side of the road, while squat, three-story brick buildings of the VA hospital stood sentinel on the right.

As Mom drove slowly down the street, I leaned my head on the window and looked at the silver-haired veterans standing outside their buildings smoking and talking. I wondered how long they'd been here.

The road curved hard to the left at the end of what looked like a parade field, and a tall, white flagpole stood at the top with a large American flag blowing gently in the wind.

Dad's building was the last one on the right, Building 212. On the opposite corner of his building was a large parking lot, and Mom pulled in there and parked the car.

Dad's room, room 110, was located on the side of the building over-looking the parking lot, and that location allowed him to see us every time we came to visit.

Grandma was right, Daddy did remember me and the rest of the family in time, but he still seemed to have problems with his short-term memory.

"Am I retired?" he would ask constantly, worried about being AWOL (Absent Without Leave) from the Army.

The doctors assured us that as his brain healed and made new con-nections, my father's short-term memory would improve. But it never did. Looking back, I can see that all we had was hope, and we held on tightly to it.

Dad's hair had grown back after the surgery, and to anyone who saw him he seemed "normal." He was able to walk around and talk just fine, unlike some of the older veterans in his ward who were wheelchair bound and rarely spoke to anyone. But Dad lived a life plagued by discontinuity and dementia—and anyone who has expe-rienced that with a loved one knows that's no "life" at all.

It was clear that Daddy was the youngest Veteran in the hospital at age 45. There was even a World War I veteran living in his ward.

Soon, my father would be known as the "young man" amongst his fellow veterans.

"When can I go home," Dad would ask each time we visited. That broke our hearts, and each time we'd say, "Soon." We kids learned how to answer his questions by listening to the adults, but it never got any easier to lie to our own father.

Daddy smiled when he saw us, and he immediately walked over to my mother and gave her a kiss. She still turned her cheek every time.

"Hi!" he said to Grandma, as if it were the first time he'd seen her since his surgery. "When did you come in?"

Grandma was expert at handling his questions and changed the subject to something else.

We all got on the elevator and went down to the basement level where the canteen was. There were four or five round tables in the canteen and several vending machines containing hot canned foods, candy, and sodas.

My father preferred Snickers and a Coke. At least that's how I remember it—the rest of my family insists he was a Pepsi man. Coke it is.

"I came to say good-bye," said Grandma as we finished our snacks and prepared to take Daddy back up to his room.

"You're leaving already?" he asked.

"Yes," she said, with sadness in her eyes.

"You guys can go to the car," I said, "I'll take him back to his room." Everyone understood I wanted to be with my father, so they kissed him good-bye and left.

"Aren't you going with them?" he asked.

"Yes, but not yet," I said. "I have something for you."

"For me?" he said.

I pulled the 1978 Eisenhower silver dollar out of my pocket and handed it to him.

"What's this for?" he asked, perplexed.

"It's for you," I said. "But not yet." I took the coin back from him and he smiled, confused.

"You have to get better," I said. "Because one day I'm going to become an officer, and you're going to give me my first salute." I held my right hand up to my forehead in a mock-salute to drive home my point.

"You want to be an officer?" he said.

"I *will* be an officer," I said, "And you're going to give me my first salute," I repeated for good measure.

He understood and seemed to be studying me, measuring me.

"I'm going to West Point," I said, with a conviction that surprised even me.

That's when I knew he got it. I saw a visceral response from him when I said those words, and his eyes seemed to light up. He just stood there for a moment; then a barely perceptible smile formed on his lips and he said, "Very good."

In that moment, a vow was made between a father and his son, and I swore to myself that I would do my best to honor it.

CHAPTER 25

———

FIRST STEPS

I picked up my transistor radio from my desk and walked to my mother's bedroom to tell her I was going out for a run. When I got to her bedroom door, she was sitting on the edge of her bed with her back to me, daubing tears from her eyes with tissues. I'd never seen my mother cry before.

I backed quietly away and went down the stairs and out the door. I tuned my radio to Q-FM-96, "Ohio's Best Rock," stretched out, and jogged down Beechton Road towards Asbury Elementary School. My legs felt heavy and sluggish, and my breathing was labored. I turned onto the path leading to Asbury Elementary, and I saw the baseball diamond where I'd hit the miracle home run the previous summer. It was the moment that changed the course of my life, but it seemed like it was years ago now.

I leaned in to the slight incline that led to the school and turned right, behind the baseball diamond and the playground. I ran past all the classrooms and then glanced into the dark windows of what used to be Mrs. Miller's classroom. So many good memories of Mrs. Miller flashed through my mind as I continued running.

I left the school grounds through another trail that led to Elmira Road and passed my friend Tracy Joseph's house.

I ran through neighborhood after neighborhood, with no particular plan. I decided I was simply going to run as far as I could to test myself, and then run even farther the next time. I lost myself in the music as I ran, and I was surprised that my legs didn't feel tired anymore.

I ran all the way to Madison Middle School, then hopped up into the grass which led to the woods. I followed the levy into the woods and then dropped down onto a well-worn trail. I no longer cared about how long or how far I ran; I just wanted to run. As I reached a natural turn-around in the trail, I saw a Red-winged blackbird. The memory of the strawberry patch and Mrs. Miller made me smile as I turned for home.

Even as I chased my dream, I was also running from the nightmares of my past. Unfortunately, I'd soon realize that nightmares were not easily outrun.

CHAPTER 26

———

BATTLING THE MONSTERS

I stared at all of the Certificates of Participation on my wall and reminded myself that I wasn't good enough to do what I'd committed to do. *Who did I think I was, anyway, to dream such lofty dreams?*

Doubt crept into my consciousness as I let the nightmares of the past catch up with me, and it shamed me. *How could I win the State Judo Championships or try to get into West Point if Mom couldn't even afford to buy me weights?*

All I saw were obstacles, and despite the previous miraculous answers to my prayers, my new-found belief in God didn't translate into belief in myself. *Other than the home run, what had I ever won before?*

Gravity. I felt the weight of gravity and of reality pull me further and further back to earth, bringing my head out of the clouds.

I lay in my bed, scared.

Earlier, I'd checked out a book about West Point from the school library and realized that the people who went to West Point were the best scholars and best athletes in the nation, and I was neither of those things, nor could I ever hope to be. Even at Judo practice I was still getting beat by the other kids, no matter how hard I tried.

I was nothing but a stupid dreamer, a fraud. And that's all I'd ever be. The realization made me retreat into my shell.

All I ever wanted was for Daddy to be proud of me, and now—with his illness—he'd only remember me as a loser.

I turned over in my bed and lay face down on my pillow, berating myself for talking too much just like I had as a first grader ...

CHAPTER 27

———

BREAK-THROUGH

One afternoon, I was building a model airplane when Mom came home from visiting Daddy at the hospital. Mom visited Daddy every day while we were at school, rain or shine, and all of us went to visit him on the weekends.

She called for me with a bit of excitement in her voice as soon as she walked in the door.

"What's the matter?" I asked, concerned that something was wrong with Dad.

"When did you tell Daddy that you were going to go to West Point?" she asked.

"The day that Grandma left a few weeks ago," I said. "Why?"

Mom smiled and said, "When I was saying good-bye to him today, he asked me, 'Is Bobby going to West Point?'"

"What?" I said, smiling. "He remembered that?"

"Yes!" she beamed.

"What did you tell him?" I asked, curious.

"I said yes, of course."

We were sure this was a sign of good things to come, that soon his full memory would be restored, and he'd be able to come home for good.

Mom was right when she told me Daddy loved West Point, and this only proved it more. And now that he remembered my promise to him, my vow, I knew what I had to do.

CHAPTER 28

———

CHANGE OF HEART

Years of humiliation stared me in the face as I stood before my Certificates of Participation once again. Defeat at the hands of bullies and of monsters flashed through my mind as I stood before the symbols of my past losses. West Point only accepts the best, and to be the best—to have a chance to even be considered among the best—I had to come to terms with my past.

Slowly at first, and then with more determination, I began to remove each certificate of participation from my wall. The certificates dated back four years, and that was four years of being defeated by one opponent after another in front of my mother, father and sisters. Four years of not believing in myself and feeling like I didn't fit in because I was different. Four years of feeling like a square peg in a round hole.

Finally, I ripped the certificates of participation in half as I pulled them down from my wall, cleansing myself of the mediocrity which had marked me and mocked me for so many years.

Next, I took my velvet posters down and replaced them with an American flag and an Uncle Sam "I Want You for the U.S. Army" poster. Satisfied, I changed into my workout clothes and headed for the garage.

Despite tearing down and throwing away my Certificates of Participation, my mother found and kept one. The date on the bottom shows that it was from 1977.

PART 2

—

WALK

"Innocence, Once Lost, Can Never Be Regained.
Darkness, Once Gazed Upon, Can Never Be Lost."

—*John Milton*

CHAPTER 29

———

ARMOR

It was time to put on the armor which would see me through the battles to come. I found Phil's old weight bench folded up in the corner and moved it to the middle of the garage. Beneath Dad's workbench, I found two full one-gallon paint cans. I picked one of them up and felt the weight of it.

"Perfect," I said, as I removed the other paint can.

I held each paint can by the wire handle and proceeded to curl them. After a few repetitions, however, the wire handles began to dig into my palms, so I put them down and searched for something to pad them with. I found a few old towels on a metal shelf, folded them in half and wrapped them around the paint can handles. They worked perfectly. Eventually, I taped towels to the handles with duct tape.

Next, I found a length of white rope, about the size of a dime in diameter, and I held each end to see if it was the right size for a jump rope. It was a little too long, but I found that if I wrapped each end around my hand one time, it was perfect.

I now had both a jump rope and a "weight set," and I was ready to go.

Day after day, after school and between Judo practices, I changed into my sweats and put myself through a self-designed workout.

Music was a constant companion, and my transistor radio went everywhere with me.

At night, I'd lie in my bed with my headphones plugged into my record player, and then visualize winning the State Championships (though I didn't know it was called "visualization" back then).

Slowly but surely, I learned to reprogram my mind for winning, and I felt my inner and outer strength grow more and more each day. It was so new to me to feel strong and confident that I deliberately pushed my body beyond any limits I thought I had, just to see how far I could go. I continued to go farther, faster, higher and do more reps and weight than I ever thought I could—and the challenge fascinated me.

CHAPTER 30

———

MIGHTY OAK

I became adept at utilizing the paint cans as barbells and was able to use them for both declined and inclined bench presses, as well as bicep and triceps curls.

Jumping rope was a little harder, but in time I found I was able to jump rope for consistently longer and longer periods of time, and I liked it. For push-ups and sit-ups, I went outdoors.

The retaining walls on each side of the garage were perfect for doing push-ups, although the width of the bricks was a little narrow.

For sit-ups, I found that the light post that lit the walkway to the house was perfect. The light post was located at the top of the drop-off that went from the walkway to the driveway, and by tying my feet around the light post I was able to do decline sit-ups. When I got tired, I'd switch to the other side where the ground was flat and do regular sit-ups.

Finally, for pull-ups, our oak tree in the front yard had a branch that I could reach by jumping up to it. The branch was thick enough to hold my weight but not so thick I couldn't get a good grip on it, and soon I wore off part of the bark where my hands went each time I did pull-ups.

Sometimes I'd see Mom smiling in the kitchen window as she watched me workout; she knew I was going after my dream

In time, I began to see the results of my workouts when I stood before the mirror, and I liked what I saw. My biceps were filling out, and I'd developed a six-pack—eight pack even—on my abs. For the first time in my life, I felt my strength and not my weakness, and working out became an obsession for me.

Soon, I was running several miles a day, every day, and I developed a system of only focusing on the sidewalk blocks before me so that the distance wasn't intimidating. Eventually, I changed the sidewalk block method to the tree method, where I'd simply focus on the next branch which hung down from my neighbor's trees as I ran through the neighborhood.

People in neighborhoods miles from my house got so used to seeing me run by that eventually they waved at me as I passed, and that made me feel good.

My commitment to working out began to show at Judo practice, too, as friends/opponents who used to regularly beat me during practice no longer could, and only the higher ranking Judokas challenged me.

Mr. Ele was pleased with my progress, and he would "rondori"—or spar—with me after each practice, honing my skills and showing me some hard-earned techniques of his. My favorite was the foot-sweep, which required precise timing to execute properly. One of my best friends on the team, Kevin Miles, was a master at this.

All the while, in between working out, judo practice and studying—which I finally started to do for the first time in my life—I would go with my family to visit Daddy at the VA hospital. The progress that Mom and I had hoped for after he remembered that I wanted to go to West Point didn't happen, but he *never* forgot about West Point.

CHAPTER 31

———

SENSEI, DOWN

I don't recall exactly when it happened, but at some point the powers-that-be at Lockbourne Air Force Base decided they no longer wanted Mr. Ele to use the Youth Center to teach Judo. Undeterred, Mr. Ele converted his two-car garage in Obetz, Ohio, into a Judo studio, and the Skyhawk Judo Team became "Ele's Judo Team" and continued to thrive.

One day after regular practice ended, Mr. Ele and I continued our routine of fighting with no time limit to increase my skills and to work on my technique. Several minutes into our fight, I managed to foot sweep him and take him down. That was the first time I'd done that, and he was very proud of me.

The competitor side of him came out, however, and Mr. Ele decided to show me what a black belt could do. He gave me all he had and to my surprise, I put up a good fight. He began sweating profusely and so did I, but we kept going at it.

Marvie and Marissa told their father we'd gone far enough, but he wouldn't listen. Suddenly, he had an asthma attack and fell to the floor, gasping for air.

The ambulance came and found that Mr. Ele was suffering from a severe asthma attack that required immediate medical attention, and they put him on a gurney and drove away. I felt responsible for pushing him too far and chased the ambulance to the corner, shouting for them to stop and take me, too.

I heard a horn beep and turned around to find Mom and Karen already in the car. We followed the ambulance to the hospital, and waited in the lobby with Marvie, Marissa and Mrs. Ele (Virgie) to learn of Mr. Ele's fate. It was well after midnight when a doctor came out to see us.

"We're going to have to admit him," the doctor said. I was devastated, but glad he was alive. I was sick and tired of hospitals, though I appreciated what the doctors and nurses did for their patients.

Eventually, Mr. Ele was transferred to the Chillicothe VA hospital, and somehow his room wound up being right next door to my father's room. I don't know if Mr. Ele arranged that or not, but when we got to the hospital to visit my dad, we were shocked to see he was playing poker with Mr. Ele.

"Your father's a card shark," Mr. Ele said, wearing his hospital pajamas and looking much better.

Eventually, Virgie, Marvie, and Marissa arrived, and it was like a little family reunion. My father seemed to recognize Mr. Ele, and that made me feel better. At least Dad wouldn't feel so lonely in between our visits.

Thankfully, Mr. Ele would not be at the VA hospital long, but while he was there, he showed me the loyalty that service members have for each other, and I appreciated that.

CHAPTER 32

———

PHIL

NOVEMBER 1978

One day, a few months before the State Judo Championships, Phil told us he was coming home for good, and no one was happier about that than I was. He accomplished his goal to get his private airplane license, but his dream to become a jet pilot never came to fruition. He gave up his dreams to come home and help my mother and our family while Daddy was in the hospital, but I didn't understand the sacrifice he'd made until much later.

I was working out in the finished basement, blasting music when Phil walked through the basement door with his flight bag.

I was jumping rope with the now-frayed and dirty rope I'd found in the garage. For some reason, Phil seemed shocked when he saw me.

I stopped jumping rope, turned down the music, and walked over to him, sweat dripping from my brow.

"Hi, bro," I said, happy to see him.

"When did you learn to jump rope like *that?*" he asked, smiling.

I was about to answer when he grabbed my biceps and said, "And when did you get these?"

I laughed, appreciating the compliment.

"Why do you have paint cans in here?" he asked, studying the now beaten up paint cans that had duct tape on them to keep the handles from coming apart.

I told him that I was training for the Judo State Championships.

"That's great," he said. "Now get out of my room!"

Dorothy, the girl Phil met in Florida, would eventually become his wife, and they would give me my first niece, Stacy.

Phil took a job at an Omega gas station and quickly rose to the position of manager. Meanwhile, he put in his application to become a Columbus police officer.

CHAPTER 33

———

BEADS

One day, while Phil was at work at the gas station, I got home from school and changed into my workout gear. I walked down to the basement to begin my workout and saw a red and white beaded jump rope hanging on the nail where my frayed jump rope used to be. I took it off the hook and felt the smooth plastic handles as well as the nice weight the beads gave the rope.

I smiled at my brother's thoughtful gesture. Typical of Phil, there was no note to accompany it. When I turned to where my paint cans should have been, I saw that my brother had replaced them with his curling bar, dumb-bells, and a straight bar, with all of the individual weights stacked neatly beside them.

I got a lump in my throat and smiled.

This gear would enable me to take my training to a whole new level, and I couldn't wait to get started.

CHAPTER 34

LAST SEED

FEBRUARY 1979

The car smelled of fried chicken as we drove towards Wright Patterson Air Force Base for the Judo state championships. My mother always made enough food to feed an army when we went on road trips, and this day was no exception.

My stomach growled from hunger, but I couldn't eat until after weigh-ins. All I had that morning was an avocado, which Mr. Ele insisted was the *true* breakfast of champions. I had butterflies in my stomach, and I was tense with nervous energy. All the months of working out, of pushing myself like I had never pushed myself before, came down to this day. But would it be enough?

Mom exited the highway at Grove City, so we could fill up with gas at the Omega Station that Phil managed. It was a cold winter day, and Phil was standing outside near one of the pumps when we pulled in. He had on a heavy Omega gas station winter coat and a Russian style hat with fake fur ear flaps which were in the up position.

Phil saw us and waved, then walked over to Mom's side of the car. Mom rolled down her window and said, "Fill it up."

Phil laughed and walked around the back of the car to put the gas in. I watched through the side view mirror as Phil used the squeegee to clean the back window, all the while teasing Karen who was in the backseat, laughing.

A moment later, he came up to my side of the window and tapped on it. I rolled my window down, and brisk air and snow dust blew in on my face.

"Can you come with us?" I asked.

"I wanted to, but someone called in sick, so I have to work another shift," Phil said.

I was bummed, but I always admired my brother's strong work ethic.

"How do you feel?" Phil asked.

"Good," I lied. I was more nervous than I had ever been in my life. My stomach was in knots and I felt like I was going to throw up.

Phil smiled and said, "Go get the gold, Rob. You've earned it." I was grateful for his confidence and support, and his words lifted my spirits.

"I will," I said, feeling myself get choked up.

Phil tapped me on my shoulder and smiled, then said bye to Mom and Karen as he went to the back of the car to remove the nozzle. He tapped on the car and Mom pulled out.

Wright Patterson Air Force
AAU State Judo Championships

A noisy buzz filled the air as Judokas from all over the state surrounded the poster boards taped to the gymnasium walls. The poster boards showed the brackets for the weight divisions. I had just turned thirteen in early February, so I was in the 13-year old heavyweight division, which had some of the best fighters in the state in it.

The reigning champion was an African-American kid from the Dayton Martial Arts Center, or DAMAC (pronounced Day-Mac) Judo Team, Robert King. DAMAC was Ele's Judo Team's greatest rival, and I admired their sense of unity as they entered the mat clapping in unison and chanting their team name before the tournament started. They were intimidating.

Robert King was a fierce competitor who dominated our weight division from the first time he arrived on the scene. He was calm and cool and had a tall lean body that gave him an advantage over his shorter opponents—like me. I was glad to see that King was in Bracket B, the bracket opposite from mine.

I didn't have to search far for my name, I knew where I would find it based on my past record. I was all the way at the bottom of Bracket A, the last seed. The guy I was scheduled to fight first pointed at my name and said, "I drew Paley in the first round, that's like having a bye!"

I was used to being laughed at and made fun of, but unlike my past experiences where I felt humiliated and weak, I felt something different stir within me this time...

"Ippon!" the referee shouted after I pinned the guy who had laughed at me. He didn't know what hit him, and I finished him off in less than a minute. Karen was my loudest cheerleader, as usual, and Mom smiled as I walked over to her and sat down. I wasn't even sweating.

Meanwhile, Robert King won his first match on a different mat and looked as strong as ever.

My name continued to advance up the bracket as I defeated one opponent after another, decisively. Robert King continued to advance in the opposite bracket, and it didn't take long to see where things were heading.

Guys who had beat me regularly over the past several years now eyed me with curiosity, as if they were trying to figure out which version of Wheaties I'd eaten that morning.

I jumped rope in between matches to ensure my muscles were nice and loose before each match. The whole team gathered around the mat to cheer me on for each fight, and Mr. Ele was smiling from ear-to-ear as I continued to advance towards the semi-finals.

There was a break before the semi-final and championship matches, and I found myself fighting my demons once again. I was in the stall of the bathroom dry-heaving, when I heard the announcer call my name. A victory in the next match would assure me a Bronze medal and my *first-ever* tournament victory. Normally, this is where I'd fold and take fourth place—content to take home my Certificate of Participation. But not this time. Not this day.

In a hard-fought match, I defeated my semi-final opponent as my whole team cheered. Robert King won his match on the other mat as well, and the dye was cast. I would fight the champ for the championship—just as it should be.

When Robert King and I bowed to each other in the championship match that day, it was the beginning of a rivalry that would last for years.

But on this day, against the odds, the winner would be a boy on the verge of manhood, a boy who was fighting for his ailing father, a boy who was fighting for a dream.

CHAPTER 35:

GOLDEN MEMORY

Chillicothe VA Hospital
Chillicothe, Ohio

I couldn't wait to get to the hospital the next day to visit my father and to show him my gold medal. When we pulled into the parking lot, he was standing at his window, as if he were expecting us. His right hand came up when he saw us, like he was taking an oath, and we waved back at him.

"Look, Daddy," I yelled as soon as we walked into his room. "I won!"

Daddy took the medal and studied it, then said, "Very good."

His highest compliment. I was about to tell him all about it when he looked at my mother and said, "Am I retired?"

I put the medal back in my pocket, disappointed that he didn't understand the magnitude of what just happened. But that was okay, I decided, because he *would* understand what giving me my first salute at West Point would mean someday ... then he would know his son was a winner.

CHAPTER 36

———

THE CHASE

After winning the State Judo Championship in February, I went on to win several more tournaments followed by the AAU Tri-State Judo Championship in October of the same year. Slowly but surely, I began to put my childhood trauma behind me as I raced towards my dream of getting into West Point.

To deal with the pain of the loss of my father from my daily life, I pushed myself continually to ensure I was in better condition than any opponent I would face, and I reveled in reaching new peaks of physical fitness.

One day, while I was jogging down a country road in Groveport as the sun was setting, an incredible feeling of calm came over me. The warm summer air felt good on my face, and my legs felt lighter with each step I took. I felt a peacefulness I'd never before known, and when I asked my legs to give me more, they responded effortlessly. I was in a dead sprint for what seemed like miles, running past grazing cows and horses in the farm fields, and I didn't feel a thing. It was the first time I experienced the "runner's high," and I continually went back for more.

By the time 8th grade wrestling season began, I no longer feared competition, I craved it. Though I had never wrestled before, transitioning from Judo to wrestling was relatively seamless, and both sports made me a better all-around fighter.

Where I once was satisfied to put up a good fight, I now found satisfaction only in dominating and defeating each opponent I faced, as quickly as possible. And if a quick victory wasn't possible, then I would relentlessly wear each opponent down, until my superior conditioning would give me the edge I needed to win.

After years of losing, 1979 marked the turning point for me.
After winning the State Championships, I went on to win the
Regional/Tri-State Championships later that same year.

To me, they weren't just opponents; they were tests of my worthiness to become a future West Point cadet, and I fought or wrestled each one as if my father's life depended on it—and deep down, I believed it did.

CHAPTER 37

——

COACH NOBLE

FALL 1979

Madison Middle School
Groveport Madison School District

Coach Noble exuded a natural athleticism that eluded me. He walked and talked with an air of confidence that inspired our team of first-time wrestlers to great heights during the season, making us one of the best middle school wrestling teams in the Columbus area.

"In life, your greatest opponent is yourself," he asserted. But with West Point looming over me in my future, I questioned the truth in those words. Nothing, I knew, was going to be a greater "opponent" than West Point. Years would pass before I finally understood what he meant.

Another Noble-ism was "Nobody can work harder than you unless you let them!"

That's not going to happen! I thought to myself.

I didn't know who my next opponent would be, but I was determined to work so hard that it wouldn't matter. Little did I know that during the season I would soon clash with an undefeated wrestler who had been wrestling since he was a child--an opponent who would put my conditioning to the test.

Coach Noble gave me my first experience as a leader by naming me Team Captain several times throughout the year. This experience taught me to think as part of a team rather than as an individual, and it built my self-confidence immensely.

If I didn't do as well as I hoped to do in practice, however, I would get upset with myself and push myself even harder. One day, I pushed myself too hard while we were running the halls and I lost my balance and ran right into the side of the wall lockers, nearly knocking myself out.

Did I mention that I never was a natural athlete?

Undeterred, I continued to "forge my body in the fire of my will," as Han said in Bruce Lee's, *Enter the Dragon* movie (I sought wisdom and inspiration from wherever I could find it.)

My greatest test as a fighter and a wrestler came on the day we traveled to Blendon Middle School for a wrestling meet. It was there that I would face the undefeated Todd Globe.

CHAPTER 38

—

GLOBE

Blendon Middle School
Westerville, Ohio

Wall lockers slammed, and wrestlers from both Blendon and Madison Middle schools shouted over one another as weigh-ins commenced. I had my singlet on but didn't pull the straps onto my shoulders in case I was overweight and had to remove it.

I was standing in line to be weighed when a couple of wrestlers from the Blendon team came up to me and asked me, "What weight class are you?"

"One twenty-six," I said.

They turned to each other then turned back to me and one of them said, "Man, this is going to be *good* match!"

That's when I got the first hint that I was about to face one of the biggest individual challenges of my young life.

"What's your record?" the other wrestler asked me.

"Seven and Oh," I said.

They walked away, and I thought I heard one of them laugh, then mention that my opponent was like "seventy and oh" or some ridiculously high number like that. Maybe even One-hundred-seventy and oh.

I should have been concerned or intimidated, but I wasn't. Now, looking back, I can truly say that I wasn't fazed at all. It was well and truly the last time in my life I can remember having such supreme confidence in myself—in a way I'd never before had and have never experienced since. I'd reached the peak of physical, spiritual, and mental conditioning in a way I would never again attain, which is why what Todd Globe did to me when we got on the mat came as a complete and total shock.

"Globe! Globe! Globe!" My opponent actually had a following. And on the wall of the gymnasium was a poster of Atlas holding up the world, but instead of Atlas, it was my opponent, Todd Globe.

Who is this guy? I wondered as I led our team through warm-ups. There were more fans there for Todd than I'd seen at high school wrestling meets, and it reminded me of one of those televised wrestling shows.

I recall the gym being very nice, and that we had the use of the basketball scoreboard and clock for each match—something that would prove crucial to me in my upcoming match.

I led my team onto the mat and put them through calisthenics to warm-up for the meet. Our fans were outnumbered by Blendon fans by at least five to one. But my most important and loyal fans were there—Mom and Karen—and that's all that mattered to me. They were seated in the bottom row of the bleachers, surrounded by Blendon fans.

Todd Globe was the team captain for his team, too, and it was clear from his physique that he had been wrestling for a very long time. He was built for wrestling, powerful and well-defined with a shock of blond hair sticking out of his headgear. I was looking forward to our match.

When we squared off, there was a buzz of excitement in the air on both sides. We shook hands and clashed in the middle of the mat. That's when I felt Todd's brute strength, and before I knew it, he took me down. Ten seconds into the match, and I was already in trouble!

Time has erased most of the details of the beating Todd gave me during the first two periods, but suffice it to say that I had to fight for every point just to make sure he didn't win by a majority—

which basically means that there's only one person wrestling/scoring, so what's the point in continuing the slaughter?

At the end of the second round, Todd and I went out of bounds and had to jog back to the middle of the mat. That's when I noticed that he was breathing hard from throwing me around like a rag doll for two periods, and I concluded (hoped?) that he wasn't used to anyone lasting this long with him in a match.

Knowing I was in serious trouble, I decided to resort to psychological warfare to give myself a chance. When Todd and I squared off in the middle of the mat, I smiled at him. That's right, I smiled!

I also forced myself to look as un-winded as possible from the beating I'd been taking, to make him think I had a lot more gas in the tank than he did.

Bad idea. Todd must have taken my barely-perceptible smile as an insult to his manhood, and he came at me in the third and final period with a whole new ferocity than he had during the first two periods. I narrowly avoided being pinned on several occasions, and I scored just enough to keep the score within 8 points or so, and it seemed clear to all that it was only a matter of time before Todd would rack up his zillionth victory. For those who anticipated a battle of Titans, they were surely disappointed.

The clock on the wall showed that there were only thirty seconds left, and I found myself being pinned by Todd again. Todd didn't have to go for the pin with his superiority in points, but he was a warrior, and warriors always go for the pin.

It took all that I had to keep both of my shoulders off the mat. Todd was as strong as an ox, and his teammates were chanting, "Pin! Pin! Pin!" as his fans went wild with excitement.

My teammates assumed it was all over for me, so they stopped watching my match and surrounded the next wrestler to encourage him before he went out.

As the basketball clock wound down to fifteen seconds, I leaned in to Todd as hard as I could, making him think I was trying to wriggle out of the headlock he had me in and to get to my stomach. He had no way of knowing how much time was left, but I did.

When the clock showed about ten seconds left, I felt Todd push against me to try to get my left shoulder back down to the mat.

Coach Noble must have seen what was happening and sensed my strategy as he yelled, "Now!" just when I rolled hard with all my might in the direction Globe was pushing me, flipping Todd onto *his* back and shoulders. I lifted his head off the mat so he couldn't use it for leverage and I squeezed with everything I had, forcing his shoulder blades down to the mat.

"Can't...breathe," he said, but I continued to squeeze harder.

To everyone's great shock and surprise—including mine— the ref shouted, "Pin!" just as the buzzer went off.

Todd's team and fans were stunned into silence.

I was exhausted, and so was he, and there was a mutual respect between us when we shook hands at the end of the match. No celebrating on my part.

I looked over at Karen and Mom as I unsnapped my headgear, and the pride I saw in my mother's eyes has never left me.

On the way home, I asked Mom, "Were you worried?"

"No," she said matter-of-factly, "You always win in the end."

And those words, too, inspire me to this day.

CHAPTER 39

LIGHTS OUT

SEPTEMBER 2, 1982

3 years later
Columbus, Ohio

It was a beautiful fall day when I arrived at Marvie Ele's house for a Kung-Fu lesson. A few years earlier, Marvie married Jim Pendergast, who was a black belt in Kung-Fu, and he took me and my buddy Tom Lascola on as his first students. Jim had brown hair and blue eyes, chiseled facial features, and the build of a welterweight boxer.

Jim was planning to open a martial arts school, and he hoped that Tom would be one of his assistant instructors. I had my eye on West Point still, so that wasn't an option for me. I was taking Kung-Fu to better prepare myself for my future as a soldier.

"Hi, guys," Marvie called when Tom and I arrived for our lesson. Marvie was as pretty as ever, and she still had that mischievous spirit that made her so much fun to be around. Unfortunately, Ele's Judo Team was no more. Mr. Ele was told to move to a better climate for his asthma, so he and his wife Virgie moved to Florida.

Nonetheless, Marvie and Marissa were like family to me, and we remained in constant contact.

"Aren't you joining us for practice?" I asked as Marvie headed for the house.

"Not me," she replied, "I don't want any part of what you guys have gotten yourself into."

"Okay," I said, smiling.

"Don't hurt yourselves," Marvie chuckled as she went into the house.

Jim's martial arts studio was located in his detached, two-car garage which was in back of the house. Tom and I went in through the side door and greeted Jim, who was already stretching out.

"You guys ready for this?" Jim asked with a grin.

"We'll find out," I said.

Like a scene out of a bad Kung-Fu movie, Jim, Tom and I were preparing for our first full-contact Kung-Fu match against students from a rival school. These students had challenged us because Jim used to train with them but had left to start his own school. All we needed now was bad music, mismatched voice dubbing, and a few pairs of nunchuks.

After we finished warming up, Jim asked, "Who's first?"

"I'll go," I said, eager to test out my skills.

"I'll keep time," Tom volunteered.

Tom Lascola was a few years older than me, and he was one of my best friends. He was a star half-back on our high school football team, and Kung-Fu seemed to come easy to him.

I put my mouthpiece in, then Tom helped me put on my full-contact finger-style gloves. We wore shin and upper foot guards as well, but they did little good when a black belt delivered the blows.

I bowed to Jim, put up my dukes, and prepared to spar.

"Begin," Tom yelled as Jim and I closed the distance with each other.

Jim threw a few jabs and front kicks to test my defenses, and I threw a few back. I decided that the best defense against someone as good as Jim was an aggressive offense, so I attacked him with a series of punches and kicks. He blocked or parried them all, but his smile told me he liked my aggressiveness.

Jim counter-attacked with a flurry of punches and kicks of his own, and to my surprise I blocked or parried most of them as well.

"Very good," Jim commented, as he brought his hands up and started to concentrate more.

I was in the best shape of my life, and my feet felt light as I moved around the garage sparring with Jim. I'd come a long way since Daddy first showed me how to fight in the living room all those years ago.

"30 seconds!" said Tom.

"Give me all you've got!" I said to Jim, wanting to get the most out of the remaining time.

Jim smiled and closed the distance with me quickly, cutting off my escape route as I backed up towards the garage door. I put my hands up to guard myself from the attack I knew was coming. I saw Jim throw a hard right at my face followed by a front kick, a move that stopped me from counterattacking. I ducked because I expected a high roundhouse kick to follow the front kick, but instead, another front kick came just as I was ducking, and Jim's foot kicked me in the face with the full force of an uppercut from a professional boxer.

I felt myself floating up and backwards through the air as I hit the metal garage door full force; then I felt my body falling forward but I couldn't see a thing. I landed hard on the mat face-first, and my head bounced a few times before I realized what had happened.

"Holy shit!" blurted Tom as he and Jim came running. I felt them turn me over and lay my head on one of their laps, and then I heard Marvie come in the side door and scream.

"That bad?" I asked, still unable to see anything.

"Open your eyes, Rob," said Jim.

"They are opened," I said, but I still couldn't see anything.

Marvie was by my side immediately, and she told me that I had to try to open my right eye, which seemed to have taken the brunt of the kick.

By now, I could see out of my left eye, but everything was hazy.

The look I saw on their faces when I forced my swollen right eye open told me that something was very wrong.

"Sit up, Rob," someone said. "We have to take you to a hospital right now."

I felt someone lift me up from under my armpits and guide me towards a car, while someone else pulled the gloves off my hands. Worried whispers were exchanged between them, and I heard them decide on Rickenbacker.

Lockbourne Air Force Base had been renamed Rickenbacker Air Force base, and they were rushing me to the emergency room.

I was lying down on my back, dizzy and confused, when my right eye began pounding with pain.

"Hang in there; we're almost there," someone said.

The attendant at the Air Force hospital took one look at my eye and said, "We can't treat that here anymore, you're going to have to take him to Mount Carmel."

CHAPTER 40

———

FADING DREAM

Mount Carmel East Hospital
Columbus, Ohio

Jim apologized to me profusely as the staff at Mount Carmel sat me down on a gurney and rushed me into the emergency room. I think I told him not to worry, that everything would be okay, or something like that, but I don't recall clearly because everything becomes a little hazy in my memory at this point.

I felt the presence of doctors and nurses all around me as they consulted about what to do. I heard them mention a certain doctor's name, apparently an eye-specialist, but then someone else said he was on vacation.

"Call him," said a male doctor, "now."

That's when I knew that something *really bad* had happened to my eye, and just like when I was a kid, when doctors talked about me like I couldn't hear them, I overheard one of them say, "He could lose his eye."

I tried to speak, to tell them, "I can't lose my eye because I'm about to apply to West Point," but the pain in my eye was too severe and it hurt me to exert myself.

"I've got him on the phone now," said a female voice.

I heard some muffled conversations, and I could make out the description the male voice gave to whomever was on the other end of the phone line. "His right eye is completely red, no sign of his pupil or iris at all." *That didn't sound good.*

The doctor hung up the phone and told the nurses they needed to lower the gurney I was sitting up in all the way to the down position.

"Robert," a voice said, "we're going to lower your bed so you're lying completely flat on your back, okay?"

"Okay," I said.

I felt the bed being lowered as the same voice continued. "Your right eye has experienced severe trauma, and we're trying to prevent it from hemorrhaging; do you understand?"

"Hurts bad," I said.

"Okay, we'll give you something for that soon. But for now, we're going to wrap a bandage around both your eyes. You must do your best not to move your eyes, okay?"

"Okay," I said.

"We have an eye specialist on the way; he'll be here soon. Just try to relax. Is there anyone you want to call?"

"My mother," I said.

I must have fallen asleep, or I was given something to make me sleep; I can't recall, but I was awakened by the sound of another male voice telling me he was doctor so-and-so and that he was an eye specialist.

"Now, I'm going to remove your bandages, but when I do, I need you to continue to look straight ahead, okay? No eye movement whatsoever; it's very important," he cautioned.

"Okay," I said.

I felt the wrap come off my head, and I thought I could make out some lights above me through my closed eyelids.

"Now, open your eyes," said the doctor. "But continue to look straight up."

I did as I was told, and I was happy to be able to make out the fuzzy outline of a fluorescent light in the ceiling.

"Now," said the doctor, "I want you to close your left eye and tell me what you see."

"I can't see anything!" I said, alarmed. "Is my right eye open right now?"

"Yes, it's open. Just keep looking straight up so I can take a better look at it."

My heartrate increased as I finally realized the severity of the situation. I was blind in my right eye. Pitch black, blind.

"Now, I'm going to take my light and approach your right eye from different angles, okay? But first, I'm going to need to put a patch over your left eye," said the doctor.

For the next few minutes, the doctor passed his bright doctor's light over my right eye from several different angles, but I didn't see a thing.

The doctor told the nurse to go ahead and place an eyepatch on my right eye, too, and then he left.

My dream of West Point was fading from sight.

CHAPTER 41

——

CROSSROADS

Later that day, I pulled up the bottom of my left eye patch a tiny bit so that I could see my feet. I didn't move my eyes, I just continued to stare at my feet so that I wouldn't feel like I was completely blind.

The doctors decided to see if lying on my back for several days would allow the blood which had built up inside of my eyeball to drain back into my body and relieve the pressure. Surgery, they told me, could cause permanent damage to my eye and even to my sight. They still couldn't tell me if I would ever see again from my right eye.

I was staring at my feet when I saw Mom stop at the foot of the bed and look at me. She looked so worried, so I said, "Hi, Mom!" to let her know that I was okay.

Her eyes lit up and she said, "How'd you know I'm here?"

I pointed to the left eyepatch and told her, "I opened this patch up a little, so I can see the pretty nurses."

"Bobby," she said, relieved.

"Did you see Marvie?" I asked.

"Yes, I saw all of them in the waiting room," she said.

"So, they told you what happened to me?" I asked.

Mom got a stern look on her face, and said, "No more martial arts!"

I didn't want to argue with her, so I nodded my head and said, "Okay, Mom."

Late at night, while nobody was around, I had plenty of time to reflect on the journey I'd been on up to this point in my life. Everything was going so well, I thought, and West Point seemed like a real possibility for me. I was doing everything in my power to meet West Point's stringent requirements of a "well-rounded person."

Academically, I was still struggling with math and science, but I was getting mostly As and Bs in my classes. Athletically, I continued to wrestle but my success rate had dropped considerably after I'd dislocated my right elbow freshman year. I'd quit wrestling before I earned my varsity letter, and that worried me a bit. But I'd gone on to win another Judo state championship, and I was honored that my classmates had seen fit to elect me class president two years in a row.

For community service, I volunteered at the Leo Yassenoff Jewish Center, where my mother took a part-time job as an assistant in the physical therapy department for the senior citizens. It was there that I first met survivors of the Holocaust, and the tattooed numbers on the arms of some of the residents unnerved me.

I'd also joined every club that I had an interest in to strengthen my extracurricular activities profile. *What more could I have done?* I wondered.

And now, everything that I'd worked so hard for since I was twelve years old was at risk.

Yet, despite my current condition, I refused to believe that my dream was over. Daddy was still in the VA hospital in Chillicothe, and though his short-term memory still hadn't returned, he never forgot the promise I made to him to give him my first salute.

"Are you going to West Point?" he would ask whenever I visited him.

"Yes," I would answer, with all the conviction I could muster. And then he would smile and nod his head. It was as if he, too, were picturing that special day in his mind.

That's what continued to fuel me each and every day, and why I wouldn't, why I just couldn't, give up on my dream.

CHAPTER 42

———

DARKNESS

"Anything?" asked the eye doctor, as his light passed over my right eye.

I wanted to see something so badly, but I saw only darkness.

"Nothing," I said.

I heard the doctor sigh and click off his penlight. Then I felt a nurse place the patch back on my eye.

Two days had passed, and my eye was showing no sign of improvement. I knew the doctor would have to consider surgery in the next few days if nothing positive developed, and that scared me.

"Let's give it one more day," said the doctor.

I lay in my darkened room and finally faced the reality of the situation. *I may never see out of my right eye again.*

No amount of optimism, of idealism, or wishful thinking could save what might already be lost, I realized, and that defeat wasn't in my plans. I was so sure that the inspiration that I'd gotten when I was twelve years old, to go to West Point, was "meant to be," because it had come to me with such vividness and clarity.

How could a loving God give a boy a vision only to allow him to lose his sight?

As I lay in my bed, my mind wandered back to a day that had so moved me, so inspired me that I believed *anything* was possible. It was such a sacred experience, that I'd never shared it with anyone, afraid that if I did, I would break whatever spell it put me under.

I kept what I'm about to relate a secret until I was twenty-one years old, when I finally told it to my whole family while we were eating Thanksgiving dinner one year.

It was the day that my father was rushed to the hospital for emergency brain surgery, and the day that I asked God for a sign...

CHAPTER 43

———

THUNDER

"The God of glory thunders."
—Psalm 29:3

Desperate and in fear of losing my sight, my mind returned to the night my father was rushed to the hospital five years earlier. The night I asked God for a sign...

FALL 1978

"Lord, I have to know if you're really there, please...give me a sign," I begged, desperate to know if God was with my father in his greatest time of need.

"If you let me know that you're there, even if my father dies, then I'll know that he's okay," I pleaded. Finally, I summoned the courage to ask God for a loud, distinct clap of thunder that would leave me no doubt that He was real, and that He heard my pleas. Then I thought about it again and changed it to, "Three thunders. Please, God, send me three loud thunders so that I'll know that what happened on the baseball diamond that day was *real.*" Tears streamed down my cheeks as I continued. "If you do this, I promise that I will *never* question you again for as long as I live." Mrs. Miller told me to pray from the heart, and that's what I did that night.

I don't recall if I said, "Amen," or not, but I fell asleep, emotionally drained. The next memory I have is of awakening to a loud clap of thunder that shook the whole house. Even Fi-fi heard it, and she ran downstairs with her tail between her legs.

Did that just happen? I asked myself as I sat up on the couch. I sat still, as if I were in a dream and I held my breath. *Was I dreaming?*

The second one came and it was louder than the first, and it sounded angry as it clapped and shook the house again, causing the glass in the china cabinet to vibrate.

"Oh...my..." I stood up and felt the hairs on my arm and the back of my neck stand up, and I walked to the window. The skies were still gray, but there was no sign of storm clouds anywhere.

I knew in my heart that the third and final thunderclap was on the way, so I placed my hands on the window sill and looked towards the sky.

"One more, God," I said, smiling, "please."

There was a moment of complete silence and stillness in the air, and then I heard it. Rolling thunder. It sounded as if it were coming from miles away, rolling and rolling like a bowling ball or a freight train as it got closer and closer. It seemed to come from the front of my house and then pass directly over the top of my house, culminating in an ear-splitting, *Boom!* behind my house as a brilliant white bolt of lightning shot from the sky and lit everything up for a brief, shining moment, then faded away.

Complete stillness and silence followed.

"Oh my God," I whispered as tears of joy streamed down my cheeks. "Oh my God."

Never did I mean those words more than I did in that moment!

I leaned against the wall under the window sill and slumped down to the floor, crying tears of joy that God was with my father, one way or the other, and that live or die, Daddy would be okay.

Then, the bigger picture struck me. *God is real.*

And somehow, he heard a twelve- year-old boy's prayers and answered them. *What was I supposed to do with this knowledge?* I wondered.

I looked at the phone and then walked over and picked up the receiver. I called my friend who lived three doors down from me to the left, Roy Nichols. He answered the phone and I asked him, "Did you hear any thunder?"

"Of course I did," he said.

I grabbed the receiver with both hands and said, "How many? How many did you hear?"

"Three, why? Are you okay?" he asked.

"Never better, thanks." I said as I hung up the phone.

Then I called Tracy Joseph, who lived a few miles behind me. When she got on the line, I asked her the same question I asked Roy, and she said the same thing.

"Three," she said, then, "The lightning struck in a cornfield behind our house somewhere."

She saw the lightning too!

"Never forget this day," I said.

When I hung up, I walked up to my room knowing I'd just experienced a life-changing event, but I had no idea what I was supposed to do with this new knowledge, this amazing realization.

I sat at my desk trying to figure out how to draw or depict what had just happened, but I was having trouble figuring out how to draw thunder. I finally decided on the lightning bolt, instead. I didn't ask for that lightning bolt, but it sure was impressive! I wondered if it meant anything.

A few minutes later, Mom and my sisters came home from visiting Daddy at the hospital, and that's when Mom told me about Dad's dream to go to West Point and the tradition of the silver dollar... and that's when the dream was born, in the glow of a bolt of lightning and the echo of rolling thunder.

CHAPTER 44

———

LIGHT

"Open thou mine eyes, that I may behold
wondrous things out of thy law."
—Psalm 119:18

Mount Carmel East Hospital
September 5, 1982

My whole family, minus my father, was by my bedside to support me "just in case."

The nurse removed the patch from my right eye and the doctor told me to open it.

I opened it, felt a moment of fear, then saw a very dim square of light right above me.

"The ceiling light!" I said, "I can make it out," I said, pointing.

I heard my family members sigh with relief.

I moved my right arm to the left and right and I got the impression that I could see a shadowy version of my arm passing before the light.

"Put your hand down and tell me if you see my hand," said the doctor.

It was like looking up from a dirty river, everything was so brown and mushy, but there was no doubt that I could make out the feint outline of the fluorescent light.

A shadow passed from my left to my right in front of the light and I said, "There it is."

"Very good," said the doctor.

"Will I see again? I mean, *really* see?" I asked.

"We can never be one hundred percent sure," he answered, "But I'm optimistic that you will."

CHAPTER 45

―――

TURNING POINT

After recovering from my eye-injury, I applied to West Point for the Early-admission program, but I received a rejection letter in the fall of my junior year in high school. Frustrated and out of options, I finally had to accept the fact that I might not be "West Point material" and decided that it was time to tell my father that our mutual dream was over. It was one of the hardest discussions of my life.

Chillicothe VA Hospital

"Hi," my father said when I walked into his room. "Where's Mom?"

"I came by myself today," I said. I walked over to the skinny wall locker beside his bed and took out his navy windbreaker.

"Let's go for a walk," I said.

We walked across the street to the picnic table on the corner and sat down. Dad pulled out his filterless camel cigarettes and lit one with a snap of his Zippo lighter.

"So, what brings you here today?" he asked, tapping my knee with his right hand.

"You," I said, smiling. I didn't know where to begin.

Dad seemed to be in a good place, and I hated to ruin his day. "I got a letter from West Point," I said.

"Yeah?" Dad asked, a look of anticipation on his face.

I frowned and shook my head. "I didn't get in," I said flatly.

Dad's head went back slowly as if he had just been hit, and then he took a drag of his cigarette.

"Did you do everything you could?" he asked.

I thought about that for a moment and answered honestly. "I think so," I said.

We sat in uncomfortable silence for a minute, each of us lost in our own thoughts.

"Dad, why did you go to Vietnam when you didn't have to go?" I asked.

My father had a medical profile from his wound in the Korean War which exempted him from Vietnam, but I found a letter he wrote asking for a waiver which would allow him to deploy with his unit. I didn't understand why he would do that.

He thought about it for a moment and said, "You see that flag?" He pointed to the large flag visible in the distance at the parade field.

"Yeah," I said, as I looked at it.

"Where that flag goes, I go," he said.

That sent chills up my spine as soon as he said it. I so desperately wanted to understand the love he had for our country. Not even his illness could take that away from him. Dementia cannot take what's in a man's heart.

"Let's go back in," Dad said as he flicked what was left of his cigarette.

I hopped off the top of the bench and walked beside my father. It was nice to have a conversation like this with him, and I was surprised that he took the news about West Point as well as he did.

We crossed the street and stepped up to the grass when Dad stopped, turned to me and said, "Don't give up."

I was stunned that he remembered, and I studied his face.

"Don't give up," he said, softer this time, almost like it was a plea.

"I won't," I said, feeling the connection to him and to West Point that had nearly smoldered flare-up again deep inside of me.

CHAPTER 46

———

LONG-SHOT

Dad's words reignited the flame that had nearly gone out inside of me, and I thought about his question all the way home. "Did you do everything you could?"

As I thought about it, I realized that there was one more option. It was a long-shot, but it was worth a try.

My pride got in the way during the application process, and I purposely didn't fill-in the part of the Candidate Questionnaire that asked if a family member had served in the armed forces or was disabled as a result of service in the armed forces.

I'd worked hard to get into West Point on my own merits, and I didn't want to use my father's service or sacrifice as a means to getting in. So, when I came across that part of the questionnaire, I simply skipped it. Now, I realized that I was wrong to do so.

I pulled into Howard's Office Supply when I got back, and I purchased stationary with an American flag on top, and then I went home to write the most important letter of my life.

Instead of the requisite format prescribed for normal letters of inquiry or applications, I threw away all pretexts of formality, sat down at my desk, and wrote a letter by hand telling West Point about the promise I made to my father when I was a kid.

I finally told them that my father was a 100% disabled veteran, and that everything that I had done to prepare myself for West Point was done on my own, from the age of twelve, and that should stand for something, shouldn't it? I respectfully requested that they reconsider my rejection and take another look at me, because I believed I was worthy of consideration.

I sent the letter off, not knowing whether it would do any good, and I continued to do everything I could to be ready if West Point called.

West Point, New York

Meanwhile in Nanuet, New York, just thirty minutes south of West Point, my father's brother Bernie and his wife Dee had departed for West Point on their own initiative. After learning of my rejection letter, Uncle Bernie scheduled an appointment with the head of the Admissions office, who was a full-bird Colonel. Later, he conveyed this story to me.

Upon their arrival, Uncle Bernie and Aunt Dee got the sense that the Colonel was used to handling visits and phone calls from people whose son/daughter/niece or nephew didn't get an appointment letter to West Point, and he was polite but firm with them.

"Sometimes, even a Senator's kid doesn't qualify for admission to West Point," he said. "It's not personal."

Frustrated, Uncle Bernie said, "It's very personal to me. My brother is a one-hundred percent disabled veteran and fought in two wars. Shouldn't that mean something? Doesn't his son at least deserve a chance?"

Suddenly, the Colonel's demeanor changed and he opened my cadet file, which was on his desk. "I'm sorry, but your nephew didn't indicate anywhere in his application that his father is a disabled Veteran, let alone a career soldier."

Uncle Bernie and Aunt Dee exchanged looks, flabbergasted at my apparent over-site.

"Would it have made a difference?" Aunt Dee asked.

"Might have," said the Colonel. "Children of disabled veterans compete for appointments in a different category than the general population does."

Later that day, I received a phone call from Uncle Bernie. He was not pleased.

"So why didn't you tell them that your father is a disabled veteran?" he asked.

"Because my father's not the one applying," I said, meaning it. I wanted to know that I was good enough to get into West Point on my own merits. I believed that I had earned that privilege.

Uncle Bernie sighed on the other end of the phone and said, "You're as stubborn as your father."

I took that as a compliment.

CHAPTER 47

_____

THE CALL

I later learned that my handwritten letter landed on the desk of one Captain Belton, an admissions officer who took a personal interest in my story. While I struggled to keep my focus and try not to lose hope, Captain Belton was advocating for me with the Admissions Board behind the scenes.

More than any other person, it was Captain Belton who cracked open the doors of West Point just enough to cast light on my dream. His efforts led to the most fateful call of my life from the Columbus, Ohio, based West Point liaison officer, Lieutenant Colonel Don Lair, who was working at the Ohio State University ROTC program.

I will never forget that call.

"Hello?" I said as I walked over to the refrigerator to get a snack.

"Good afternoon, is this Robert Paley?"

"That's me," I said, as I scanned the refrigerator shelves.

"This is Colonel Don Lair from the Ohio State University ROTC—"

"Thank you—Colonel, did you say? I appreciate your call, but I already told my counselor that I have no interest in applying to ROTC at this time."

"As I was saying, Robert, I work at Ohio State, but I am also the Central Ohio West Point Liaison officer," he said.

"You are?" I said, suddenly paying attention. "I'm sorry, Sir—"

"And the reason that I'm calling is that I received a call from a Captain Belton of the Admissions Office, and West Point is interested in re-opening your file."

Chin-drop-to-the-floor moment.

"They are?" I said. It took all that I had not to shout for joy.

"Yes, but first you'll need to report to the Ohio Highway Patrol Academy to take what's called a P.A.T., or Physical Aptitude Test. I'd like you to come this Saturday at 8 o'clock if that'll work for you."

"Yes, Sir. I'll be there, Sir, and…thank you!"

Ohio Highway Patrol Academy

I don't recall the exact date I reported to take the P.A.T., but I do recall how nervous I was going in. There were about twenty other candidates there to take the test, and it was clear by the size of a few of them that they were football players. It was my first glimpse of the caliber of athletes that West Point was seriously considering, and I wondered how I'd stack up against them.

"Good luck," my mother said, as I turned to join the others.

The first event, if my memory serves me correctly, was the standing broad jump, followed by a basketball throw across the gym from the kneeling position. Then came the sprint, where we had to run a certain distance between two lines back-and-forth in under one minute. In each event, other than the standing broad jump, I kept up with the top-performers, and I was pleased with myself for that. Once again, my years of intensive physical conditioning were paying off.

The final event was pull-ups, and I was so amped-up to have my foot in the door on a possible path to West Point that I broke my personal best, doing about 25 pull-ups. Years of doing pull-ups on the Oak Tree in the front yard paid off hugely, and I did more pull-ups than anyone there that day. I was trying for 26 pull-ups, but I couldn't quite make it, and I hung in the halfway-up position for about 30 seconds as I tried to squeak out one more. Then my arms gave out and I dropped to the mat.

As soon as I hit the mat, a door to an office with reflective windows opened and a tall, slightly gray-haired man walked out and approached me.

"You did a good job out there today, Robert."

"Colonel Lair? Thank—thank you, Sir," I said, finding myself getting momentarily tongue-tied. I had no idea that he was in the office watching us, but I was glad I'd performed so well now that I knew he was. He was West Point's eyes and ears in the field, and whatever he witnessed would be reported directly back to West Point and Captain Belton.

"I'd like for you to meet my mother, Betty," I said. "Nice to meet you, Ma'am," he said as he shook her hand.

"Thank you. You too," my mother said.

"I understand your father's a veteran?" said Colonel Lair.

"Yes, Sir, he is," I said. *So, he knows*, I thought to myself.

"Well, you did a good job, today, Robert. I'll be back in touch with you soon"

"Thank you, Sir," I said. "You don't know how much this means to me."

"I may have some idea," he said, giving me a knowing look.

Colonel Lair was the first direct contact I had with West Point, and his presence at the P.A.T. was the first visible sign that I was finally on a path that could lead me to West Point. There was only one thing left to do.

CHAPTER 48

WEST POINT

1983

"Ain't no sense in lookin' down!" barked my father, smiling as he called cadence again for the first time in ten years.

It was just like old times as we sped east on I-70 towards New York and West Point for a school visit. Mom signed Dad out of the hospital, so he could accompany us on my first, and only, college visit the summer of my Junior Year.

"Ain't no sense in lookin' down!" we repeated. Karen and I looked at each other and smiled.

"Ain't no discharge on the ground!

"Ain't no discharge on the ground!"

"Sound off!"

"One-Two!"

"Once more!"

"Three Four!"

"Break it on down!"

"One, two, three, four, one two (pause) three four!"

It was great to get out of Ohio and to travel as a family again, and the trip didn't seem to bother Daddy at all. In fact, it seemed to reinvigorate him.

"Where are we going?" he'd ask multiple times along the way. And our answer, it seemed, was music to his ears.

"West Point."

Highland Falls, New York
West Point

As we entered Highland Falls, I felt my heartrate increase, knowing we were just minutes away from entering the main gate at West Point.

Family photo albums contained pictures of our family at West Point dating back to the 1950s, and even though I was in a few of the photos, I had no recollection of it at all.

I leaned forward from the back seat and crossed my arms between the headrests, anxious to get my "first" glimpse of the place that I'd seen only in books and my imagination for the last five years.

A granite structure with a guard standing outside of it told me that we had finally arrived. My mother slowed the car down, and the guard smiled and waved us through.

"That's the Thayer Hotel," my father said, pointing to the redbrick building that sat on a hilltop to our right.

"He remembers," Mom said, smiling. I looked at my parents, and they both had smiles on their faces, and I wondered how many memories they shared between them about their visits to West Point over the last thirty years.

As we approached the start of a low stone wall that ran the length of Thayer Road for as far as the eye could see, Dad inhaled deeply and said, "You can feel the history here."

I wondered what he meant by that.

I studied my father's face as we continued along Thayer Road, and he seemed to be at peace.

To the left, large brick homes overlooked the Hudson River, and a huge brown rock jutted out from the hillside.

Suddenly, as we drove around a gentle curve leading to Cullum Road, the gray, granite structures of the academic buildings came into view and they took my breath away. They looked like castles and conveyed a sense of power and permanence, citadels of American freedom.

"Wow," I whispered to myself as we descended a slight incline that took us directly under one of the granite structures. As we ascended the hill on the other side, we were surrounded by huge gray walls and bridges made of stone. I almost expected to see a Knight on his fiery steed cross in front of us at any moment.

At the top of the hill everything opened up and spread out before us as we passed the cadet library, where an imposing statue of General George Patton stood.

I felt like my heart was going to leap out of my chest. West Point was more beautiful and more intimidating than I'd ever imagined it would be, and I loved it.

We passed Cullum Hall, where a 1950s photo in our family photo album shows my brother Phil, crawling in the grass while my father looks on.

My father, standing to the right, looks down at my brother Phil while
Uncle Bernie and Aunt Dee pose for the camera. Cullum Hall is directly
across the street from where my father is standing. Circa 1956.

"Trophy Point," my father said, pointing to the right where rows of
old patina colored canons lined the road leading up to an oversized
flagpole. Below and to the right, an incredible view of the Hudson
River was visible for as far as the eye could see.

"Look," said Karen, pointing to the left.

My eyes widened as we passed some bleachers and saw the expanse
of the famous Plain, or parade field, stretch out before us. In the
distance stood the cadet barracks, and high above them silhouetted
against the sky was a dark gray granite building with a tower pointing to the heavens. I later learned that this was the Cadet Chapel.

My father smiles broadly as he leads our family along Trophy Point.
Behind my father is Nancy, my cousin Marilyn, and behind
Marilyn is my brother Phil trying to pick me up (we are partially
blocked from view). Circa 1969.

Mom pulled over and stopped the car so that she and Dad could look at the parade field, too.

"This is where we came to watch parades," Mom said, reminiscing.

"Really?" I said. I looked over at the parade field and tried to imagine them sitting in the bleachers. I looked at Dad and he was deep in thought, taking it all in.

"When was your first visit to West Point?" I asked.

"When Phil was a baby," Mom said. "The first time I went to New York to meet Daddy's family, we came here to watch a parade. That's when Daddy told me that he gave this up to marry me."

"Why?" asked Karen.

"Because cadets can't be married," I said, "and a long time ago Daddy wanted to be a cadet."

A blurry photo of Nancy and me sitting on the patina colored canons of Trophy Point. Circa 1969.

We continued on and took a left up a steep hill called Stony Lonesome Road. It was so steep that my mother's car seemed to strain from exertion. Near the top of the hill, we saw the tower of the Cadet Chapel sticking up over the trees, and Mom pulled into the parking lot. We got out of the car to look at the magnificent Chapel, and then we stood on the balcony and took in the expansive view of the Hudson Valley below.

It was difficult to discern from above where West Point began and the mountains ended, so skillfully was the one carved into the other.

We drove the rest of the way up the hill where the road curved hard to the right and saw Michie Stadium, the home of the Army football team.

"Cadets!" Karen cried.

Cadets wearing black shorts and white T-shirts with the academy crest emblazoned on their chests jogged by, hugging the stone wall that surrounded a beautiful body of water, called Lusk Reservoir. From that day on, every time I ran, I imagined myself chasing cadets.

I turned and watched them run by with a sense of awe.

These guys made the cut, and I envied them for that. They were lean and muscular, with tight haircuts, and all of them were tall.

"See how tall they are?" my mother said.

"I see that Mom, but I'm not going to get any taller between now and next year," I said.

"Hang from a tree," she joked.

"They're not measuring my arm length, Mom."

We pulled in to the parking lot outside of the stadium and went into a gift shop. I bought two T-Shirts that said West Point on the front of them, one was yellow and black, and the other was navy and light blue.

On the way out, we passed another group of cadets running. "They have girls here now?" my father asked, surprised.

He got sick in 1978, two years before the first female class graduated from West Point, so I wasn't surprised he didn't know about that change.

By the time we drove back out Thayer Gate, my desire to attend West Point had grown even stronger.

CHAPTER 49

BOYS' STATE

My German teacher, Herr Robert Peters, was a tall, lean bespectacled man who served in the Army during World War II. When I told him during freshman year that I wanted to go to West Point, he made every effort to help me.

At the end of freshman year, he asked, "Do you want to be a leader?"

"Yes," I responded.

"Then lead," he said, as he slid a blank petition to me to run for class president. I ran and won and had the honor of serving my classmates as their president for the next three years.

In the spring of Junior year, Herr Peters nominated me to attend the American Legion's Boys' State program, called Buckeye Boys' State in Ohio. He was an active member of Groveport's Robert Dutro American Legion Post 486, and his nomination of me would have far-reaching consequences for me and for my family.

SUMMER 1983

"You know," said Ms. Bea Barnett, my assistant high school principal, "Winning governor at Buckeye Boys' State could put you back in the running for West Point." Ms. Barnett was the first female administrator in our district, and she was tough as nails but always had the student's best interest in mind.

"Do you really think so?" I asked.

"Absolutely! It's a highly respected program," she said.

I trusted Ms. Barnett a lot. We'd grown closer after I'd received my rejection letter from West Point. I was feeling down about it, and I withdrew into myself like I used to do as a child. Everyone saw the change in my personality.

One day, when I was walking by her office, Ms. Barnett pulled me aside and said, "Can I ask you a personal question?"

"Sure."

"Are you taking drugs?"

Drugs? I was shocked by her question. "No, it's worse. I got rejected by West Point."

Ever since that day, she too, had taken an interest in helping me, so I never took her advice lightly.

"Thanks," I said. "I'll think about running for governor then."

On the day of my departure for Buckeye Boys State in June 1983, I heard someone shout my name as I was walking out of the high school. It was Ms. Kathy Benson, the pretty high school French teacher whom I'd never had as a teacher.

I turned around to see what she needed.

"Hi, Ms. Benson," I said.

"Robert, I'm glad I caught you before you left. I just wanted to wish you luck if you decide to run for governor at Boys' State. If anyone can do it, *you* can."

I was sincerely moved by her kind words. Even more so because she'd chased me down just to tell me that.

"Thank you," I said. "I appreciate it."

It's amazing, really, how a word of encouragement from a teacher can stay with you for the rest of your life.

Bowling Green State University
June 14, 1983
Flag Day

"This came in for you, Governor," said Luther Liggett, the spunky, gray-haired president of the Ohio American Legion who was my mentor and advisor at Buckeye Boys' State.

It was a yellow Western Union Telegram from Ms. Barnett. It read, "Congratulations, Governor Paley. The Class of '84 thinks you're great!"

I'd never received a telegram before, and it brought tears to my eyes. I folded it and placed it in the pocket of my gray tuxedo.

"Are you ready?" asked Luther.

"Ready," I said, checking myself in the mirror one last time.

"Are my Mom and brother here yet?"

Luther smiled. "Your mother just got here."

I walked outside where I was greeted by Highway Patrolman Robinson, the Ohio State Highway Patrolman of the Year, who was my "driver."

"Mr. Governor," he said, smiling, as he opened the back door for me.

"Patrolman," I said, smiling back. It was a little over-the-top, but I'd be lying if I said I wasn't thoroughly enjoying myself.

Luther got in the front seat, and Patrolman Robinson turned on the lights on his highly polished Highway Patrol cruiser.

Minutes later, I stood outside the entrance to Anderson Auditorium. Flags lined the way in honor of "Flag Day," and 1,426 screaming Boys' State delegates could be heard inside rocking to the band's rendition of "Hang on Sloopy."

My stomach was tied in knots at the spectacle.

I leaned to my right to get a look at the stage and saw my mother seated in the place of honor, right behind the podium with Bill Welsh, the Director of Buckeye Boys' State.

When the band struck-up "Stars and Stripes Forever," Luther held his hand out and said, "It's time." I walked in to a warm welcome and made my way to the stage, waving at my Smith City brothers and shaking a few hands along the way.

When I got on the stage, I gave my mother a hug, and she smiled at me and said, "Wow!"

"I know," I said, enjoying our private moment. Then, I looked around for Phil, but he was nowhere to be found.

"Where's Phil?" I asked.

Mom's face briefly changed from happy to concern, then back to happy again as she said, "He couldn't come. Work."

The American Legion gave my mother a beautiful bouquet of red roses, and then I gave my inauguration speech. My first words were, "My thoughts turn now to my father, who is a disabled Veteran, and couldn't be with us tonight..."

After the exciting evening, Mom was heading home, and I walked her to her car.

"I thought Phil changed his schedule?" I said, disappointed that he couldn't be here with us. "Why didn't he drive you here?"

Mom's concerned look returned.

"What's wrong, Mom? Is everything okay?"

"He's at the hospital," she said.

"What? Why?" I gasped, fearing the worst.

"He's okay," Mom said. "His gas station got robbed, and someone shot the assistant manager five times. Phil's at the hospital with him."

"Is Phil okay?" I asked, just to be sure.

"Yes, he left a few minutes early to come and get me. Five minutes later..." Mom stopped talking as we both thought that through. If Phil hadn't left early...

"Is the assistant manager alive?" I asked.

"I don't know," said Mom.

I was walking back to my dorm room, shocked at what Mom had just told me, when a delegate from the Boys' State newspaper, *Hetuck*, called out for me.

"Governor! Do you mind coming back inside, so we can take a picture of you for tomorrow's paper?" he asked.

"Not now," I said, "Sorry. Just use any picture."

When I got back to my dorm room, I thought about the poor man who'd been shot five times, and I realized that if I hadn't run for and won governor, it would have been Phil who got shot.

I took out the bible that I carried with me throughout my entire campaign at Boys' State, and I got on my knees and cried and prayed for the assistant gas station manager as if he were my own brother.

When I returned from Buckeye Boys State the following weekend, I gave my brother a big hug, so grateful that he was okay. Then I looked at him and said, "Is he—"

"Alive!" Phil said. "Shot five times and he's still alive. I guess it just wasn't his time."

"Thank God," I said.

When I finally saw a picture of the newspaper the day after the inauguration, I smiled. The reporter submitted the worst picture he could possibly find of me, and it wasn't in the Hetuck. It was in a local paper that served thousands. *Never snub a reporter*, I noted to myself.

Phil's application to be a Columbus police officer was accepted, and he spent the rest of his career chasing bad guys.

Now, back to Buckeye Boys' State for one more story.

CHAPTER 50

─────

WHAT THE FORK?

Buckeye Boys' State
Friday, June 17, 1983

Certain events that have occurred over the course of my life have
made me believe there are no coincidences. This is one of them.

LANDS AT BG — U.S. Secretary of Defense Caspar Weinberger (second from left) arrives at Bowling Green State University to address the 1,425 delegates attending the annual Buckeye Boys State convention. To his right is Bill Welch, director of the convention. Weinberger told the young delegates — including many from the Defiance area — that a nuclear freeze will not result in world peace. Instead, he called for U.S.-Soviet arms negotiations. (UPI)

Page 10 of the Defiance Crescent News on Saturday, June 18, 1983
NewspaperARCHIVE.com

Luther Liggett told me that we had a "surprise guest" coming to Buckeye Boys' State, and for security reasons, he couldn't tell me who it was. Instead, he told me to put on my suit and meet him outside.

It must not have been too big a secret as to who was coming, however, because as I stood with Luther Liggett and Bill Welsh, the Director of the convention, protesters were lined up behind us with signs saying things like, "No more nukes!" and "Make love, not war!"

It was all very exciting, as we stood on the sidewalk adjacent to a grassy field. Minutes later, I heard the rumbling of helicopters in the distance; then suddenly two Huey helicopters appeared just above the tree line and pulled up into a hover, before gently setting down.

Stepping out of one of the helicopters was the Secretary of Defense, Caspar Weinberger, Jr., followed by a two-star general who was carrying a heavy briefcase. Mustached Secret Service men scanned around and talked into their sleeves.

The VIPs were quickly escorted into a nearby building, and I tagged along, closely behind. Secret Service agents were everywhere. "How cool," I thought to myself.

Before I knew it, I was standing at a table set for lunch with Luther Liggett, Bill Welsh, and the most powerful man in the Department of Defense—just months after I'd received my rejection letter from West Point.

Surely, God and the universe love irony!

Standing to my left was the two-star general. He smiled at me politely but didn't seem to "get" why this 17-year-old with non-matching pants and suit jacket was there at all. He grinned cordially and nodded at me, so I grinned cordially and nodded back.

To his left, and directly across from me was Secretary Weinberger, smart in a navy-blue suit and tie. To my right stood Luther Liggett and beside him, Bill Welsh.

The table was set with white linen and lots of silverware. *Why in the world would anyone need so much silverware?* I wondered.

I started to pull my seat out to sit down and Luther shot me a quick look and shook his head "No".

I was completely out of my element and felt my temperature begin to rise.

The SECDEF and Bill Welsh shared small talk, and the General and I just continued to nod and grin at each other.

Finally, the SECDEF pulled out his chair to be seated, and we all followed suit.

"Note to self," I thought. *"Always wait for the senior person to sit before you do."*

I had a busy morning and hadn't eaten breakfast, so I wasn't surprised to hear and feel my stomach rumble. I couldn't wait to eat.

I sat down and came face to face with the ridiculous amount of silverware spread out on each side of my fine china dishware. I was used to Chinette.

In a jiffy, a delicious looking salad appeared in front of me, and I couldn't wait to dig in to it. I grabbed my fork and started to dive in when I sensed Luther looking at me again. I gave him a sidelong glance and saw him shaking his head "no". As if to say, "Not yet."

I put my fork down, then smiled and nodded again at the General next to me. He seemed amused.

Finally, after copying everyone else by laying my napkin ever so lightly across my lap, I picked up the same fork they did and began to shovel forkful after forkful of salad into my mouth. I'd never had a better salad in my life!

I didn't put my fork down once, which I realized was not how the others were doing it, but I didn't care anymore. I was hungry!

The last thing left on my plate was a little cherry tomato...it sat so lovely and shiny, drenched in olive oil and reflecting the lights above. Normally, I would just grab it and pop it into my mouth, but something told me that now wouldn't be the right time to do that.

My stomach growled again, so I gripped my fork tighter and I moved to stick the tomato.

The darned thing slipped out from under my fork and slid to the other side of my salad plate. *No problem. Just stick it in the middle,* I thought to myself. But the darned thing slipped out from under my fork again, this time catching the lip of the plate and going in circles.

I thought I heard a pause in the very serious conversation the adults were having, but when I looked up, they all politely resumed their conversation and acted as though they weren't watching me.

I made one more attempt and grew frustrated when the tomato slipped again. Hoping no one would notice, I slowly reached up from below the table with my left hand, pinned the tomato down with my fingertips, and then slowly, surely stuck my fork deep into the meatiest part of the tomato.

"I got you now!" I thought to myself in my best Darth Vader voice. My fork plunged deeper and deeper.

"Victory was mine!"

I moved my hand and lifted the delicious looking tomato to my mouth when I heard a strange, high pitched sound coming from… my plate!

I had apparently pushed down on the edge of my plate too hard and lifted it when I was stabbing the tomato, and now the plate began a slow-motion spin cycle.

I plunged the tomato into my mouth and watched in horror as the little plate spun slow at first, then with each dip and roll gained speed and increased in pitch. I sat frozen with the cherry tomato stuck in my cheek like a chipmunk, and all eyes focused on me and my plate.

Surely it would stop soon, I thought, as it began to spin faster and louder.

Surely, anytime now, it would just…stop!

But it didn't stop, in fact, it got faster and faster, louder and louder and everyone, the General, the Secretary of Defense, and my very embarrassed mentors just watched the little plate spin.

I forced the tomato down and felt my temperature rise, as beads of sweat appeared on my forehead.

Finally, I laid my left hand on the plate and it came to an abrupt halt.

I smiled and nodded. They all smiled and nodded back.

A waiter saved me when he removed my plate and replaced it with the main course—chicken dumplings.

The Secretary of Defense said something about how hungry he was as he stuck a dumpling with his fork. As he brought it towards his mouth, the gravy from the dumpling dripped onto his tie.

"Look what I just did," he laughed. "I'm so clumsy!"

The General and the others laughed on cue, too. So, I joined in. From the partial wink Secretary Weinberger gave me, I was sure he'd done that on purpose, and that made me respect him more than I already did.

"So," Secretary Weinberger asked me, "What do you want to do after high school, Little Governor?"

I nearly choked on my dumpling.

For a moment I saw another chance at West Point appear miraculously before my eyes. Surely, he saw my persistence with the tomato and thought, "You're just the kind of guy we need leading our Soldiers, son!"

So, it was with great pride that I said, "Well, Sir, I'm hoping to go to West Point."

The Secretary of Defense smiled and said, "Let me know if you need any help with that."

CHAPTER 51

———

URGENT FURY

Groveport Madison High School
October 25ᵗʰ, 1983

"We just invaded Grenada," said Mr. Milless as he walked into the lunchroom. Mr. Milless was a big, burly man who was one of the high school social studies teachers.

"Grenada?" asked Mr. Sexton, another social studies teacher with a walrus-like mustache. I was standing within earshot and was fascinated by their conversation. From what I could gather, American college students were in danger on the island of Grenada due to some kind of Communist insurgency, and President Reagan ordered one of America's most elite unites, the 82ⁿᵈ Airborne Division, to go and rescue them. *How awesome!*

"Where's Grenada?" I asked.

"In the Caribbean," said Mr. Sexton, who was standing with his arms crossed in front of him in his usual pose.

I was familiar with the 82ⁿᵈ Airborne Division from my military history studies, and I couldn't wait to get home to watch the news to learn more about what was going on.

Less than one year later, I would meet some of the heroes who fought at Grenada.

CHAPTER 52

———

WEST POINT PREP SCHOOL

SUMMER 1984

I'll never know if becoming Governor of Buckeye Boys' State helped me or not, and I'm sure that the Secretary of Defense forgot to put in a good word for me, but none the less in the spring of my senior year in high school, Lieutenant Colonel Don Lair called me with great news: I had been accepted into the U.S. Military Academy Preparatory School, or USMAPS, located at Fort Monmouth, New Jersey. Captain Belton's advocacy for me had paid off.

Although it wasn't West Point itself, it was certainly the next best thing, and it was a cause for celebration within our family when I was accepted. Dad couldn't have been happier.

Each year, the West Point Admissions Office chooses about 300 cadet candidates to attend the prep school in order to help prepare them for the academic, leadership, and physical demands of West Point. Roughly half came from the Active Duty, Reserves, or National Guard, while the other half—including me—came from the civilian sector, better known as "Fort Living Room."

I heard that by the end of each year, one out of three cadet candidates either wash-out of the program or opt-out on their own. I didn't plan to do either.

Fort Dix, New Jersey
June 1984

I in-processed into the Army at Fort Dix, New Jersey, with roughly 150 other cadet candidates from Fort Living Room, USA. My father also in-processed at Fort Dix when he joined the Army en route to the Korean War in 1951.

It was here that I first met my peers who would become my friends, enemies, and classmates for the next five years on our journey to and through West Point. I had never been part of a more accomplished group of student-athletes in my life, and I wondered how any of them hadn't gotten into West Point on their first try.

This is also the place where I first "met" the drill sergeants who would mold us from civilians into "lean, mean, fighting machines." I was pleased when a barrel-chested African American drill sergeant wearing the dreaded "Smoky the Bear" hat hopped onto our bus, called us "maggots," and demanded that we disembark "his" bus by "one minute ago."

It was a mad scramble and within minutes, he and his other friendly instructors had us in some semblance of a platoon formation. I was loving it.

Then things slowed down a bit, as the Senior Drill Instructor, or DI, told us that we would generally be left alone while we in-processed at Fort Dix, but that would *not* be the case once we got to Fort Monmouth. I couldn't wait.

While I was in the finance section, I remembered a scene in the movie "Superman" with Christopher Reeve where he sent half of his check home to his mother, so I decided to do the same. Mom never knew where the U.S. Treasury checks came from, and I didn't tell her.

The most unpleasant station was the "rubber glove" station, where a female doctor ... well, you get the picture.

Flash forward to lunchtime, where we are standing in line at attention and we see the same doctor eating lunch amongst her peers. Someone whispers, "How can she eat after doing *that* to us all morning?"

That's when I learned that situational humor in high-intensity situations is ten times funnier than it would be otherwise. And if there's one thing true about American soldiers, they can make a joke no matter how stressful or absurd a situation is.

Fort Monmouth, New Jersey
USMAPS

"Look at that old man!" someone shouted from the bus as we pulled into our new home for the next year.

I looked out my window and saw a very old man, hunched over, "jogging." It was a funny sight, but impressive at the same time.

During the first few weeks at Fort Monmouth, the Senior Drill Instructor and his posse put us through a mini-boot camp, and during that time they molded 150 civilian-types into something that resembled an efficient military organization. Once mini-boot was finished, we all felt pretty pleased with ourselves ... until the *real* soldiers arrived.

We were standing around getting to know each other in the barracks hallways when the Active Duty soldiers arrived. They were decked-out in their Class A's, and several of them wore the famed red berets of the 82nd Airborne Division.

The men I'd seen on the news during the invasion of Grenada in 1983 were now walking through the doors of our barracks. There was Scott "Scotty Mo" Morrison—who was the epitome of an Airborne Ranger in the way he carried himself—John Nelson, and Bill Nyfeler. Bill Nyfeler would be my first roommate.

Bill was tall, slim, and had dark hair cut high-and-tight. He helped me get "squared away" in all things military, though my youth, immaturity, and propensity to talk too much often got on his nerves.

"You're showing your age, Paley" he would say to me if I got a little too excitable at times. I'm sure that the unexplainable miracles I'd experienced when I was twelve went a long way towards my delayed development in the usual sense. How could I live in "reality" after that?

What he didn't know, what he couldn't know, of course, is how happy I was to just to be there! I was literally "living the dream!" Sometimes, this made me outright giddy, and I had to force myself to contain that side of me.

The soldiers coming in from active duty, many of whom were combat veterans, had to sanitize their uniforms from all signs of previous Army life, and wear only the prescribed Cadet Candidate uniform. Thus, those who fought only via video games joined those who fought in America's most elite units. Somehow, no one ever got us confused.

The veterans brought maturity and experience to our battalion, held most of the key leader positions throughout the academic year, and went on to become some of the future leaders of the Corps of Cadets and the Active Duty Army. I was honored to have served with them.

Perspective

One morning, when I was standing by my wall locker for a morning inspection, SFC Frank Withers, the company Tactical Non-Commissioned Officer (NCO) walked into my room. SFC Withers was a badass Airborne Ranger Vietnam Veteran with down-turned eyes that made him appear sad, even when he smiled. He wore the combat patch of the 101st Airborne on his right shoulder, and a Purple Heart Ribbon on his left breast.

"How are you this morning, Sergeant Withers?" I asked as he entered my room.

"I woke up in a dry bed, in my own house, and I wasn't getting shot at. In my book, that's a good day," he said.

SFC Frank Withers

I started to laugh but then I realized that he was being completely serious.

From that day on, I learned to be grateful for the little things in life, and to appreciate those who had been through hell in order to gain such an appreciation for the things which I took for granted every day.

Post Chapel

I continued my spiritual quest to find meaning in what I'd experienced over the past several years by going to numerous churches and synagogues. I liked the atmosphere I found in different churches of all faiths, but I never experienced an "a-ha!" moment that told me I'd found my spiritual home.

One evening, I decided to go the small post chapel located right around the corner from the barracks for Friday night Jewish services. To my great surprise, that very old man we'd seen "jogging" the first day we arrived at USMAPS was the Rabbi.

His name was Rabbi Dana, and he had a newspaper clipping hanging in his office showing him saying a prayer over an Army Air Force bomber crew prior to a mission.

"This is me," he said, "and this is the crew who dropped an atomic bomb on Japan."

I couldn't believe the irony of it all. Here was a Rabbi who represented the faith of my father telling me about blessing a crew who dropped an atomic bomb on the people of my mother. I had absolutely no qualms about it, however, because when it came to my country, there were no divided loyalties.

I *did* find that the spirituality of the Jewish service, though it was nearly all in Hebrew which I didn't understand, resonated with me deep down, and from that day on, I identified as a Jew. Little did I know there would be a price to pay for this decision.

Battalion Activities Officer

When I found out that there'd be an election for a Battalion Activities Officer (BAO), it seemed only natural for me to run. I felt I'd done a decent job planning activities for my high school class through the years, and I looked forward to doing the same for my new USMAPS classmates.

My tactical officer, Captain Schwegman, was a West Point graduate with reddish hair, a prominent nose, and chiseled facial features. He called me into his office and said, "If you're going to run, I expect you to win. You represent Charlie Company."

"Roger, Sir." I said. "I plan to run, and to win."

He smiled and dismissed me.

I went to the room of my good friend John "Bear" Rodriguez, who was a jolly guy from a California ranching family, to tell him about my decision to run for BAO, or class president. John was an artist, and he volunteered to draw my likeness on posters, so we could post them throughout the battalion area.

Then I went door-to-door throughout the barracks introducing myself and telling my classmates what I would do if elected. On the day of the election, we made public speeches in front of the whole battalion and then waited for the results.

To my shock, I was elected class president. I considered this a huge honor because everyone was a leader at USMAPS, and to be picked as their activities leader made me feel especially good.

I received a letter from Captain Belton that read, "Congratulations, Cadet Candidate Paley. We already know you're a leader, now show us you can make the grades!"

Although this letter was more of an admonition than a congratulation, it still made me feel good that they considered me a leader. Eventually, I took the hint and stepped down mid-year to focus on my grades, which weren't very good. Especially in math.

Academics

I continued to struggle in all things math, and after failing too many tests, I noticed a tall, brown-haired guy with glasses studying in the library. *Glasses!*

His name was Curt Herwig. I tried to make small talk with him, but he was too into whatever he was studying to pay me any attention. I finally cut to the chase.

"I was wondering if you could tutor me in math."

"Sorry, I don't think so," Curt said without even looking up at me.

"I'll give you fifty bucks," I said.

"Sit down," he said.

And that's how I began my comeback in math.

My USMAPS class portrait, 1984.

CHAPTER 53

—

TOO LATE

USMAPS
September 11, 1984

I was seated in math class with my blouse off due to the heat when a runner knocked on the classroom door and told the instructor that he had an urgent Red Cross message.

Red Cross messages usually mean one thing—a death in the family.

"For who?" asked the instructor.

"Cadet Candidate Paley," he said.

Dad? I thought to myself.

My heart jumped out of my chest and I stood up and ran out of the classroom towards my company area. I was in such a panic about the message that I completely forgot to put on my blouse and my cover (patrol cap). I ran across the grass and past USMAPS headquarters to my Tactical NCO, SFC Withers' office.

"Where's your blouse?" he asked me instinctively, then he told me to go and see Captain Schwegman.

Coral Gables, Florida

I wore my Class-A uniform to my grandmother's funeral because I didn't have a suit at the Prep School, nor did I need one.

We met at Grandma's condo where she lived with her brother, Sam. Their next door neighbor was the mother of "Kit," the voice of the car in the hit series *Knight Rider*. We always got a kick out of the fact that the mother allegedly kept a picture on the wall not of her famous son, but of the black car.

Uncle Sam told us that Grandma died peacefully in her sleep, and that gave me some consolation.

A few days earlier, I'd written Grandma a letter just as I'd promised her I would, and I was so glad I had. But when I walked into her bedroom to stand in the last place she was alive, I saw my letter lying on top of her dresser, unopened and realized I'd sent my letter too late.

At the showing, Grandma lay in her open casket, as everyone paid their respects. A few minutes after the others had finished, Dad walked over to the coffin and stood by his mother's side, deep in thought. Then we heard him say, "Goodbye, Mom," as he bent down and gave her a kiss on her forehead.

There wasn't a dry eye in the house.

When we returned to the condo, all the mirrors were covered with black sheets and we sat Shiva for Grandma on the floor, as is the custom.

I recalled the talk that Grandma and I had when Dad didn't recognize me after his surgery. She told me how very proud he would be if I graduated from West Point, then she said, "It's too bad that I won't be there to see it." *I wonder how she knew.*

As we shared cherished memories of our indomitable grandmother, Nancy brought me a cup of coffee. In the midst of our grief, I sipped the coffee in tiny, consecutive sips, so fast that Nancy started to laugh at me. And I started to laugh, too. Grandma would have wanted it that way.

CHAPTER 54

———

DEAN BEAL

"Bring your books."

SPRING 1985

USMAPS

Dean Beal was a no-nonsense retired Colonel and former Associate Director of the Office of Admissions at West Point. He spoke with clarity and conviction, and he scared the hell out of us.

It didn't take long to learn that those who weren't cutting it academically would soon be called-out. Literally. In the middle of an academic day, a "click" would indicate that Dean Beal was about to speak over the intercom.

In his raspy voice he would say, "The following cadet candidates report to my office...*bring your books.*"

This statement was the kiss-of-death for a cadet candidate, and anyone summoned to Dean Beal's office in this manner was literally never seen or heard from again.

By the time we returned to the barracks, the unfortunate souls who were summoned by Dean Beal were gone without a trace. Their wool blankets were folded on their bunks, the sheets were gone, and their wall lockers were left opened and empty. Aliens couldn't have done a better job.

Despite my improvement in math grades under Curt Herwig's incredible tutelage, my overall GPA and SAT performance did not inspire confidence in Dean Beal. He was the ultimate arbiter for recommending a cadet candidate to West Point based on their academic performance and potential.

One day, during class, came the "click" of the intercom. "Cadet Candidate Paley, report to my office…"

Click.

I stood up, my heart sinking. I reached for my books and "Bear" said, "He didn't say bring your books. So don't!"

That's right, he didn't say to bring my books. Maybe there's hope?

I reported to Dean Beal who directed me to sit down. In a very impersonal and businesslike manner, he said, "Cadet Candidate Paley, based on your overall academic performance to date I cannot in good faith recommend you to West Point. Do you have any questions?"

I admired his candor, but I didn't know what that meant for my chances to get into West Point.

"Sir, does this mean—"

"It just means that I can't recommend you because I'm not sure you can handle West Point's curriculum. But that doesn't mean that you won't receive an appointment," he said.

Hope. When that's all you have, you take it.

"Thank you, Sir," I said.

CHAPTER 55

THE FINAL CUT

APRIL 1985

USMAPS

In springtime, selections are made for appointments to West Point. Three lists are posted one day apart, and if your name isn't on one of the lists, then chances are you are *not* going to West Point and that you will eventually evaporate into thin air like the other poor souls did.

The days of the lists were the longest three days of my life.

On day one, excited cadet candidates who excelled in academics and athletics celebrated being on the first list. My name wasn't there, but pride made me check it anyways. Twice. I was happy for those who'd made it, and I waited for the next list.

Day 2. Same result.

Tomorrow will be my day, I thought. I was so nervous that I knocked on Captain Schwegman's door and reported to him.

"What is it, Paley?" he said.

"Sir, tomorrow's list…is there anything more I can do to ensure I'm on that list?"

Captain Schwegman looked at me as if he were trying to read between the lines of what I was saying. He was probably half-expecting me to give him a "Chicago handshake" and slip him a folded twenty dollar bill for his troubles.

"What's done is done, Paley. You'll either be on the list or you won't, there's nothing else you can do now."

Of course there wasn't! What was I thinking? That was stupid of me.

The next day, I walked down the stairs towards the wall where the third and final list was posted, and I saw my friends celebrating. I smiled and imagined how I would react when I saw my name there.

As soon as someone stepped away from the list, I stepped towards it and scanned for my last name alphabetically. It wasn't there.

My heart sank, and so did I. I literally slid down the wall, defeated. I had been weighed and measured and found wanting.

"Sorry, Rob," someone said.

"Tough break," someone else said.

I got up and walked up the stairs to my room to pack my gear and go home. How humiliating it's going to be to return home to my family and friends.

As I emptied my wall locker of its contents, I felt a bit of relief as well. I truly gave it my best, and I didn't have anything to be ashamed of. I simply didn't meet West Point's stringent and unbending standards. Now, I could find a new path.

"Paley," called Sergeant First Class Frank Withers, my tactical NCO.

"Yes, Sergeant?" I said, trying to hide my sadness and disappointment.

"Don't pack your gear yet," he said.

"What?" I asked.

"You're not leaving yet," he said.

For the next several days, I was one of the walking-dead whose name was not on a list but who still wasn't told to leave. *Why couldn't something be easy for once?* Friends who were on the list would stop talking about West Point whenever I came around, and I soon felt like a leper.

April 26, 1985

I sat alone in the cafeteria so as not to dampen my friends' spirits, and I waited, and I waited some more. By the third or fourth day, an announcement came over the intercom in the cafeteria.

"Cadet Candidate Paley, please report to Captain Schwegman's office."

I took my tray of uneaten food to the counter and could feel all eyes on me. Though I had friends who supported me, there were many others who would just as soon see me leave. My time as the Battalion Activities Officer put me in near-daily contact with the Commandant of the Prep School, Colonel Drisko and several other high ranking officers, and it didn't take long before I heard people referring to me as a "Cheeser," which I learned was right up there with a "Brown-noser." I was just trying to do my job.

Now, as I walked towards Captain Schwegman's office, I no longer cared which way it went. I just wanted to get out of limbo.

Captain Schwegman's door was closed, so I straightened up my uniform and reminded myself that no matter what happened, I was the son of a Sergeant Major and would conduct myself as such.

I knocked twice on his door.

"Enter!" said Captain Schwegman.

I posted to the front of his desk, my eyes looking above him, and saluted. "Sir, Cadet Candidate Paley reporting to Captain Schwegman as ordered."

Captain Schwegman returned my salute.

"At ease," he said. "Paley, sorry about the last few days. I know it's been hard on you."

"Yes, Sir." I said. *Just get it over with, will ya?*

"How long have you wanted to be a cadet, Paley?" he asked.

"Sir, for as long as I can remember."

"Well, you gave it a good shot, and all I can say is—"

He reached into his upper right hand drawer and produced a green Army certificate portfolio; then he slid it towards me.

"Congratulations, *Cadet* Paley!"

"What? Are you serious, Sir?" I said, losing all military bearing and motioning with my hands.

Captain Schwegman raised his eyebrows at me, but he was smiling. I returned to the position of attention.

"I mean, thank you, Sir!"

"Now get out of here and go call your family," he said.

I couldn't believe it. I could barely see through my tears of joy as I ran outside to the phone booth to call my family. I felt like I was going to burst from trying to hold in the pure joy I was feeling inside.

I opened the appointment letter as soon as I got into the phone booth to make sure that my name was really on it. And there, in the center of the page I saw it: Robert Holden Paley.

"Thank you, God. Thank, you."

This was no Certificate of Participation!

I called home collect, and Phil answered the phone.

"Hi, bro," I said, nonchalantly.

"Hey, Rob," Phil said. "Any news?"

"Yeah," I said, again nonchalantly.

"And?" Phil said, knowing that it could go either way.

"I'm going to West Point!" I shouted.

"What?" Phil shouted back. "Are you kidding me?"

"No, I'm not, I'm really going," I said, crying as Phil cried right along with me.

"Tell Daddy."

PART THREE

———

RUN

CHAPTER 56

———

THE DAZE

West Point, Bradley Barracks
Delta Company, 2nd Regiment
Home of the D-2 "Dragons"

As a "Prepster," I arrived at West Point one day before Report Day, or "R-Day", along with the other Cadet Candidates, so for 24 hours I had my room all to myself. I recall my squad leader pointing me towards my room. I pinged along the wall towards my door, executing sharp turns as I went. As Plebes, we were required to "Ping" at a pace of 120 steps per minutes, walk along the walls and square all corners. Not only did this identify us as Plebes—as nobodies—in the Corps, but it served to remind us of our place in the pecking order.

As I approached my door, I noticed that a white paper nametag with black lettering was already slid into the metal plate which was hung eye-level on the door. The tag read, "PALEY, RH '89". Above my name was someone else's nametag, it read "Curly, HG '89." I paused an extra second before I turned the doorknob just to take it in. *They're expecting me*, I thought to myself. That was the moment I felt like I belonged at West Point, that I had officially made the cut. I smiled and went into my room, shutting the door behind me.

Inside the room, there was perfect symmetry as one would expect of West Point. In the far corners, perpendicular to the large windows which overlooked Central Area below, were wall-mounted bookshelves with a desk and chair below each one. Butted up to the desks were two single, gray metal framed beds with folded linen lying at the foot of each one.

Butted up to the bed on the left was a single sink with a medium oak-colored storage cabinet below it, and above the sink were two medicine-cabinet style mirrors.

In the left-hand corner—behind the door when it was in the opened position—was an open closet with an empty rifle rack attached to the side of it, which could hold two rifles.

To my immediate right, on the wall shared by the door, were two side-by-side built-in oak closets. There were two long, narrow drawers under each closet, and two large sliding doors on top of each closet.

Soon, I knew, I would finally get my cadet uniform issued, the famous Dress Gray, and I smiled at the thought of that.

Since I had first-dibs, I chose the bed and desk on the left side of the room. Then I walked to the window and looked down at Central Area, which was three stories below me. I saw an old stone, three-story building in the middle of central area, and to the left of it an old, patina four-sided clock which looked like it could have been there since the days of Grant and Lee.

Granite barracks surrounded central area on all sides, and I knew that the barracks directly across from mine was the one that could be seen from the road that we drove in on the first time I laid my eyes on the parade field. Those who got to have the rooms facing the parade field and the Hudson River were lucky, indeed.

But I was just happy to be here. We were generally left alone on that first day, but all of that was about to change. R-Day was just hours away, and in the morning my peaceful introduction to life as a "New Cadet" at West Point would come to an abrupt end.

CHAPTER 57

BEAST BARRACKS

The first day of Cadet Basic Training (CBT)—better known as "Beast Barracks"—was a blur. We started off in the morning wearing black shorts with yellow trim, white T-shirts with the Academy crest on the left chest, black Low-quarter leather shoes, and calf-length black socks. To add to the humiliation of this outfit, we had tags safety-pinned to our shorts indicating a series of stations we were required to go to in order to get measured for our uniforms, collect our gear in green Army laundry bags, learn the knowledge required of Plebes, and become proficient in drill and ceremony in preparation for a parade at the end of the day.

We learned to fear the "Cadet in the Red Sash," whose sole job, it seemed, was to confound us.

In the midst of the chaos of screaming Cadets in the Red Sash, we learned that we were only allowed to speak with four responses: "Yes, Sir!" "No, Sir!" "No excuse, Sir!" and "Sir, I do not understand!" (Woe be it to the cadet who didn't replace the "Sir" with a "Ma'am" for the female Cadet in the Red Sash!)

At one point, I returned to my room in between stations where I tried to catch my breath. I stood near the window (but not *too* close) and watched my classmates ping back and forth across Central Area, being directed to and fro by the Cadets in the Red Sash. In all the chaos, I hardly noticed that there was the constant sound of a lone drummer tapping away on a snare drum. And then I saw him, standing at attention at the corner of the stone house near the four-sided clock. He tapped out a steady beat over and over again, and I smiled.

This is *exactly* what my father would have expected the first day at West Point to be like.

Suddenly, a dreaded Cadet in the Red Sash opened my door without knocking and I came to attention. The upperclassmen said, "In here. Be back downstairs in five minutes." Then, my roommate came in and stood at attention in front of me. The upperclassmen left and shut the door.

"You must be my roommate," I said, smiling.

"Yes, Sir!"

"Relax, I'm not an upperclassmen," I said, "I'm Rob."

My roommate let out a sigh and rolled his eyes. He was sweating and nervous.

"Holy, shit!" he said as he finally relaxed and smiled.

Then he shook my hand. "I'm Harry," he said.

I glanced at his last name which was above the academy crest on his white T-Shirt and said, "Harry Curley?" I had to fight a smile.

"The second!" he said.

I laughed and said, "No kidding?"

The Army always puts the last name first on documents, and I mentally noted that his name would read "Curly, Harry". Oh, well, it's better than *Lobert*, I thought to myself.

"Where you from?" I asked.

"Akron," he said, still sweating and breathing hard.

"No kidding! I'm from Groveport—it's just outside of Columbus."

Harry smiled and looked at his wristwatch. "We better go."

"Wait, let me give you a dress-off," I said.

Harry turned around and I pulled the sides of his shirt back above his waistline, using my thumbs to fold the sides of the shirt neatly back to remove the excess material. Then I turned around and he did the same for me. Loose, baggy shirts were a strict "no-go" at West Point, regardless of what shirt we were wearing.

We stood near the door, looked at each other, then opened it and pinged back down to the swirling chaos below.

As I pinged to my next station, the Superintendent of the United States Military Academy, General Willard Scott—a three star general and the highest ranking Soldier on post—was standing in the middle of Central Area with his hands behind his back, observing R-Day activities with a smile, as if he were reminiscing about his first day at West Point so many years ago.

As I neared him, several New Cadets in front of me pinged right past him without saluting, only to render sharp salutes to the Cadets in the Red Sash who were a few feet away.

General Scott saw what happened and smiled, amused.

When I got within six steps of him I rendered a sharp salute and said, "Good morning, Sir!"

General Scott returned my salute with a smile and I overheard him say as I pinged by him, "Perhaps I need to get a Red Sash." This was just one example of the down-to-earth nature that General Scott was known and loved for, and it took all I had for me not to smile. Smiles are not an issued-item to Plebes at West Point, and are therefore strictly forbidden.

By the end of the day, the Cadets in the Red Sash managed to process the largest Plebe class in West Point history, the Class of 1989.

Finally, we changed into our white-over-gray cadet uniforms and put on the gray epaulets of a "New Cadet." Then, we marched onto the Plain for the first parade of our cadet careers.

In the distance, the American flag waved on a large white flagpole at Trophy Point. The bleachers were filled with proud parents who remained to see their kids one last time before they would be swallowed up by the Academy, not to be seen again until Labor Day.

I didn't get a chance to enjoy my first day at West Point because I was too busy trying not to get in trouble with the Cadets in the Red Sash, and there was always something that had to be done. But at the end of my first day as a West Point cadet, as I stood on the parade field with my classmates, I was able to finally appreciate the moment.

When the National Anthem played, images of the American flag waving on the screen in the movie theaters when I was a kid flashed through my mind, and my childhood desire to stand amongst giants was now a reality. *How proud Dad would be to see this moment,* I thought. A chill went down my spine, and in that moment, I felt Dad was somehow with me.

I excelled during Beast Barracks, and I enjoyed the tough physical conditioning we underwent. I did my best to remember as much as possible of my experiences so that I could tell my father all about them when I got home.

CHAPTER 58

GAZELLES

There was a sense of excitement in the air as we marched to the Apron—the cement area in front of the barracks and adjacent to the parade field— to begin Physical Training (PT). Motivational music—much of it the same music I had listened to on my Sony *Walkman* while running or working out over the past several years—blasted from the speakers. I recall *Survivor's* "Eye of the Tiger" being one of the songs played each day, and that made me feel right at home.

One morning, as we marched to the Apron to form-up for PT, we were divided into ability groups for a long-distance run. The Gold group was for the slower runners, the Gray group for intermediate runners, and the Black group for the gazelles. I chose to join the Gray group, but someone in the Black group called me out.

"Paley, you should be over here!" shouted a Random Voice from the Crowd.

No, I shouldn't be, Random Voice from the Crowd! I thought to myself as I tried to ignore him.

An upperclassmen near me overheard the Random Voice from the Crowd and said, "Get over there, Paley."

At the Prep School, I came in fourteenth place in my age group during a half marathon, so I guess someone considered me a runner. I reluctantly jogged over to the Black group, where every single cadet had the look and build of a marathon runner. After a few minutes of stretching out, we began our run, and I immediately knew I was in big trouble.

Instead of jogging, we took off in an all-out sprint, which would have been fine if we were doing a 100 yard dash, but this was supposed to be a *distance* run. The group pulled away from me before I even had the chance to let my muscles warm up, and by the time we got near the Superintendent's large white house I was twenty feet behind the gazelles. If this were a nature show, I'd be the one that the lions caught as the rest of the group made their escape.

"Close it up, Paley!" shouted Captain Colpo, who would be my D-2 Tactical Officer for the next two years. Colpo was an infantryman, and he had the hard, lean build of a runner.

I did as I was told, but I was already hating whoever called me out to join the Black group. *I couldn't keep up with these guys if I had a bicycle!*

For years, I'd imagined chasing West Point cadets while I ran—but I never could have imagined this.

We took a left on Washington Road and the pace seemed to moderate a little, enabling me to finally rejoin the group at the rear of the formation. *Ok, maybe this won't be so bad,* I thought to myself as I tried to get into a rhythm.

I focused on the feet of the runner just ahead of me. *One step at a time,* I told myself. *One step at a time.* It was the sidewalk block method I had used as a kid when I first started running so that I wouldn't think about how much further I had to go. It seemed to be working when all of a sudden, the group and the person in front of me turned left, up a steep hill.

It was Stony Lonesome Road, the road my mother's car barely made it up when we first toured West Point a few years earlier.

Ohio didn't have hills like this when I ran hundreds, if not thousands of miles back home, and I was in deep trouble. The upperclassman who ran to the side of and centered on our group called cadences as we ascended the hill. Everyone responded to his cadence call, while I just mouthed the words, unable to breathe.

My legs began to feel like lead, as if I had never run before in my life. I kept churning and churning, hoping the top of the hill would come soon. I was relieved when I noticed the entrance to the Cadet Chapel on my left. *Not much further now*, I thought to myself.

Hang in there.

At last, we reached the top of the hill where the road curved to the right near the beautiful reservoir and Michie Stadium.

I did it! I thought to myself as the road flattened and I caught up with the rear rank. *It should be downhill from now on.*

Just when I was getting too proud of myself, the group continued forward toward what looked to be another hill, which sloped up and to the right behind the football stadium. I looked forlornly to my left, knowing that the downhill part of the run was that way. *Guys,* I wanted to say, *weren't you supposed to take a left?*

I leaned in and accepted my fate. I thought I was ready for West Point's physical demands, but I was being humbled.

The group took a right hand turn up Delafield Road, and I did my best to keep up with them. As we made a slight left toward the entrance to Fort Putnam—an historic Revolutionary War sight—I began to dry-heave and fell out of the formation. As I tried to pull myself together, I noticed the sign to Fort Putnam and noted to myself that I'd have to come back and check it out sometime. *Squirrel!*

"Let's go, Paley!" shouted Captain Colpo. "Stay focused. Mental toughness!"

I'll give you mental toughness, I said to myself as I wiped spittle from my mouth with the back of my arm and started jogging again. By now, I'd lost sight of the group over the crest of the hill. My legs felt like lead but I continued to grind it out. As I crested the hill, the group was at least a hundred yards away and already making a turn to the right, toward Delafield Pond.

I was all alone, and as I started the descent I uttered my favorite prayer, Isaiah 40:31.

"But they that wait upon the Lord shall renew their strength..." I continued to run, and to pray. "They shall mount up with wings as Eagles..." *That's it*, I felt the lead feeling drop off my legs like I was shedding armor. "They shall run and not grow weary..." *Lighter. Faster!* "They shall walk and not grow feint."

Suddenly, I was alone on that country road in Groveport again, with grazing cattle and horses on each side of me as the sunset created a golden sky.

I was no longer running—*I was flying!*

Captain Colpo glanced back and did a double-take as he saw me closing the distance to the group at a full sprint. He grinned and shook his head as I caught up with the rear rank just as the formation turned right onto Merritt Road.

I caught my breath as I rejoined the formation, sweat poring off of me, but my muscles were warm and loose now. To my right, the newly-built Jewish Chapel caught my eye. It looked like a granite Bible supported by granite bookends on each side, and it gave me comfort. As I passed by it, I noticed the golden tablets with Hebrew writing on them, and I assumed it must be a reference to the Ten Commandments.

Little could I have known then that someday I would be forever linked with that Chapel in an historic way.

The group turned left near the entrance to the Cadet Chapel and we descended Stony Lonesome Road. It was so steep that we basically sprinted down as a group, and then eased our way to the right onto Washington Road at the bottom of the hill, heading back to the barracks.

As soon as we got to the road in front of the Supe's house, the upperclassmen shouted, "Free sprint to the finish!" and we took off. To my surprise, I wasn't the last one to make it back to the original assembly area.

The next day, I tried to hide in the Gray group again, but this time I smiled when I got called out. There is no going backwards at West Point. By the end of the week, I managed to keep up with the Black group and never fell-out again.

APFT

The smell of sewage wafted through the air of the hot summer day as we gathered along the banks of the Hudson River for our first record Army Physical Fitness Test, or APFT. Because flat ground is so hard to find in the West Point environs, it was commonplace to use a one mile stretch of flat road which just happened to be located near the West Point sewage treatment facility. My classmates and I concluded that it was just one more way that West Point tried to "haze" us and to weed out the weak (officially, there was no more hazing at West Point, though anyone or anything that annoyed or frustrated us was referred to as a "haze.")

I was excited to see how I would fare against my classmates. I was now going up against some of America's best athletes, and I was anxious to see how I would measure-up.

I did quite well on the push-ups and sit-ups, though I can't recall how many of each I actually did, and now I set my sights on the 2-mile run. The course was one mile out and one mile back, and if not for the smell of the sewage treatment facility it might have been a pleasant run with its view of the Hudson River to the east.

When it was my group's turn to go, I set off on a strong pace but there were several New Cadets who leapt out ahead of me and left me in the dust. I held myself back, determined to catch them on the way back, and I focused on the road and on my breathing.

About mid-way to the one mile mark, I felt strong so I picked up the pace a little more, creating distance between myself and a gaggle of other New Cadets. At the one mile turn-around, I leaned into the run a little more and set my sights on the guys who had jumped out to an early lead at the start of the run. They were about fifty to seventy five yards ahead of me, and they seemed to be flagging. My time running with the Black group gave me the confidence that I could catch up with them, and little by little, I closed the gap. I felt stronger with each step I took. With about a half mile left, I finally caught up to them and picked them off one by one, feeling as strong as I ever have in my life.

With about a quarter mile to go until the finish line, I went into an all-out sprint. I was feeling quite strong as my legs churned relentlessly toward the finish line and the screaming upperclassmen and cadets who awaited us there.

Suddenly, I heard voices and footsteps coming from my left and rear, and I glanced back in time to see my good friends and fellow-Prepsters Tonya Cheek and Patrice Boemio blow right past me, talking to each other in a casual tone as if they were taking a walk. For a moment I tried to keep up, but I was at the peak of my running capability, and all I could do was maintain my stride and marvel at their grace and stamina as they continued to increase the distance between us.

CHAPTER 59

———

BOODLE CALL

I was assigned to Delta Company, second platoon, or D-2. After Beast Barracks, this designation represented the Company I would join for my remaining four years at the academy—Delta Company, 2nd Regiment, better known as the D-2 "Dragons."

One day, during Beast Barracks, we were standing in company formation on the Apron when a cadet in the Red Sash told us that we were going to be given time to observe our faith at either the Cadet Chapel or the Holy Trinity Church.

"If you are protestant or Christian, move to the left," said the Cadet in the Red Sash. Numerous cadets moved to the left.

"If you are Catholic, move to the right," he said. More cadets moved to the right.

I continued to stand by myself at the front of the formation. The Cadet in the Red Sash didn't seem to have an answer for this situation, so he consulted with a few other Cadets in the Red Sash. Finally, he said, "Fall in on this New Cadet," to someone who must have been standing behind me.

I felt someone fall in to my left. The Cadets in the Red Sash stepped out of earshot to discuss this apparent dilemma amongst themselves.

I caught the scent of perfume when the wind blew and I whispered, "You smell good," to whomever it was beside me.

I saw her laugh out of my peripheral vision but then quickly regain her composure. And this is how I met my first Jewish friend, Sherri Langston.

The Cadets in the Red Sash returned and said, "What religions are you guys?"

"Jewish," said Sherri.

"Jewish," I said as well.

"Look," said a Cadet in the Red Sash, "we don't have any Jewish services today, so why don't you two just pick one of these others and go with them. I hear you'll be well fed."

Say no more!

"You can speak amongst yourselves to decide," he said.

"Who do you think has the most food?" I asked Sherri.

We considered it, and then we both said, "The Catholics." And that's where we went for Sunday services.

Later, we were told that Mr. and Mrs. Sweberg, whose sons had both graduated from West Point, were going to host the Jewish cadets each week, and from then on we joined them at the newly-constructed Jewish Chapel.

CHAPTER 60

CAPTAIN BELTON

A day or two before classes were scheduled to begin, I was summoned to the Admissions Office. For a moment, I thought they were going to tell me they'd made a mistake—that I wasn't supposed to be here after all. Then I remembered they'd already printed out a paper nametag for my door as well as my PT shirts. They couldn't afford to let me go now!

When I reported to the admissions office, I had the pleasure of meeting the man who'd fought so hard to get me into West Point. Captain Belton. I reported to him, and he told me to relax.

I went to parade rest.

"No, I mean, really relax, Cadet Paley. Rest."

I did as I was told, and he stood up and shook my hand.

"Nice to finally meet you," he said.

"You, too, Sir."

He ordered me to take a seat, and he sat down, too.

"Cadet Paley, the reason I called you here is because I've put a lot of my personal credibility on the line for you," he said. "And I appreciate that very much, Sir."

"So now I need you to do something," he said.

"Anything, Sir."

"Pass all of your classes this year. Fail none of them," he said. "You will have 18.5 credit hours of classes each semester, and if you can pass all of your Plebe classes, then you'll be able to make it through West Point," he said.

It sounded like academics were going to be real challenge for me. "Cadet Paley," he said. "I'm not sure if I should tell you this or not— but every year, we make one exception. This year, you're it."

I didn't know if I should thank him or apologize, so I thanked him.

As difficult as it was, I passed all my classes Plebe Year.

CHAPTER 61

———

HAZED AND CONFUSED

Sometime during first semester of Plebe Year, I reported to dinner formation in my White over Gray uniform. I failed to button my right epaulet correctly and by the time I reached formation, my right epaulet and gray shoulder board that was attached to it were hanging down off my right shoulder, flopping up and down with each step I took. Naturally, this attracted the ire of the "hazes" from the upper class—Cadets Ring, Clukey and Haislop—and before I knew what was happening, I had all three of them in my face.

They yelled at me simultaneously, letting me know what a dirt-bag I was for daring to come to formation in such a sorry state. They were quite creative with their insults and sometimes I had to do my best not to smile at their witty remarks. One of them unbuttoned my left epaulet and made it hang off my left shoulder to match the one on my right, forming little wings.

"Are you trying to fly away, Paley?" asked Cadet Haislop. "Do you think you're at the Air Force Academy?"

"No, Sir!" I barked, trying my best not to smile.

"There are ten others who applied for this spot you're standing in right now, Paley," said another. "And I guarantee you they would have buttoned their epaulet!" *Ouch.*

At one point, their faces were so close to my face that it felt like a group hug. *Come on, bring it in guys. Let's stop all this yelling.*

Finally, the Company First Sergeant, Cadet Palka, put his face next to my left ear from behind me and said, "Listen to me, Paley. I want you to reach up and button your epaulets right now. Do it!"

And so I did. And finally, the hazing stopped and I was left alone, rattled.

A moment later I felt the presence of another upperclassmen approach me from my left rear, though I couldn't see who it was, nor did I recognize his voice.

"Hang in there, Governor," the voice said. Then he walked away.

Governor? Then it hit me. Whoever this cadet was must have been at Buckeye Boys State with me back in '83.

"Yes, Sir!" I said, as I felt a rush of adrenaline. I didn't know who it was who buoyed my spirits on one of my worst days, but it sure was great to know that there were other Boys' Staters in the ranks. Whoever this was obviously made it directly into West Point, so he was now a Yearling.

I didn't know the name of the person who offered me those encouraging words for a long time, but then one day a Yearling cadet from another company in my regiment, G-2, stopped by and introduced himself to me as Mark Steele, from Granville, Ohio. He would become one of my best friends at the Academy, and still is to this day.

CHAPTER 62

———

YUK YUK

1986-1987

Yearling Year

Having survived Plebe Year, I was looking forward to being an upper-classman with a little bit of rank and the responsibility for developing a squad of Plebes.

Yearlings, also known as "Yuks," were the kinder, gentler upper-classmen of the Corps, having only months ago been mere Plebes, or "Smacks," they identified more with the Plebes than with the Cows or Firsties. Juniors are called "Cows" because tradition has it that a long time ago, cadets didn't get to leave West Point until after their Yearling year. Then, they would enjoy extended leave before returning for their junior year. While on leave, they would eat too much and return to West Point overweight, as big as a...you get the picture.

And "Firsties" is simply short for "First Classmen," the leaders of the Corps.

One day, I was studying in my room when I got a message from the Charge of Quarters, or CQ, telling me to report to a Major Melton.

Who's Major Melton? I wondered. I figured I'd done something wrong and I'd find out what soon enough.

I located his office and reported to him.

"Cadet Paley," he said. "Why aren't you on my Judo team?" *Oh, so that's why I'm here.*

"I hung up martial arts a few years ago, Sir," I said, "After a serious eye injury."

"Your record states that you were a state Judo champion."

"Twice," I said. Remembering to add, "Sir."

"Here's the situation Paley," he said. "We have a tri-meet against Navy and Air Force in a few weeks; I'm light at the 138- pound weight division, and I'm not willing to take a loss at that weight without putting up a fight."

"Roger, Sir," I said, agreeing with his point.

"So, what I need to know is—"

"I'll do it, Sir," I said.

Major Melton sat back and crossed his hands on his stomach. "Good."

Two Weeks Later

It felt good to be back in a Judo uniform again, but because I no longer had the timing or the skills of the Brown belt that I once had been, I insisted on wearing a yellow belt.

I liked the people on the Judo team, and I especially had fun taunting our heavyweight, Ken Johnson. Ken was amused by me and could crush me at any time, but instead he tolerated my constant pushing and shoving as a big brother would a runt little brother.

I also had great respect for Al Yazawa, who was in a weight class above mine and was smooth as silk with his technique. Try as I might, I could never best Al on the mat.

By the time the Tri-meet arrived, I was still shaking off cobwebs and didn't have high expectations. My job was to show-up and put up a fight so we wouldn't have to forfeit in that weight class.

Perhaps it's because I had such low expectations that I was loose on the day of the meet, and I ended up beating both the Air Force and the Navy Judokas. The Navy guy was a Black Belt, and he smelled a rat after I beat him. We would meet again.

Ken grabbed me after the tournament, put me in a headlock, and rubbed my head with his knuckles.

"I thought you were a chump, but now I *see* you're a champ!" he said.

Although I'd promised my mother not to do martial arts anymore, my team needed me and that left me no choice. I was back on a Judo team, and I asked my Mom to send me my Brown belt from Ohio.

"Just be careful," she said.

Jewish Chapel Choir

I'd never tried out for a choir before, but during Plebe Year when I heard the Jewish Chapel Choir was one of the best Trip Sections—meaning they could leave West Point on official, extracurricular business without having to take leave—I was inspired.

When I met with the Choir conductor, he asked me two questions. "Can you read music?" and "Can you keep a tune?"

I answered "No," to both questions.

"Welcome to the Jewish Chapel Choir!" he said.

Several Months Later

I don't recall how much later it was when I met the Navy Black Belt in a tournament again. It may have been in the Eastern Collegiate Judo Championships, I can't recall anymore, but suffice it to say he wasn't surprised when he saw me wearing a faded Brown Belt this time. He looked at me with a bit of disdain, as if I had violated a code of honor when we last met. And though that implication would normally have led me to fisticuffs, I understood how he felt. When we met in the Championships, he exacted his revenge, and my bloody lip was my penance.

CHAPTER 63

———

THE WESTS

I was sitting at my desk studying with gauze in my mouth when the CQ knocked on my door.

"Cadet Paley," he said. "Major Kaplan called and said for you to get your Full Dress over Grays ready ASAP."

"For what?" I asked.

"The Jewish Choir is singing at some place in New Jersey, and there weren't enough cadets there last night. A van will be here to pick you and a few others up at 1600 hours for tonight's concert."

"Roger that," I said, frustrated. I had an exam I needed to study for.

Watchung, New Jersey
Synagogue

I stood amongst the choir trying to sing along with my bloody lip stinging me. I already sang bad enough without a sore lip, and now I was throwing off the whole choir.

Halfway through our songs, we would take a moment to introduce ourselves to the adoring audience and try to say something funny or clever. One cadet always said, "I joined the choir so I could visit beautiful temples like this one and meet your daughters." The reaction ranged from shock to outright laughter, and tonight his line was a hit.

"Check out that one in the yellow and white sweater," said one of my friends.

We all agreed that the brunette in the yellow and white striped sweater was the prettiest one in attendance that night. The guys in the Jewish Chapel Choir had an informal competition to see who could meet the prettiest girl on our road trips.

When my turn came to introduce myself, I said, "I'm sorry I was late getting here, but I was at a *Jew*-do tournament today. Thus, the swollen lip." I got the smiles I was hoping for, and then I said, "I don't even know who I'm staying with tonight," and a handsome couple sitting in the middle of the synagogue raised their hands and said, "You're staying with us."

As soon as the concert ended, I went out to the hallway where I was introduced to Doctor and Mrs. Gerald West, and they in turn introduced me to their son Robert, and their cute little daughter Danna. And then the girl in the yellow and white sweater that we noticed during the concert walked up to me and introduced herself as Rachel West. I saw a couple of the other cadets staring at me and shaking their heads, jealous.

Dr. West was handsome and soft-spoken and carried himself with a dignified air. Mrs. Joanie West had jet-black hair and her eyes seemed to sparkle as she looked at me with a mischievous smile, as if she were amused by me. We hit it off instantly.

The Wests were unlike any other family I'd stayed with before. They were so much fun and they welcomed me into their home like I was a member of their family.

They traveled to West Point on several occasions to spend time with me, and through them I also met the Mathews, the Erdays, the Robustellis and the Bergers—all of whom I am still friends with to this day. To distinguish me from their own son by the same name, the Wests called me "Robert Cadet" and still do to this day.

Dr. Gerald West was an ENT doctor, and he had a private practice with his wife Joanie's brother, Arthur. Joanie was an interior designer, and their houses reflected her taste and her style beautifully.

The Wests often invited me to spend Passover and other holidays with them, and through them my Jewish education continued. Part of the Jewish education, apparently, was how to dress better!

I wasn't the sharpest dresser, and one morning there was a note on the kitchen table with a credit card from Joanie telling the kids to take me clothes shopping. I protested at first, but as a cadet I didn't have much spending money for luxury items like new clothes, and the kids told me that it would make their parents happy to be able to treat me.

"Don't worry," said Rachel. "You're part of the family."

We had so much fun as I tried on new clothes, selecting the ones the kids gave me a thumbs-up to and rejecting those that received the thumbs-down. It was like a montage from so many movies I've seen before, and we had a blast.

My company-mates noticed my improved appearance, and a few of them often came to me to borrow sweaters or dress shirts. One of my future roommates, Guy Moore, made such an impression on a girl while wearing my clothes that they got married after graduation, and he jokingly credits me to this day for helping him to win Peggy's heart. Glad I could help!

I grew to love the Wests and their extended family, and some of my best memories with them were spent at their summer home in the Hamptons. Through them, I learned to appreciate what hard work and generosity meant, and I admired how Robert and Rachel took summer jobs to learn the value of money.

I recall with fondness driving to Main Beach at East Hampton one summer while the kids and I sang "Born in the U.S.A." at the top of our lungs, while Dr. West and Joanie just smiled and shook their heads.

The Wests introduced me to a whole new world that I didn't know existed. They accepted me not because of my social status, but because of my character, and that too taught me an important lesson.

What I didn't know, however, was that my character was about to be put to the test.

CHAPTER 64

TRIAL BY FIRE

West Point Jewish Chapel
Shabbat Services

Rabbi/Lieutenant Colonel Marc Abramowitz was an Orthodox Jew who had a beautiful family consisting of his wife, a daughter, and twin sons. His wife could trace her family's lineage directly back to Moses himself, and that fascinated me. The Rabbi wore a mustache and glasses and carried himself with a quiet dignity. I never saw him get ruffled or excitable.

One day, my good friend David Santo and I were speaking to the Rabbi when the subject of Bar Mitzvahs came up. It turns out that neither David nor I had had a Bar Mitzvah when we turned thirteen, and this surprised the Rabbi very much. He asked if we would like to become Bar Mitzvahs—or Men of Duty/Blessing—as adults. The idea fascinated us, and David and I agreed that we would.

The date was set for May 1987, and I took one more step towards learning about God and my heritage.

Boiling Point

Sometime around the end of first semester of Yearling Year, my roommate Paul Sariego, and his good friend Charlie Stone told me some disturbing news. They'd overheard a cadet—let's call him Cadet Mark Boyle—saying some disturbing things about me. "I don't care what Mark says about me," I said, defensively. But the

truth was I cared very much what he or anyone else said about me-
-perhaps *too* much.

One day, Mark went too far and started spouting blatant anti-Semitic comments about me, and both Paul and Charlie knew that
this wasn't okay.

I was struggling with academics again, and I didn't need to deal with
this kind of ignorance, but the comments were beginning to esca-
late in tone and severity.

Soon, anytime I saw someone sitting with Mark in the library or
speaking to him in the hallways, I'd wonder if they, too, shared his
anti-Semitic views. I pushed these thoughts out of my head because
I realized my thinking seemed paranoid and wasn't fair to the others. Still, as I continued to be made aware of these comments by a
reliable source, I took the time to record in my journal each and
every allegation, and my journal was filling up quickly.

Mark was overheard saying things like, "Jews never serve in America's wars," and "Jews shouldn't be allowed in the military," and so
on.

His comments disturbed me but didn't spur me to action. What
disturbed me more than Mark's comments was his cowardly hypoc-
risy. Every time I passed him in the hallway, he'd force a fake smile
and say, "Hey, Rob."

I'd always gotten the sense that several of my classmates didn't like
me for some reason, and though I'm sure some/most of it was my
own fault, I couldn't help but wonder how much had to do with
Mark.

As Mark's comments continued to get people's attention, I started
going to the synagogue and studying anti-Semitism and the holocaust in the chapel library. I asked the Rabbi for the key, so I could

study in peace and quiet on the weekends, and I'm sure he thought I was studying for my upcoming Bar Mitzvah.

Left to right: Paul Sariego, me and Charlie Stone.
When not on duty, we tried to dress as "civilian" as possible.

By the time second semester started, Charlie and Paul told me Mark's antics were not only continuing, but were also escalating in nature. Apparently, while Mark was riding on a bus to the Newark airport with other cadets over the Christmas holiday, a Hassidic Jew drove up beside the bus and Mark yelled something like, "Hey, driver, run the Jew off the road!"

Charlie said that he heard this with his own ears, and several cadets who were on the bus gave Mark a dirty look, but Mark seemed to thrive on the attention and in pushing the boundaries.

My grades started to drop across the board as I dug into Psalms to find the wisdom and strength to deal with Mark. I simply couldn't understand his mindset, and I decided the time had come to talk to the Rabbi about Mark.

CHAPTER 65

——

THE JOURNAL

After services ended, I stood outside the synagogue and waited for the Rabbi to come out. I knew he'd be making the one mile trek back to his house on foot, and I decided that would be a good time for me to talk to him.

He locked the door to the synagogue and turned around, illuminated by the walkway lights.

"Rabbi?" I said.

"Who's there? Robert, is that you?" the Rabbi asked as he crossed the road to the sidewalk.

"Yes, Rabbi," I said.

"Why aren't you back at the barracks?" he asked.

"I need to talk to you about something," I said.

"Is everything okay?" he asked.

"Not really," I said. I proceeded to tell him about all the things that Mark Boyle had been saying over the past several months, and he was completely shocked by what I told him.

"I have this all in writing," I said. "Dates, times, places, everything."

Rabbi Abramowitz stopped in his tracks. "All of this, in writing?" he asked.

"Yes, Rabbi. Not just about Mark, but a group of his friends, too."

"I'd like to see this journal," the Rabbi said.

The next day, I dropped my journal off at the Rabbi's house, and he and his wife invited me in. I observed what an Orthodox Jewish family does on a Saturday unburdened by television, radio or video games, and I was fascinated by this complete focus on God and the Torah.

The children were bright and engaged, and I realized as I observed them that my father, too, was raised in an Orthodox Jewish household when he grew up in the Bronx.

I knew I'd receive a world-class education at the Military Academy, but I had no idea I would learn so much about my faith and my heritage, too.

Jewish Council

The following week, I was summoned to the synagogue to speak to Rabbi Abramowitz, and he told me what had transpired since I'd given him the journal.

Apparently, after reading my journal, Rabbi Abramowitz summoned an emergency meeting of the Jewish Council of West Point. I didn't even know there was such a thing.

During the meeting with the Jewish Council, Rabbi Abramowitz read excerpts from my journal but insisted on protecting my privacy, so he didn't tell them who the journal belonged to.

As soon as the council became fully apprised of the magnitude of the anti-Semitic remarks being spewed by Cadet Mark Boyle, they demanded immediate action from the Rabbi. If everything contained in my journal was true—and it was—they said the situation constituted the most egregious case of anti-Semitism in West Point history.

A debate ensued, explained the Rabbi, and when it got heated, he admitted to slipping and referring to me by name.

Major Kaplan, my sponsor and academic advisor, was furious.

"Cadet Paley is in serious jeopardy of failing out of West Point right now, and we have an obligation to do something about this," he said.

The council agreed with Major Kaplan, and the Rabbi elevated the situation to the West Point Chaplain, who was a Full Bird Colonel. After he read my journal, he elevated the situation to Brigadier General Fred Gorden, the Commandant of Cadets. And finally, my journal ended up on the desk of Lieutenant General David R. Palmer, the Superintendent of the United States Military Academy.

"You're kidding me?" I said.

"I'm not," said the Rabbi, "and I've been ordered to let you know that the entire chain-of-command stands with you should you choose to press UCMJ charges against Mark Boyle."

"UCMJ?" I said. UCMJ is the Uniform Code of Military Justice which governs the armed forces. To be prosecuted under UCMJ could lead to federal criminal charges and jail time.

"I don't know if I'm ready to go that far, Rabbi," I said. "I know my sources are reliable, but I haven't even talked to Mark about this yet."

"Would he give you the same consideration if things were reversed?" asked the Rabbi.

"I don't know. May I take spring break to think on this further?"

"Of course," said the Rabbi, "I can buy you some time. But when you get back, I'll need your decision."

I nodded as I thought about the seriousness of the situation.

CHAPTER 66

———

SORROW

1987

Spring Break

I canceled my plans to go to Fort Lauderdale for Spring Break and, instead, went back home to Ohio. I visited my father and told him about my experiences as a Yearling, but I left out the parts about the ongoing anti-Semitism issue I was dealing with.

We spoke at length about West Point and I asked him more about his military career. He told me how he'd dropped out of high school and gotten involved with gangs, before deciding to enlist when Truman asked for volunteers to fight in the Korean War. He tried to enlist several times with different branches, but each time he was turned away for being under eighteen years old.

Finally, on his seventeenth birthday, his parents signed to give their consent for his enlistment. He was in combat by age eighteen, was wounded in action, and went to Japan to recover. That's where he met Mom. They were married a year later, and had their first child, my older brother Phil.

It was the most detailed and normal conversation I'd had with him since I was a boy, and it lifted my spirits immensely. He continued to ask me, "How's West Point?" and each time I tried to tell him another great anecdote about life as a cadet. He enjoyed all of them. His love and respect for West Point was beyond comprehension.

When I returned to Columbus, I went to the Ohio State University Library and pulled out a stack of books about the Holocaust. Then I found a table in a quiet section of the library and studied what they didn't teach me in high school.

I spent hours at the library each day and went back and forth between grief and anger as I learned the proud and tragic history of the Jewish people.

I was inspired by examples of extreme courage and defiance as some Jews led uprisings against their captors at concentration camps or in the Warsaw Ghetto. But they were the few, and more millions died tragic deaths.

I checked out the Congressional Record on the service history of American Jews throughout U.S. history and was pleased to learn that not only did Jews fight in combat, but they fought in combat arms branches in greater numbers (by percentage) than did any other minority population in the United States. Additionally, the first person to receive a Medal of Honor in U.S. history was Jewish. His name was Benjamin B. Levy, and he earned his Medal at the Battle of Glendale on June 30, 1862.

I was also pleased to learn that the first Jewish graduate of West Point graduated second in his class...of two.

No other minority in the United States has been awarded more medals directly related to combat than the Jews have, and their number included my father.

Having to learn this as *new* knowledge was ridiculous, yet I was compelled to research these facts by Mark Boyle's behavior. Valor is valor, and I respect every soldier who fought, bled and died for our country.

Armed with this new knowledge, I returned to West Point to face my tormentor.

CHAPTER 67

———

FACE-OFF

SPRING 1987

West Point

I was seated at my desk studying for a test when Charlie came in to visit me and Paul on the first night back from Spring Break. By now, Charlie had become my friend, too, and he told me how people in the company had me all wrong.

I knew I had my faults, however. I had trouble bonding with guys for some reason, and the "armor" I wore to protect myself made me come across as arrogant, indifferent, and too often, defensive.

Despite any animosity others felt towards me, I respected them and knew I was missing out on getting to know some great people. I regret that I never let down my guard enough to get to know them or to let them get to know the real me.

Counting Charlie as a friend, though, doubled the number of friends I had at the time, and that's pretty good math in anyone's book. To be fair, I did develop friendships with others in the company and across the Corps as well, and I value each of their friendships to this day. In general though, I recall my overall experience as one of isolation and loneliness, and now I know that I may have created this dynamic myself. Hindsight.

None the less, Paul Sariego and I hit it off from the first few minutes we were roommates after he drew the "short straw". I'll never forget a conversation we had one night as we traded stories and got to know each other.

Paul told me how he'd once dated a beautiful young lady named "Conchita."

"That's a pretty name," I said. "What's it mean?"

"Seashell," said Paul.

"Hmmm," I said, laughing, "Some things just *don't* translate well, do they?"

Paul thought about it, and then he too started laughing.

"I mean, what's her brother's name? Starfish?"

Paul busted a gut, and we started laughing so hard we couldn't breathe. It was the beginning of a friendship that would last throughout our cadet career and to this day.

After sharing stories about spring break, Charlie seemed like he had something he wanted to say.

"Rob, it's getting bad," said Charlie.

"Yeah? What now?" I asked.

"Mark said he wishes that Hitler had succeeded in killing all the Jews."

That was the final straw. I slammed my text book shut and said, "This ends now."

I recalled that Charlie and Mark are friends, or at least were friends, and I stopped. "You know that if I do this, Mark will know that you're the one who told me."

"I don't care, he's gone too far," said Charlie.

I looked over at Paul and he agreed.

I knocked on Mark's door and opened it. His roommate, the biggest guy in our company, was seated at his desk studying, and Mark was lying in bed wearing his cadet robe and reading a novel.

"Mark, we need to talk," I said.

"About what, Rob?" asked Mark, as if we were buddies.

"You know damn well about what. Follow me," I said. I walked across the hallway to the locker room, and Mark walked in behind me.

"What's this all about?" he asked again, which only made my blood boil more. *If you're going to be a bigot, then at least own it.*

"I've heard you've been saying things about me and about Jews," I said. "So, before I do what I've gotta' do, I need to know if you said the following things..." I proceeded to list all of the things that Mark had allegedly said about me, Jews, and any other minorities I'd heard about.

Mark stood silent as I listed everything Charlie had told me over the past several months. At first, I saw what must have been a feeling of betrayal that someone whom he considered a friend had gone behind his back.

But Mark was in check-mate, because to deny the allegations would mean that Charlie—the son of a West Pointer who retired as a three-star general—was lying to me, and that would be a violation of West Point's inviolable Honor Code.

Finally, I saw resignation as Mark's shoulders slumped and he said, "Yeah, I said those things."

"My next question is, did you mean them? Because if you did, you don't deserve to lead American soldiers."

"Who are you to tell me who I can or can't lead?" he asked.

"This isn't a game, Mark. You're in deep shit right now. I told my Rabbi what you've been saying, and he reported it to the Commandant and the Superintendent. They've read my journal, and know the names of you and your buddies, and they are prepared to back me one hundred percent under the UCMJ if I decide to press charges."

Mark seemed shocked, and then resigned. "Do what you've gotta' do," he said.

"You meant everything you said?" I asked, feeling the anger rise inside of me.

"I just meant it towards people like Milliken and others who take and take from our country and never give back," Mark said.

"Well not all Jews are Milliken," I said, "And with regard to your comment that Jews have never served in combat for America—I just got back from visiting my father in the VA hospital, and he's one hundred percent disabled from fighting in Korea *and* Vietnam. Fighting! So, don't you *ever* say that Jews don't fight for this country."

Mark's face changed expression, and he said, "I'm sorry, Rob."

I studied his face to see if he was being sincere, and I decided that he was.

"Now," I said, "here are your options. I'm willing to forgive you for what you've said, but I will never forget. If I hear you or any of your buddies talk about Jews, women, African Americans, or any other minority ever again, I will press charges immediately. There won't be a second chance."

Defeated, Mark looked down and said, "Okay. Thanks."

"And do me one more favor, Mark, don't ever say hi to me again between now and graduation if you don't really mean it. I hate hypocrites."

"Okay," Mark said.

As hard as it was to do, I put my hand out towards him. He seemed surprised, and then shook my hand.

"Just remember, Mark, when you look back on this someday—it was a Jew who saved your career."

Mark nodded, and I turned and walked out of the locker room, avoiding a national scandal.

My father isn't the only one who loves West Point.

CHAPTER 68

———

MEN OF DUTY

MAY 1987

Jewish Chapel

It was a packed house in the synagogue on the day of our Bar Mitzvah. David Santo and I were dressed in our India Whites and were excited to be able to demonstrate our faith in a formal ceremony that neither one of us had had when we were teens.

We looked forward to becoming "Men of Duty."

Our families had trouble finding seats due to the large number of international reporters and other guests who had shown up unexpectedly. There was an article about our Bar Mitzvah buried deep inside the New York Times, but the announcement also went out over the Associated Press and reporters flew in from as far away as Israel and Paris to witness what was supposed to have been a small, family service. Rabbi Abramowitz had to ask all those who were not part of our families to please stand up and move towards the back of the synagogue, where it was already standing room only.

When I looked out into the audience, I was pleased to see my family there all the way from Ohio. Unfortunately, my father couldn't come because the doctors recommended against the long drive.

Next to my immediate family, I saw my adopted family from New Jersey, the Wests. And I saw my cousins who came in from all around the country. I was also pleased to see some of my friends from D-2, like Donna Crouch, Guy Moore, Paul Sariego, Heather Brannon and Charlie Stone.

It was a special day, and I was nervous about reading from the Torah portion in front of so many people.

As I scanned the crowd, I wondered if this is what it was all about from the beginning. To find my place within my faith, and to honor God in doing so.

The spiritual journey that began on a baseball diamond brought me to this day, a day in which history was made by two cadets from Ohio.

The text of my speech said it all. "God, Family, Country—we are inseparable."

Trophy Point

I was giving my family and the Wests a walking tour when we got to the granite benches that lined the meandering footpaths of Trophy Point. Each granite bench has a different word inscribed on the side of it, and when we got to one of them, my brother Phil said, "This is your bench, Rob."

Everyone stopped to read what Phil was referring to. On the side of this bench, which has a great view of the Hudson River below, was the word *DETERMINATION.*

I looked at my brother to thank him, and to my surprise his eyes watered when he said, "You're the most determined person I've ever seen in my life, Rob."

Everyone was moved by Phil's unusual display of emotion, and I've never forgotten what he said that day. For the next several years, whenever I was concerned about making it through West Point, I walked to that bench, sat down, and rekindled my determination to make it through just one more day.

Bradley Barracks

A few days after my Bar Mitzvah, I was seated at my desk studying when someone knocked on my door lightly.

I looked to my left and I saw it was Wally Roy, one of my company mates whom I've always admired for his mischievous streak and Harrison Ford-like smirk. Wally was confident but not cocky, and he always seemed unaffected by West Point. He was one of the guys whom I admired but who never said more than a few words to me before. "I just wanted to say congratulations on your Bar Mitzvah," Wally said.

The fact that Wally went out of his way to say this to me meant a lot, and I nodded my head to hide the lump in my throat.

It was around this same time that Scott Morrison, a highly respected and "squared away" cadet whom I've always admired first talked to me about my father. Scott was one of the 82nd Airborne Rangers I'd met a few years earlier when we were at the Prep School, and now he was in my company.

One day, Scott noticed that in addition to carrying around the silver dollar, I also wore my father's Sergeant Major rank under the pocket of my black "as for class" shirt.

"Why do you wear that?" he asked.

"For my father," I said. Then I told him about the promise I'd made to my father when I was twelve, and he seemed sincerely moved by my story. Wearing my father's rank under my pocket made me feel closer to him somehow.

Scott never seemed to judge me and I recall discussing my father's career, Israel, and Judaism with him on several occasions.

Later, I was moved when Scott told me that he had gone to Israel and placed a prayer in the Wailing Wall for my father's health. Not many people would have gone out of their way to do such a thing.

Scott was on the West Point skydiving team and he would often drop from a helicopter carrying the American flag and land right in the middle of the football stadium during games. He was the epitome of a soldier to me, and I always appreciated the kindness he showed me.

One day, I don't recall exactly when it was, Scott came back from parachute practice and seemed shaken up.

"Stephen Miller streamered in today," he said.

When a parachute canopy fails to fully-deploy, it causes the parachute to collapse and create what looks like a streamer instead of a parachute. The protocol in such a case is to cut the main chute and deploy the reserve, but unfortunately, Stephen wasn't able to do that.

Yet, somehow he survived.

Stephen later told me what had happened as he plummeted towards the trees and hills below—how he saw his life flash before his eyes, and then felt a jolt. His chute got stuck high in a treetop and that prevented him from hitting the ground full-force, which would surely have been fatal. Instead, he hung about twelve feet off the ground and counted his blessings, knowing he was lucky to be alive.

Eventually, he cut himself loose, then leaned against the trunk of a tree until help arrived. No one could believe he'd survived.

It was this and many other stories that always made me aware of the fact that the training we were undergoing to become soldiers was dangerous at times, and accidents could and would occur. Unfortunately, not all of our classmates would be so lucky.

CHAPTER 69

JEOPARDY

SUMMER 1987

Summer Term Academic Program (STAP)

I was moved to Grant Barracks with the other cadets in the Corps who had failed one or more classes the previous academic year. I failed second semester *Probability & Statistics.*

Some called Grant Barracks the "transition barracks" because it was the last home a cadet would have before transitioning back to the civilian world after being kicked out for academic reasons.

My roommate was Ron Davis, who was a star sprinter on the track team. He had muscles on top of his muscles and he carried himself with a dignified air, proud but not conceited.

As we were getting to know each other, we were pleased to find that we were both from Ohio.

"I attended the track state championships at Ohio State University a few years ago," I said. "And there was this black guy decked out in fluorescent green shoes, shirt, and bandanna running the one hundred yard dash. He looked ridic—"

"That was me," Ron said flatly.

"—awesome." I said, "He—*you*—looked awesome!"

Cadet Ron Davis, in his prime.

Ron and I laughed, and I told him that only someone who has complete confidence in himself would be bold enough to dress like that, and on that day, I recall that Ron had won each of his events handily.

Later that evening, Ron walked into the room and found me decked out in every religious article I could wear. I had on my prayer shawl and yarmulke, and I held in my hands the Bible that the Wests had bought me in Israel. I would have worn two sets of *Tefillin* if I thought it would have helped. The only thing missing was an ark.

To determine my fate and the fate all of the others who'd failed a class, the academic board had convened in the academic building across the street. A yellow glow of lights told me where they were meeting.

"What are you doing?" Ron asked.

"Praying," I said. "For both of us."

"Do you believe in God? Ron asked.

I held up my bible and prayer shawl as if to say, "What do you think all of this is about?" But then I saw Ron smiling.

"All I'm saying is, if you believe in God, you don't need to do all of that," Ron said. "*Trust him.*"

Does God speak to people through others? I wondered. I pondered his words and they made sense to me, but I have always believed in the Power of Prayer.

Instinctively, I felt like Ron was right on some level. Basically, he was telling me to "Let go and let God."

And so, I did.

A few hours later, the academic board concluded, and I saw my sponsor, Major Kaplan, departing the building. I ran down the stairs and shouted for him—not good etiquette—and he stopped. I saluted Major Kaplan and said, "Is it over, Sir?" I meant the board, but I could just as well have meant my cadet career.

Major Kaplan had a poker face and shook his head. "I've sat on numerous academic boards, Paley, and I've never seen a board argue over a file as long as they argued about yours. It must have taken them thirty minutes to make their decision," he said. "People kept changing their votes the entire time. It was crazy." *And?*

"You've been retained," Major Kaplan said, smiling. "Retained?" I said. For some reason the meaning of the words wasn't registering with me.

"You get to stay, Paley. Congratulations."

"Thank you, Sir!" I said. Something told me that Major Kaplan had a lot to do with the board's final decision, and I appreciated it very much. I vowed to never again allow someone else to be in a position to determine my fate, if at all possible.

CHAPTER 70

————

FINAL COUNTDOWN

Two Years Later

I continued to struggle academically, and I was placed on academic probation, meaning I wasn't allowed to exercise the First Class privileges afforded to senior cadets. Basically, I was confined to West Point. To eliminate all distractions to my studies, I had quit the Judo team the previous year.

Now, I was on the home stretch to graduation and the attainment of my life-long dream. My roommate, Guy Moore, loved to highlight this fact by constantly playing "The Final Countdown," by the band *Europe.*

Guy was the Company Honor Representative. He had brown hair and blue eyes and always wore a ready smile. He was a Mormon, and he told me about the affinity Mormons have with the Jews, believing that we share a common tribal heritage.

Guy and I got along great, and we never got on each other's nerves. Well, at least *he* never got on *my* nerves. I shouldn't speak for him.

One day, I decided to go to the cadet library to listen to some music in the media center on one of the upper floors. The previous year, I'd discovered that I had a passion for musicals. I was a volunteer on the Cadet Fine Arts Forum, and as an usher, I was usually able to sneak into the back of the theater to watch Broadway musicals when they came to West Point. They were fascinating to me, and since then, I would go into the soundproof music room, put on headphones, and lose myself in musicals like "Fiddler on the Roof", "My Fair Lady," and "Hair."

I would hide the fact that I was listening to musicals, however, by placing Van Halen or Kiss albums on the top of the musical album covers, so any curious cadets who looked inside would think I was jamming to some good ol' Rock-and-Roll. There's no shame in listening to musicals, but that's just where I was "at" at that time in my life. All about the ego and the "rep"!

One day, as I was leaving the media center, I discovered a door in the middle of the library and decided to see what was behind it. It was dark inside the room, and it had a bit of a musty smell. When I flipped the light switch, I was amazed to find archived books dating back to the time of Eisenhower and Patton.

I was in the "Stacks", and when the door shut behind me, I noticed that it was almost vacuum sealed, so quiet was it. I looked around and saw there was a single desk and chair sitting along the wall. I made a note to myself that I would have to come study here in the future, where there would be no distractions for me.

I continued to browse through the book collections, and I came across Hebrew writing on the spines of some books. Curious, I removed one and saw that it was The Midrash. I went over to the desk, sat down, and began reading. I learned about some compassionate Jewish customs of leaving one's door open a crack on Shabbat so that anyone who was hungry could come in to eat a Sabbath meal. I learned it was compassionate to only take the egg from a nest when the bird wasn't there. And I learned why one doesn't "seethe a lamb in its mother's milk." It was all about compassion. Being Kosher. Correct.

What were the chances, I wondered, that I would happen to pick the stack that had the Midrash volumes in them? I decided I would return more often and randomly pull one out to learn something new. And so it was, in my final academic year, that I would study alone in the quiet of the stacks with a volume of the Midrash by my side. I needed all the help I could get.

CHAPTER 71

——

EPIPHANY

I was in an especially good mood one fall day, and I decided to go for a walk. I'd never gone for a walk before, but West Point's campus was about to undergo a dramatic change as the Hudson Valley transformed into a jewel of reds, oranges, and yellows that would attract visitors from hundreds of miles away.

Studying in the Stacks was paying off, and for the first time in my cadet career—my life even—I was learning how to *truly* study. No longer were the engineering classes confounding me. I had changed my attitude about math, science and engineering to one of interest and curiosity. I purged myself of my first-grade memories of Mrs. Minor's red pen marks all over my paper, and whenever I heard my subconscious remind me that I was a "dunce," I rejected it. I was coming into my own and just in time. I was even appointed the Battalion Operations Officer by our new Air Force Tactical Officer, Captain Dart, who was a great mentor to me. Things had never looked better for me in my entire cadet career, and I was looking forward to graduation day.

I stepped out of the huge, castle-like wooden doors of the Cadet Mess Hall and saw the most beautiful purple and orange sky I'd ever seen at West Point. I inhaled deeply and took it all in.

"Beat Navy, Sir!" a female Plebe said as she pinged by.

"Yeah, beat 'em," I said, distracted by the beauty that surrounded me.

"Good evening, Sir," another cadet said as he pinged by me, raising his elbows parallel to the stairs as he ascended them. "Yes it is, Cadet," I said. "Yes it is."

Where to? I wondered as I scanned the grounds before me. I looked up and saw the statue of George Washington sitting on his fiery steed and pointing off to the distance—toward Trophy Point.

Trophy Point it is, George. I walked past the statue and looked up to see George Washington's likeness silhouetted in dramatic fashion by the multi-colored sky. If only I could talk to him or show him what his courage in gaining America's freedom had produced.

It was Washington's vision to create a military academy at West Point to train engineers who could fight America's wars and build her infrastructure, but he never saw his vision fulfilled. He died in 1799. Instead, it was President Thomas Jefferson who finally gained the support of the public and of Congress to establish the United States Military Academy at West Point in 1802, and the rest is history.

I walked across the Plain and neared the bleachers, and images of my parents flashed through my mind as I imagined them sitting together over the years watching parades. A chill went through me, as I pictured them sitting in those same bleachers for my graduation parade which was now just months away.

I crossed the street to Trophy Point and walked over to "my" bench, Determination. I sat down and took in the beautiful portrait created by the sky as it was reflected in the Hudson River below. For the first time in a long time, I felt at peace with who I was, where I was, and where I was going.

I removed my wallet from my back pocket, and I removed the silver dollar that was carefully tucked inside. I had carried this silver dollar for so long that Eisenhower's likeness was now even more bald than usual.

I studied the silver dollar and marveled at how it symbolized the dream which was born inside of me when I was just twelve years old. How ignorant I was then about the things that I would have to go through in order to get to this very moment in time. Had I known then what I know now, would I do it all over again? I wondered. I looked at the silver dollar again and smiled. In a heartbeat!

As I pictured myself saluting Dad on graduation day, a terrible thought began to creep into my consciousness, threatening the peace I was feeling inside. When I was a kid and imagined giving my father my first salute as an officer, I imagined him well and living at home again. Suddenly, the reality of the situation began to sink in. After all these years of pain and sacrifice devoted to giving Dad my first salute, I realized that when it was all over, he wouldn't even remember it.

That thought saddened me, and I realized that my need to make him proud had blinded me to the fact that he wasn't getting any better. I got so involved in my selfish dreams and goals that I completely overlooked the fact that all he wanted, all he *really* wanted, was to come home.

And getting home is what it's all about.

I heard the words he spoke to me at the hospital the last time I visited him. *"I'm sick and tired of this damned place."*

And then, I recalled the disappointment in my mother's eyes and the haunting words she said to me when I was a kid and failed to catch my father when he was falling down. *"Why didn't you help him?"*

I stood up to try to shake that horrible memory and the shame it brought me, but it was no use. I studied the silver dollar in the palm of my hand. What once inspired me, now mocked me.

Everything I thought I was, everything I wanted to be...suddenly seemed like an illusion. Like a ship breaking away from its moorings, I felt the tethers that held me to my dream snap and break from the very foundation of who I thought I was.

If it were me in the hospital for ten years, my father wouldn't rest until he found help for me. I owed him just as much.

When I turned towards the barracks, I knew what I had to do.

CHAPTER 72

―――

RECORDS

"Hi, Mom," I said when she answered the phone.

"What's the matter?"

"Nothing," I said. "Everything is fine. I just called to ask if you still have Power of Attorney for Dad."

"Yes, why?"

"Because I need you to write a letter to the records department in Saint Louis and ask them to send a copy of Dad's medical records. I'm going to try to find help for him in New York City."

"Which ones?" she asked.

"*All of them,*" I said.

Instead of going home for Christmas break, I decided that I would take Dad's records to the best neurologist I could find to see if there was anything that could be done to help him. Surely, after ten years, there must be some kind of new medicine or procedure that could help him, I thought.

It was time to bring Dad home.

CHAPTER 73

———

MICHELLE

OCTOBER 1988

Cadet Mess Hall

"Sir, the dessert for this meal is German Chocolate Cake. Is there anyone who would not care for a piece of German Chocolate Cake, Sir?" bellowed Cadet Jones, the Plebe who sat opposite me at the foot of the table.

"Cut it evenly this time, Cadet Jones," I said.

Cadet Jones put the cake down and said, "Yes, Sir!" and got to work cutting the cake.

"So when will they be in?" asked Paul, who was seated to my right.

"Not sure," I said. "It could take months. He's got twenty-three years of records."

"And you plan to find a doctor for him how?" asked Paul.

"I don't know yet," I said. "I'll figure something out."

"And you plan to do this over Christmas break, while everyone's gone for the holidays?" asked Paul, smiling.

"Okay, so maybe I didn't think it all the way through," I said. "But I've got to try something."

Paul nodded.

"Sir!" said Cadet Jones, holding up the now-cut cake. "The German Chocolate Cake has been cut. The German Chocolate Cake to Cadet Paley for inspection please, Sir!"

"Send it," I said.

The cake was passed down the table from one cadet to another as it made its way to me for inspection. Each cadet studied the cuts and shook their heads as they passed it along. I knew it wouldn't be pretty.

Paul handed the cake to me and frowned. Cadet Jones had missed the center of the cake causing different sized pieces to be cut. This meant that someone would be cheated out of their fair portion of the cake, and that is simply—

"Unacceptable, Cadet Jones! Did you even use a template?"

"Yes, Sir!" said Cadet Jones, worried.

I picked up my fork and identified the smallest piece of cake. Then I stuck my fork into it and mangled it.

"I marked your piece, Cadet Jones," I said, as the cake made its way back to him.

"Yes, Sir!"

Suddenly, Cadets started shouting and waving their white, linen napkins in the air, which meant that a civilian female or females were joining us for dinner. They usually came from the sports teams of opposing schools, and they had to endure a gauntlet of male testosterone to get to their dinner tables.

The hooting-and-hollering with napkin waving was a (barbaric) form of welcome, Cadet-style.

That's when I heard the clink-clinking of forks on the water glasses, which was a ritual reserved only for the prettiest of guests.

All the upperclassmen at my table turned their eyes toward the sea of rising white napkins which followed the special guest in waves as she passed by their tables.

That's when I saw a beautiful brunette walking with her cadet escort, my good friend Bob Barush, who was one of the top shooters on West Point's rifle team.

I grabbed Paul by the arm and leaned in so he could hear me above the din of screaming cadets.

"I know that girl," I said to Paul. "She owes me money!"

Paul smiled knowingly and said, "No, you don't, Rob. Don't do it."

As she walked past my table, she was smiling ear-to-ear from all the attention.

"Michelle?" I shouted as soon as she walked by me.

She turned her head and said, "No, Mindy!"

"I'm Rob—" but she was too far away to hear me, so I just shrugged my shoulders. Paul shook his head.

The hollering only stopped when Mindy sat down a few tables behind mine.

"Anyway," I said. "Doesn't hurt to try."

"You're a slut," said Paul.

"Sir! May I make a statement?" asked Cadet Jones.

"What?' I said.

"Sir, she's looking at you."

"Who is?" I asked. "And why are you gazing around?"

"Mindy, Sir," said Cadet Jones.

"That's Miss Mindy to you." I said, shaking my head and smiling. Paul had his elbows on the table with his chin resting on his hands, and he glanced to his left.

"Jones is right, she is looking this way." Paul said.

I didn't want to turn around to look, so I came up with another plan.

"Cadet Jones, bring me the chocolate cake."

"Yes, Sir!" said Cadet Jones. He brought the cake to me and I carved my name into the largest piece with my fork. Then I took it out of the pan and placed it on a dessert plate.

"Cadet Jones, this mission is strictly voluntary, but should you accept it, I would like for you to take this to Miss Mindy."

"Yes, Sir. I'll do it," Jones said. And off he went.

Paul gave me the play by play as Jones executed his mission. "Ooh, he's surrounded by upperclassmen," Paul said. I could hear the upperclassmen hazing my Cadet.

I pushed away from the table and said, "I'd better go save him."

When I got to Jones, he was holding his own, and I told the upperclassmen who were shouting at him that I sent him. The group broke up giving me dirty looks.

"Good job," I whispered to Jones, who pinged back to our table with a slight smile.

I looked at Bob and he was smiling, clearly entertained by the whole thing. I tried to discern if Mindy was his girlfriend or date by asking, "Do you mind?"

Bob shrugged and held up his hands, giving me the go-ahead.I turned to Mindy and said, "Sorry for the drama."

"You must be Robert?" she said, pointing towards the cake.

"Right," I said, suddenly getting tongue-tied.

"Did you come to take your cake back?" she asked.

"Actually...I came to ask you for your phone number."

"I see," she said, smiling. "I'll have to think about that. But thanks for the cake!"

Crash and burn! I should have sung, "You've Lost that Loving Feeling," instead.

I nodded and turned to walk back to my table as several cadets from another company saw me get rejected and started to tease me on my return walk of shame. I felt the heat rise as I sat down as quickly as possible.

The Plebes at the end of the table were barely hiding their smiles, concluding that I had struck-out judging by the sound of the laughter coming from the other tables.

"Good job, Jones," I said. "But you can't win 'em all." The Plebes smiled noticeably, and I said, "Smirk off!"

I looked at Paul, and he just shook his head.

About fifteen minutes later, I had almost forgotten about my humiliating incident when Cadet Jones said, "Sir, Miss Mindy is walking this way."

"Stop gazing around, Jones!" I said, though I appreciated his heads up. I decided that the most dignified thing to do would be to ignore her as she walked by. Don't even look at her.

I sensed her walking by with my buddy Bob, and then I looked up, only to see her stop at Cadet Jones' chair and hand *him* a note, presumably her phone number.

"Oooh!" I heard all around me as other cadets noticed what had just happened, too. I felt the blood rush to my head in humiliation. How would I ever live this down if Mindy had given a Plebe her number instead of me? I'd be the laughing stock of the entire Corps!

Mindy looked back at me as she walked away and smiled.

I lowered my head in embarrassment. Suddenly, Cadet Jones got up without my permission and pinged over to me. "Sir, she told me to wait one minute then bring this to you."

As soon as Jones handed me the yellow Post-It note, the previously jeering cadets clapped for me. Reputation, saved!

CHAPTER 74

——

FIRST DATE

Our first date was at Eisenhower Hall. Aunt Dee and Uncle Bernie bought tickets for a symphony and told me I was welcome to join them if I wanted to. I had absolutely no interest in symphonies, until Mindy said she'd love to go. Immediately, I changed my mind and called Aunt Dee to ask if she could buy two more tickets.

"Two, why two?" asked Aunt Dee.

"Well, I'm bringing a girl. It'll be our first date."

"I thought you said you didn't want a girlfriend while you were a cadet?" Aunt Dee said.

"I don't. I mean, I didn't, but this one's…"

"Special? Is she Jewish?" asked Aunt Dee.

"Half," I said. "Her name is Mindy Lazarus."

"We look forward to meeting her."

Eisenhower Hall

The concert was about to start, and I thought I was going to get stood up. Aunt Dee and Uncle Bernie saw my concern, and Aunt Dee said, "Don't worry, I'm sure she's just running late."

A minute later, Mindy showed up in a dark skirt and a light blouse, and she smiled that big runway smile when she saw us.

We'd been talking on the phone for weeks and were getting along great, so now it was time to figure out if there was chemistry in-person.

"Hi!" Mindy said as I gave her a hug.

"You must be Uncle Bernie and Aunt Dee," Mindy said, commanding the moment.

"That's right," said Uncle Bernie, clearly impressed. "It's nice to meet you." Uncle Bernie was tall and carried himself with a gentlemanly dignity. He looked like a smaller version of Orson Wells with his facial hair and general features.

"Robert hasn't stopped talking about you for two weeks," Aunt Dee said.

Mindy smiled, flattered, and looked at me.

"Aunt Dee!" I said.

"We can chat later. We'd better go in now," said Aunt Dee.

I'd never been to a symphony before, so I wore my issued cadet blazer with an embroidered class crest on the left breast just to be sure I was dressed properly for the occasion. It was a nice change from the Dress Gray with its high collar. Mindy sat to my right and Aunt Dee and Uncle Bernie sat to my left.

As soon as the symphony began, the vibrations from the Bass and Violins penetrated deep into my bones and I sat up in my seat. The sound of a live symphony was nothing like it was on the radio, and I instantly became a fan. Through song after song, I felt gratitude for being alive and able to enjoy such cultural awakenings. I placed my hand down on the seat by Mindy's hand, and our pinkies touched. Neither of us looked at each other, focusing on the symphony; then I took her hand in mind. She squeezed my hand tightly, all the while continuing to focus on the concert, and we communicated our feelings without saying a word.

CHAPTER 75

———

THE LIBRARY

NOVEMBER 1988

I continued to study in the library, and it paid big dividends. Despite getting the best grades of my cadet career on the mid-terms, my overall GPA was still dangerously close to just 2.0, and I wasn't authorized to leave post during the academic week. I wasn't pleased to be one of the cadets hoping for a "Two-Oh-And-Go", but unfortunately that's where I was.

This allowed me to see Mindy only once or twice a week, and on weekends I would visit her at her family's house. Her father Les was a Korean War Veteran who had earned three Purple Hearts. Her mother Julia was Italian and was tall and elegant. Her younger sister Cindy was pretty and very smart, and she loved to hang out with us. It was nice to get off-post and see what life was like outside of the Gray walls of the Academy, and I managed to keep my grades up despite my growing relationship with Mindy.

Mindy's father wanted sons, but he was blessed with two daughters instead, so he taught them both how to shoot, and shoot well. Both of them went to college on scholarships for their shooting ability. On the day I met Mindy, she had taken third place shooting against West Point cadets in a rifle match, and that was very impressive by any standard. She was in pre-Law at Saint John's University, and she was already a senior at the age of nineteen.

Mindy traveled between her home in New Jersey and her internship at the New York Statehouse in Albany, New York, and whenever she was passing West Point, I'd park my car on a hillside adjacent to the highway, so we could talk to each other via CB radios for as long as we had range.

One day, I asked Mindy to stop by the library at 1900 hours and to wait for me by the main entrance. As soon as she pulled in, I got in her car and told her to drive.

"Where are we going?" she said, laughing, as her little brown mustang made its way south on Thayer Road.

"I want to get something to eat," I said. Then I pulled my civilian clothes out of a bag and started to change out of my uniform while Mindy was driving.

"What are you doing?" she said.

"Just drive. This is going to be how we manage to see each other during the week from now on, but I can't be in uniform."

"Won't you get in trouble?" she asked.

"Only if I get caught!" I said.

Cadets are required to mark their whereabouts on a card which hangs by the door of their rooms. Options are Library, Gym, and so on. To mark your card for one place but to go to another is a violation of the Honor Code. But to *not* mark yourself at all is simply a violation of a Regulation, which states that you should mark your card.

In this manner, Mindy and I had a secret rendezvous each week, and we had fun going to dinner and trying not to get caught.

One day, when I was driving home for Thanksgiving and Mindy was heading home from Albany, we were talking on the CB radio, when our radio connection weakened.

Without realizing what I was doing, I said, "I love you," to Mindy over the CB Radio in front of the whole world of truckers who shared our station.

The radio crackled, and then I heard Mindy reply, "I love you, too!" before we lost communication.

A burly sounding trucker with a deep voice and an amplifier came on and said, "Aw, now ain't that sweet."

CHAPTER 76

REVELATIONS

DECEMBER 1988

Two weeks before my Term End Exams (TEEs), Mindy told me I needed to focus on my studies and suggested we shouldn't talk until exams were over. I respected her for that, and other than a quick call to catch up now and then, we followed her suggestion. I dove into my studies like I never had before, and I'd often work right up to closing time at the library. The desk in the Stacks was perfect for me, and I continued to learn how to learn.

In the days leading up to the TEEs, I felt my confidence in my abilities growing exponentially. Just as I did when I was training for the first Judo state championships I'd ever won, I sold-out and did what I had to do to ready myself for the exams.

On the day before the first exam, I received a box in the mail that my older sister Nancy had warned me was coming.

At last, my father's records had arrived, and after my last exam, I planned to seek out a neurologist in New York City who would be willing to look at my father's records and tell me if there was any hope for further recovery. All we had was hope.

I walked into my room and Guy's face lit up when he saw what I was carrying.

"It came!" he said, happy for me.

"Sure did, and it's heavy."

I removed the letter that Nancy had taped to the top of the box and read it. Nancy was a Physician's Assistant at the time, and she was able to review the contents with a critical eye.

In her letter, Nancy warned me against opening the box until after my final exams. She told me that the records were difficult to read, but she didn't elaborate. I decided she was probably right, and I placed the box next to my desk and sat down to study for my first exam, which was on the Vietnam War.

After dinner, Guy left to take his first exam, which was scheduled from 1800-2200 hours. I studied under the lamplight of my desk for about an hour, but the more I studied for an exam on the Vietnam War, the more curious I became about the illness that Dad had contracted while fighting in Vietnam.

Soon, I was so curious about the contents of the box that I found myself unable to concentrate. Ever since I was a kid, all I'd known about Daddy's illness was that Mom called it a "bug" and Grandma said it was a form of Meningitis, but that's all I knew. The answers to all the questions that had formed in my mind over the years were inside that box. That darned box that was sitting right there on the floor beside my desk. That darned box which, once opened, could teach me more about my father than I'd ever before known.

Before I knew it, my pocket knife was out and the blade exposed, glistening in the light of my desk lamp. I looked at my open book about the Vietnam War; then I looked at the box that contained actual documents from the Vietnam War, and I rationalized in my mind that reading my father's records would still be "studying."

I picked up the box and set it down on my bed. Then I cut the tape around the edges and opened it. I pulled out the first record lying on top, and I was surprised to see that it was from the Korean War. *No wonder it took so long to get the records.*

I sat down on my bed cross-legged and proceeded to read each and every paper one by one, placing them in piles based on the topic. It was a painful journey through time.

I tabbed each and every record with Post-It notes to make it easier for a doctor to find whatever he might need to assess my father's chances of recovery. Along the left side I tabbed anything to do with Prognosis, along the bottom edge of the papers, Diagnosis, and along the right side, Surgeries.

Nancy was right, reading about all the things my father went through—the painful spinal taps after Vietnam, the three brain surgeries to install or repair a Shunt, and all the exams and follow-ups—was too much.

Three things surprised me as I read his records. The first was the revelation that my father spent his first two years after Vietnam as an inpatient of Walter Reed Hospital in Washington, D.C. All the while, my family lived on the grounds of Walter Reed. Could this be why I didn't speak until I was six years old, I wondered, surrounded as I was by so much death and suffering?

The second thing that jumped out at me was the fact that my father had started taking sleeping pills regularly only between the years 1976 and 1978, only stopping when he fell ill due to the return of the Vietnam "bug." Why then? I wondered. And why not at any time before that?

And the third thing that jumped out at me was my mother's absolute devotion to my father through it all. The records showed that from the time my father went into the VA hospital in 1978 all the way through the present, she had visited him every single day, with few exceptions, no matter the weather or time of year.

On one particular day, which I recalled her talking about, she drove to the Chillicothe VA hospital and was told that my father had been transferred to the Cincinnati VA hospital for tests. So she drove to the Cincinnati VA and just missed him. He had been driven to Dayton for another battery of tests at Wright Patterson Air Force Base, which is where she finally caught up with him. Apparently, she knew that he wouldn't understand what was going on and she couldn't bear the thought of him not knowing where he was or, worse yet, where she was.

Even though it's unlikely that my father would even remember the frustratingly long day filled with confusion on his part, my mother made it clear to the hospital staff that my father was never to be transferred anywhere again without her knowledge or her ability to accompany him.

One time, Nancy and I asked why she went to see Daddy every day when he didn't even remember if she had been there or not, and she gave us a look that shamed us.

"He's my husband," she said. And that was enough.

That was the first time I realized how much my mother truly loved my father, and how absolutely devoted she was to him.

For years I had hero-worshipped my father and his example, but for the first time in my life I realized that my mother was just as courageous as my father in her own way. She never once complained, and when my father went down from his illness, her iron-will was revealed as she fought to keep our family together. I felt pride just in being their son.

After three hours of reading my father's records, the weight of what I had just read finally hit me, and it seemed as if my heart literally broke for him. My grandmother was right—he had been through so much. I placed my head in my hands and fought the feelings welling up inside of me. Nothing seemed more important to me now than finding help for my Dad. *Nothing.*

Reading the nurse's reports in the records revealed a common plea uttered by my father. *"I want to go home."*

Tears streamed down my cheeks as I finally understood why my father was so sick and tired of hospitals.

In the glow of the lamplight from my desk, I made another vow to my father. I vowed that I would find him help, no matter what, to try to bring him home at last.

CHAPTER 77

DEATH OF A DREAM

Thayer Hall
Exam Room

The next day, I reported to Thayer Hall to take my first Term-End Exam. Of all my courses, this one should have been the easiest test for me to do well on. I was ready.

The course was an honors' history course taught by the Dean of West Point himself, Brigadier General Roy K. Flint. I was chosen to be in his class based on the strong recommendation of my sponsor, Major Kaplan. Proctoring the course for the Dean was Colonel Hamburger, who was a helicopter pilot in Vietnam.

On my desk was a composition notebook that would be used to write our answers in. To the left of that was a blank sheet of paper that we could write on to help us formulate our thoughts. This paper had to be turned in with the notebook at the end of the exam.

After reading some administrative announcements, Colonel Hamburger told us that we could turn over the test question and begin.

An audible response could be heard throughout the exam room as everyone read the question. It was a single, open-ended question that we would have to answer for four straight hours. The question read, "Knowing what you know now about the Vietnam War, what would you have done differently if you were President Johnson?"

It should have been easy. Simply expound on everything that you could remember about the mistakes which were made and offer an alternative course of action to those mistakes.

As I started to write a quick outline on the blank paper which was provided for us, I began to have flashbacks to the things that I had read in my father's file the previous evening.

Suddenly, the question hit me as absurd. Vietnam was not a hypothetical situation. Over 57,000 men had died and hundreds of thousands more suffered from injuries or illnesses. My eyes teared up, and I didn't understand what was happening to me.

As I struggled to pull myself together, more images of the things I'd read passed before my eyes. *"I want to go home."*

Finally, I had my answer. I opened the composition notebook, and wrote, "If I were President Johnson, I would not have deployed MSG Jerome Paley and the 25th Infantry Division to Vietnam in 1966."

With conviction, I closed my notebook, grabbed the blank sheet of paper and laid it on the corner of Colonel Hamburger's desk, just four minutes into a four hour exam.

Colonel Hamburger must have thought I was going to the latrine or something, because he didn't even stop me when I walked out of the classroom.

As soon as I passed the threshold of the door, I felt a huge weight lift off my shoulders. I had failed my first exam, and now there was absolutely no way I would graduate on time and give my father my first salute.

It was all over.

My silly, childish notion to give my father my first salute as if it were a panacea for all that he had endured throughout his career in the Army was now squashed for good.

I killed what I created as a boy to do what I needed to do as a man.

CHAPTER 78

NEW MISSION

I drew an "X" through another doctor's office in the Yellow Pages and soon there were pages of "Xs". No one would see my father's records on such short-notice, and I was getting frustrated. My second exam was coming up in the afternoon, and I had more work to do to find someone who could help my father.

As I reached for the telephone receiver, the phone rang, but I didn't pick it up. It rang several times and finally stopped. Then I picked it up to make more calls.

When I wasn't making calls, I took the phone off the hook so I wouldn't be disturbed.

My next exam was in engineering, and I stayed in the exam room only long enough to review each problem, just to see how I would have done. Though there were a few problems that I wasn't expecting, I felt a sense of satisfaction that I could have done well enough on this exam to maintain my current grade which was a B- or a C+, either one being the best grade I'd ever made in an Engineering class. I wrote my name on the top of the exam, looked around at everyone focusing so hard on their tests, and then turned my exam in to the proctor. I had just failed my second class.

West Point does not tolerate mediocrity, and it is a firm rule that if you fail a final exam, even if you go into the exam with an A+, then you fail the entire course.

I returned to my room and continued making phone calls, but with no success. This continued for two more days, as I continued to fail exam after exam, unable to focus on anything but finding help for my father. Finally, on the last day of exams, I failed another honors' history course, one taught by the Superintendent of the United States Military Academy himself, Lieutenant General David R. Palmer. I was one of only five cadets in the entire Corps selected to be in his honors history course, which spanned the period from the Korean War through the Vietnam War.

I wrote the same thing in the composition notebook that I had in my first Vietnam exam. "I would not have deployed Master Sergeant Jerome Paley to Vietnam in 1966."

There was nothing left to do now but pack my bags and go home for good. I was packing my bags when there was a light knock on the door from the CQ. "Cadet Paley, Mindy's on the phone in the orderly room," he said.

"Tell her I'm not here," I said.

The CQ noticed my phone was off the hook and said, "She won't take no for an answer."

I walked down the hall and entered the orderly room.

"Hello," I said.

"What's the matter?" asked Mindy, clearly hearing the change of tone in my usual manner.

"Nothing," I said.

"Clearly something is wrong," said Mindy. "You're not answering your phone, then it doesn't even ring—did something happen?" she asked. "Is it your exams?"

"Look, I'm sorry. I've just got some really personal things going on right now and I don't have time for—"

"Us?" asked Mindy.

"Like I said, I'm sorry."

Just then, Cadet Pfeil, a Plebe, opened the door and walked into the orderly room. I snapped my fingers and pointed hard towards the door. He quickly turned around and walked back out.

"I'm sorry for whatever's happening," Mindy said. "But I want to help if I can."

It was clear that Mindy was not going to give up easily. Pre-Law.

Frustrated, I finally said, "Look, I just received my father's medical records, and things do not look good for him, so unless you happen to know a neurosurgeon in the City or you happen to have one in your family—"

Mindy started laughing, and I was stunned into silence. This was not the response I was expecting. At first, I got mad, but then I had to smile.

"What is so funny?" I asked, disarmed now.

"Cad-*idiot!*" she said. "I don't know one neurosurgeon, I know two!"

Once again, I wondered about God's mysterious ways.

"Please tell me you're not kidding," I said, holding my breath.

"I would never kid about something like this," she said. "I know Doctor Allen Silverstein and Doctor Richard Pelosi. Do you want their office or home phone numbers?"

"Oh my god! How—"

"My father's a biochemist, and he's known them for years."

CHAPTER 79

——

ONE STEP CLOSER

The next day I was zooming towards Ridgefield, New Jersey with my father's records to meet with Dr. Pelosi. I was running late to get to a 1 o'clock appointment when I got to a busy intersection with too many cars. In New Jersey, if you want to make a left turn you first have to make a right turn into a loop. That lane was full of cars and the clock on my 300ZX read 1255. I was never going to get there on time. Doctor Pelosi made it clear to me that he only had ten minutes of spare time to give me.

Just then, the entire intersection before me cleared left and right as an ambulance came barreling down the road from behind me. I cleared the road for him, too, but as soon as he passed me, I realized he was turning left, the same way I needed to go.

Extreme situations require extreme measures, I thought to myself, so I accelerated and drove right up to the back of the ambulance and chased it into and through the intersection, following it to the left. All cars in front of the ambulance cleared a path for him and—by extension—for me. When the ambulance got to the next intersection, however, it came to a complete halt. Traffic was so tight that no one could move over for him.

I slammed my hand on my steering wheel and said, "Damn it!"

But when I looked to my left, I saw a sign for Doctor Pelosi's office. I had stopped right at his office. I turned hard left and walked in right at 1 o'clock.

Dr. Pelosi was tall and had a shock of brown hair parted to the side, and short sideburns. He put on his glasses to review my father's file, and then he looked up and said, "You did all this?" He was referring to my tabbing system.

"Yes, Sir," I said.

"Very useful," he said as he thumbed through some papers and looked at specific ones of interest to him.

"My son went to West Point," Doctor Pelosi said.

"Did he?" I asked. That's a nice *coincidence.*

I sat silently to give him time to absorb what he was reading. Finally, he said, "Your father has recovered from surgeries in the past, so I'm thinking it may be worthwhile to look at the current shunt that's in his head. A CT scan would be useful."

I picked up a large yellow envelope with my father's most recent CT scan and said, "I have one right here."

Dr. Pelosi smiled and took it from me; then he put the CT scan into his machine to look at it.

Finally, he turned to me and said, "I think it'll be worthwhile to refer you to Doctor Silverstein. He's one of the best in the nation."

"Great!" I said, "I appreciate it."

"He's a very busy man with a long waiting list, though, so don't get your hopes up. But it wouldn't hurt to call him and see if he can get you in next year."

Later that day

After calling for hours only to be told that Dr. Silverstein wasn't available, I finally got through.

The secretary covered the mouthpiece, but I could still hear her say, "It's that West Point cadet again, what shall I tell him?"

The next thing I knew, Doctor Silverstein was on the line. I gave him my best one-minute elevator pitch.

"Sir, I'm a West Point cadet and I'm calling on behalf of my Jewish War Veteran father who has been in the VA hospital for the past ten years. I have all his records and his latest CT scan, and all I'm asking from you is to look at his records and tell me if there's hope or not." Whew.

"Well, Cadet, I understand that, and I'd be happy to help, but the fact is I'm booked solid for six months out and I don't take CHAMPUS."

"That doesn't matter," I said, "Because I'll have a national collection if I have to. Please, Sir."

"Hold on a minute, cadet." He said. Then he covered the mouthpiece.

"Cadet, someone must be watching out for you because a patient who has never canceled before just called to cancel his appointment. Can you be here on December 20th at 9 a.m.?"

"Yes, Sir! Thank you so much. I can't tell you how much this means to me and to my family. I'll bring all of his records." I said.

"I don't want to see his records. I want to see *him*."

CHAPTER 80

———

DR. SILVERSTEIN

Office of Dr. Allen Silverstein
Ridgefield, New Jersey
December 20, 1988, 9 a.m.

It was like a family reunion. Dad, Mom, Phil, Nancy, and Karen came for the big event. Dad was about to meet with one of the nation's most prominent neurologists, and we all sat in the lobby with nervous anticipation. Dr. Silverstein was the President of the American Neurological Association, and his services were in high demand internationally.

And now, thanks to a piece of German Chocolate Cake and the Lazarus family, Daddy was about to meet him. Promptly at 9 a.m., the door to Dr. Silverstein's office opened, and a gray-haired man who reminded me of Albert Einstein looked down at his clipboard and called, "Sergeant Paley." He looked up and was surprised to see there were six of us standing up.

"All of you?" he asked.

"This is very important to all of us," I said.

"Right, come in then. Come in."

We entered Dr. Silverstein's office, and he told Dad to sit down in the chair in front of his desk. I stood on the wall next to Dad and the rest of the family stood behind him.

"Sergeant Paley," Doctor Silverstein said.

"Uh, Doctor, it's Sergeant Major Paley," I said.

The doctor looked at me through his glasses as if he were trying to determine if I was seriously concerned about something so trivial. He must have concluded that I was.

"Fine. Sergeant Major Paley, what year is it?"

My father looked uncomfortable and a little embarrassed. He looked to me for help, and as bad as I wanted to help him, I remained silent.

"I don't know," he said, embarrassed.

"It's 1988, I want you to remember that."

"Okay," my father said.

"Who's the President of the United States?" asked Dr. Silverstein.

Dad laughed a little and then looked at me again. He seemed to be embarrassed, and I felt bad for him. I didn't see what good it was to humiliate my father and I wanted to say something, but I reminded myself that Dr. Silverstein was one of the best.

"I don't know," Dad admitted.

"Ronald Reagan," said Dr. Silverstein.

Daddy's face registered shock and he said, "The *actor?*"

We all laughed at his reaction, but my family and I were probably more shocked that he knew who Ronald Reagan was.

"Yes, the actor," said Dr. Silverstein. "I want you to remember that."

"Okay," my father said.

"Now, I need to conduct a few physical tests on him. Who's the family representative?"

Everyone pointed to me.

A few minutes later, after Dr. Silverstein tested my father's reflexes, his gate and his vitals, we returned to the office. My father sat down in the same chair and Dr. Silverstein asked him, "What year is it?"

"I don't know," Dad said.

"Yes you do," said Dr. Silverstein.

Dad paused and then tentatively said, "1988?"

We all looked at each other in shock, then smiled.

"Who's the President?"

Dad said he didn't know again.

"Yes, you do," said Dr. Silverstein, leaning in towards my Dad.

"Reagan?" he said.

We all cheered as if he'd just won *Jeopardy* or something. It was the first and only time in ten years that we saw any sign that Daddy could be re-taught things, and it was a positive new development.

Dr. Silverstein turned to a typewriter and began to type a letter. We all looked at each other wondering what he was typing. I shrugged my shoulders.

Finally, Dr. Silverstein pulled the paper out of the typewriter and handed it to me. "This should be enough to get him into Walter Reed for further evaluation," he said.

I scanned the letter and then asked, "Does this mean..."

"There's hope!" said Dr. Silverstein. Hearing those words after ten long years was enough to make us all cheer and hug each other, tears in our eyes.

We thanked Dr. Silverstein profusely for his time and for his optimism, and then we went out to the lobby. Phil pulled out his checkbook and said, "How much do we owe you."

The receptionist, a red-haired lady with cat eye glasses said, "No, put that away. It's a Mitzvah."

We were one step closer to bringing Daddy home.

CHAPTER 81

———

BRITTNEY

LATE DECEMBER 1988

Columbus, Ohio
The Gold Rush

When you stop chasing your dreams, your nightmares catch up to you. That's what I found out the hard way one evening when I was at a local dance club trying to drown my sorrows.

My family was ecstatic about Doctor Silverstein's optimistic assessment of Daddy's chance for recovery, but I now had to figure out what I was going to be when I grew up.

I nursed a beer while I sat at a high-top round table just off the main dance floor. My high school classmates kept trying to get me to join them on the dance floor, but I was in no mood to dance. Occasionally, I thought I saw Kim Spaulding, a beautiful brunette who was voted the best looking girl in her high school class, looking my way. Kim had married my buddy David, who was voted best looking male in my class, and together they'd had the best looking baby girl whom they'd named Brittney.

As I was wallowing in my sorrows, Kim approached me and gave me a hug.

"Welcome back," she said.

"Thanks," I said.

"I need to talk to you," Kim said, shouting over the loud dance music.

"Have a seat," I shouted back.

"Can we go somewhere else to talk?"

"Sure," I said, and I got up and led her to the hallway doors.

As soon as the double doors shut, it was quiet enough to hear each other without shouting.

I was a little confused about what she wanted to talk to me about, but I guessed it was about David. Maybe he was having trouble at boot camp?

Kim seemed a little nervous, but she took a breath and steeled herself. "Okay, I'm just going to come out and ask you this. Okay?"

"Sure," I said. Anxious to hear what this was all about.

"Do you know anyone named Mr. Hodge?"

I froze when I heard his name again for the first time since I was ten years old. I was trying to process her question, but my face already gave her the answer.

"Oh my God," she said, tears forming in her eyes. "Oh my God." Kim started crying, and I finally snapped out of my shock.

I placed my hands on her shoulders and said, "Did that bastard do something to you, too?"

Tears came down her cheeks as she said, "No, it's Brittney. He's been babysitting my baby for a year."

My shock was immediately replaced by rage, as I imagined the warped pervert harming an innocent child, an infant.

"You have to take her to the hospital immediately," I said. "You have to get her checked."

Kim cried as I fought to control my rage. My hands started to shake as I geared up for battle.

"We already did," she said, "They couldn't find anything."

"Well, that's good then," I said, knowing that they wouldn't necessarily find anything physical.

"I can't believe that bastard's already out of jail. But how in the hell is he still allowed to be around children?"

"I don't know," Kim said, sobbing.

I pulled her close to me and wanted to cry with her, but all I could see was revenge.

"Where does he live?" I asked her.

Kim stepped back and saw the look on my face. "No, Robert, I can't tell you that," she said, reading my mind. "You've got too much to lose."

I knew she wouldn't tell me, so I asked if she was okay. When she nodded her head, I held the door open for her as loud music blasted into the hallway and she went back inside.

I turned around and headed for my car. I kicked the entrance door open and thought of all the ways the Army had taught me to kill a person. I drove to the nearest pay phone by the Burger King and called my brother Phil, who was a Columbus policeman.

"Phil, if I give you a name, can you get me an address."

"You better have a good reason for asking me this, Rob, because what's your asking me to do is illegal."

"Walter Hodge," I said.

"Absolutely not," Phil said. "I won't let you ruin your career."

CHAPTER 82

————

LIES

I retreated to my world of silence for the next few days, and I brewed over the injustice of our legal system. How could they possibly let a serial child kidnapper and rapist out only to continue to molest innocent children? *It just doesn't make any sense.*

A few days later I went to visit Ms. DeWine, as was my custom whenever I came home on leave. Ms. DeWine lived a few houses down from my parents and always had fresh baked bread for me when I visited her, and she was always very nice to me when I was growing up.

We sat at her kitchen table enjoying the bread when Ms. DeWine muted the television and said, "Can I ask you something personal?"

"Of course," I said, as I stuffed my mouth with the delicious fresh bread.

"Did what Mr. Hodge do to you as a child affect your relationships?" she asked.

I nearly choked on the bread. For the second time in as many days I was hearing Mr. Hodge's name, which I hadn't heard prior to this for over twelve years.

"I don't think so," I said, "I mean, I've had girlfriends, if that's what you mean?"

"You've always been the strong one," she said. "All of the kids that were molested have grown up to have difficulty adjusting."

That's when she told me that her son was in the middle of a divorce from his high school sweetheart.

"I'm sorry to hear that," I said. Trying to figure out what was going on. "Did you know that Mr. Hodge is out of jail?"

"Oh, dear," said Ms. DeWine.

"I know," I said, "it's crazy!"

"No, I mean, 'oh dear' your parents never told you the truth, did they?"

"What do you mean?" I asked.

"Well, Mr. Hodge never went to jail. We lied to you when you were kids so you wouldn't be afraid to walk past his house to go to school."

Suddenly, it seemed like my world was collapsing around me.

"Those were different times," she said. "Different times."

I lost my appetite and thanked Ms. DeWine for telling me the truth. Then I told her that I had to go home. As I walked to the door, Ms. DeWine said, "It's just too bad what happened to your father because of all that."

I literally stopped in my tracks, then slowly turned around. "What do you mean?" I asked, as my heartrate increased.

"Oh, dear, I've already said too much. Why don't you go and ask your mother."

"I'd like to know now," I said.

Resigned, Mrs. DeWine elaborated. "Well, after the Judge let Mr. Hodge off for time-served, your father was so mad that he began guarding the neighborhood night after night to protect us from Mr. Hodge and his family. Apparently, they were overheard in the courthouse making threats against us."

"Night after night? For how long?"

"I don't know, one, two years. The poor man would sleep all day just so he could stay up all night."

I thanked Ms. DeWine for the information and left.

As I walked home with snow swirling around me, everything began to fall into place.

The sleeping pills...the rattling back door...the missed baseball games and Judo tournaments...the discussion about shooting someone and dragging him into the house...*How did I not see this all along? God restored my sight but yet I still could not see!*

CHAPTER 83

GUILT

1989

New Year's Day

As I made my way back to West Point through the treacherous winter snow, I tried to process my newfound knowledge. At last, after years of being in the dark, I now knew the truth about Mr. Hodge and the effect he'd had on so many families. He had ruined or nearly-destroyed so many lives, and I wished him death and damnation.

Telling on Mr. Hodge and taking him to court apparently meant nothing to the judge and the jury, and in the end it was my father and—by extension—our family who paid the price. The "what-if" thoughts began to haunt me. *What if I'd never told on Mr. Hodge?* I wondered. *Would Daddy still be sick today?* The answer to this question would haunt me for the next thirty years of my life.

For years, I'd resented my father for never showing up at my baseball games or Judo tournaments, believing it was because he was ashamed of me. And now I know that he wasn't ashamed of me, that he loved me and my family so much that he sacrificed his health to protect us.

Even his last conscious act before the surgery and the dementia was selfless. He called the police on himself because he was afraid he might hurt one of us. At that time, the news was full of stories of

Vietnam Veterans with undiagnosed PTSD killing their families and themselves.

His entire life was one of service and of sacrifice, and all I wanted was his approval and for him to be proud of me. And now I'd taken away the one thing that could have brought happiness to him in his current situation—the first salute.

First Mr. Hodge took my father's health, and now I let him take my dream. As much as I wanted to help my father, I now knew that I also wanted to graduate from West Point. I had grown to love West Point as much as my father did, and as much as it was for him that I wanted to graduate, it was also for me, too. But it was too late now. I had sealed my fate.

The only honorable thing left to do now was to go to West Point and resign. I didn't have the heart to tell my family over the holidays that I had failed all my final exams and would be kicked out of West Point upon my return. But they would find out soon enough.

CHAPTER 84

―――

COLONEL
JACK GRUBBS

JANUARY 1989

I got back to West Point a day before the report date so that I could gather my gear and my thoughts before tendering my resignation. I couldn't believe it was all over, but at least I could now focus 100% on Dad's recovery.

I drove toward Thayer Gate to go to McDonalds when I noticed the gate guard standing huddled against the building, trying to keep himself warm against the biting New York winter.

I stopped my car and rolled down the window.

"MP!" I shouted.

The MP stuck his head around the corner of the guard shack and said, "Yes, Sir?"

"How many guys do you have in there tonight?" I asked.

"Three, Sir, including me," he said.

"Roger, thanks."

I drove through the local Highland Falls McDonalds and purchased four cheeseburger meals, substituting the cokes for hot chocolates.

Then I drove back through the main gate, stopping to surprise the MP with three meals. He seemed very grateful.

I was in my room waiting for the hammer to fall, and it came down on 3 January 1989. The CQ told me I was to report to Colonel Grubbs in the Engineering department at 0900 hours.

The biting New York winter penetrated my wool jacket as I pushed through the snow towards Mahan Hall. Winters at West Point are infamously referred to as the "Gloom Period," because everything—the sky, the buildings, our uniforms—are all gray and gloomy. And now, as I fought my way through the biting wind and snow to the appointment that would officially bring my cadet career to an end, the term took on a whole new meaning for me. *Gloom period, indeed.*

When I found Colonel Grubbs' office, I hung up my winter jacket and hat, dusted myself off, ensured that the gig-line on my belt was straight and knocked on his door.

"Come in," he said.

As I walked towards Colonel Grubbs' desk, I felt like a pirate who was about to walk the plank. The trip would be short but painful. "Sir, Cadet Paley reports to Colonel Grubbs as ordered."

He returned my salute and told me to take a seat. Colonel Grubbs was lean, wore his hair tight, and had the chiseled facial features so common to an Airborne Ranger.

I immediately noticed the colored combat patch on his Class A jacket hanging on the coat rack behind him, and I knew that he had fought in Vietnam. The patch was of the famed 173rd Airborne Brigade, and was unmistakable for the white, angel-like wing cradling a red bayonet on a blue background.

He's a badass, I thought to myself. Smart for the academy to send me to someone as tough as Colonel Grubbs to tell me that I'm being dismissed.

"Cadet Paley, do you know why I called you here?"

"Yes, Sir, because I failed all of my final exams."

"No doubt you already know the consequences, but do you want to tell me what happened?"

"No thank you, Sir. I'm prepared to tender my resignation instead." I laid the envelope with my resignation letter in it on the edge of Colonel Grubbs desk. He didn't take it.

"Look, what do you have to lose? You entered the Term-Ends with the best grades you ever had in your cadet career, and then you failed every exam. Why?"

"It's kind of personal, Sir." I said.

"Okay, why don't you tell me about it, anyway? The Dean wants answers."

I figured Colonel Grubbs was right; maybe it would be best to tell him the truth before I went home.

"How much time do you have, Sir?" I asked.

Ten minutes later, I finished telling Colonel Grubbs the outline of my story (without mentioning Mr. Hodge, of course). When I finished, he seemed visibly moved.

"What unit did your father deploy with?" he asked.

"Headquarters, 65th Engineer Battalion, 25th Infantry Division, Sir. In January 1966."

Colonel Grubbs grinned and said, "Cadet Paley, do you think that maybe my Yearling year roommate deployed with that unit at the same time?" he asked.

"You're kidding me, Sir?"

"No, I'm not. In fact, let's give him a call."

Colonel Grubbs flipped through his circular rolodex, found the number for his former roommate and dialed.

A moment later, Colonel Grubbs was speaking to him.

"Roy, it's Jack. Quick question. Weren't you with the 65th Engineers when you deployed to Vietnam?" he asked.

"Thought so," Colonel Grubbs said as he looked at me and nodded his head. "Did you know an NCO by the name of Paley?" Colonel Grubbs asked.

"No kidding?" said Colonel Grubbs, shaking his head.

"Well, you're not going to believe this, but I have his son in my office right now. Yes! He's a Firstie and graduating in May."

I am? I wondered, could it still be possible somehow?

"Sure. Here he is." Colonel Grubbs handed me the telephone and said, "It's Lieutenant Colonel Buckner. *He knows you father.*"

I nearly fell out of my seat.

"Good morning, Sir," I said.

"Cadet Paley, your father must be so proud. How the hell is your old man? Jacob, right?"

"Negative, Sir, but you have the first letter right. It's actually Jerry."

"That's right!" he said. "So how's he doing? I never did learn what happened to him after he was medevacked back to the states."

"Well, he's actually not doing too well, Sir. He's been in a VA hospital in Ohio for the past ten years. That's kind of why I'm in here talking to Colonel Grubbs right now."

"Is there anything I can do for him?"

"Actually, Sir, I've been trying to get him back to Walter Reed, and I've been having some trouble with that."

"I have classmates who work there. Let me give them a call."

"Thank you, Sir. I'd appreciate it very much."

"Give me your address, Cadet Paley. I've got some clippings and pictures of me and your Dad in Vietnam. I'd like to send them to you."

I didn't want to tell him that I might not be here when they arrived, but I gave him my cadet address anyway.

"Okay, I'll get back with you soon."

"Sir, can you tell me…was my Dad a good Soldier?"

"Your father was a great soldier." My heart seemed to skip a beat when I heard those words. I don't know why I asked that question, but I guess I just wanted to hear it from someone who actually served with my father in combat, and it made me proud.

Lieutenant Colonel Buckner wished me luck and hung up, and I passed the phone back to Colonel Grubbs, amazed at what had just taken place.

"Damnedest thing I've ever seen, Paley," said Colonel Grubbs as he smiled and hung up the phone.

As if speaking to Colonel Buckner wasn't coincidence enough, Colonel Grubbs said, "Did you know the Dean was an infantry battalion commander with the 25th ID in '68?"

"I didn't know that, Sir."

The "coincidences" continued to stack up. It seemed that the 25th Infantry Division was well represented at West Point. I felt a lightness in my chest as I pondered the strange turn of events which seemed to be transpiring. It took failing all of my Term End Exams to be brought before Colonel Grubbs, whose West Point roommate served in the same unit that my father did in Vietnam in 1966... once again, I found myself letting go to the mysterious and intoxicating pull of destiny.

Colonel Grubbs sat up and rested his elbows on his desk. "Let me ask you something, Paley." He looked me square in the eyes and said, "What would your father say about you bailing out of the Academy while using him as your crutch?"

Before I could answer, he continued, "Don't answer that question to me, answer it to yourself and to your dad. Now, assuming you want to graduate, let's see what we've got. I'm not saying that I can do anything for you—you've put yourself in a helluva bind. But if I can work something out, will you finish what you've started?"

Once again, in my darkest of moments, a ray of hope appeared.

"Yes, Sir. I found out some new things back home and...but I'd like to make up all of my finals, Sir."

Colonel Grubbs seemed surprised that a man in my position had the chutzpah to make any kind of demand.

"Sir, I know I can pass them."

"We don't have the time or the resources to re-administer all those exams before classes start tomorrow," he said. "I'm afraid that won't be possible."

"Thank you, Sir. Then I would like to tender my resignation."

Colonel Grubbs sat back in his chair and seemed to be studying me. "Why's this so important to you?"

"Because before I was accepted to come here, Sir, there were a lot of people who said I'd never make it in. And even after I did get accepted, they said I'd never make it through." I paused, because I was getting a little choked up.

"Go on," said Colonel Grubbs.

"Well, Sir, I decided that in order for my first salute to my father to mean anything to either of us, I would have to prove to myself that I could take everything that West Point could throw at me, which is why I don't want to get any special exceptions."

"I respect that, Paley. But I can't make you any promises on that point. Before I go and talk to the Dean, I need you to hold off on that resignation letter. Again, what would your dad say?"

The empathy that Colonel Grubbs seemed to have for my father moved me.

"You're right, Sir. I understand. I just don't know if there's time to find help for my father and to redo Firstie year..."

"I understand, Paley, but you're still missing the point concerning your father's preference for your life and its linkage to the Army."

I realized Colonel Grubbs was right. I let my emotions get the best of me, and in doing so I jeopardized the very thing that seemed to have kept my father alive all these years—the promise of the first salute.

Colonel Grubbs closed the discussion. "You'll hear from someone in the next few days. You're dismissed."

I stood at attention and gave Colonel Grubbs as sharp a salute as I could render. I instinctively knew that I would follow this man anywhere.

I did an about face, and walked towards the door, knowing that something very special had just happened that defied all odds and explanations.

"Cadet Paley," said Colonel Grubbs as I was about to exit his office. I came to attention and said, "Yes, Sir?"

"The good Lord blessed me with daughters, but if I had a son, I'd want him to be just like you."

It was the highest compliment I had ever received in my life, but I couldn't speak because of the baseball sized lump in my throat, so I nodded my thanks and closed the door.

In the silence of the hallway, tears of gratitude rolled down my cheeks.

The red bayonet on Colonel Grubbs' combat patch seemed to symbolize the end of my cadet career. He had my fate in his hands, but instead of wielding the bayonet, he donned the wings of an angel-in-disguise.

CHAPTER 85

THE DEAN

After the longest two days of my life, I was finally summoned to the Dean's office. I walked up to a skinny Major whom I'd never seen before, and he looked underwhelmed to meet me.

"So *you're* Cadet Paley," he said.

"Yes, Sir."

"The academic board held an emergency meeting to determine your status, and you've been retained."

"Thank you, Sir!" I said, feeling so very fortunate.

It seemed that the vision I had of saluting my father on graduation day was meant to be, after all, and I was filled with gratitude.

"However, you will not be able to make up your final exams."

My facial expression changed immediately. "Sir, please thank the academic board members for their generous offer, but if I can't make up my exams, then I choose to resign."

The Major looked at me like I had two heads. Then he sat back and grinned. "Colonel Grubbs said you would say that."

"He did?" That alone made me smile, because I hadn't let Colonel Grubbs down. But the Major wasn't finished playing all his cards yet.

He placed his right hand on a legal pad that was lying on top of three cadet files.

"You've forced me into this, Cadet Paley. Do you see these files?" he said.

"Yes, Sir."

"These files belong to three of your classmates who failed some of the same classes you did but by only 1 point each. The Academic Board has decided that these cadets will receive passing grades and graduate with their class if you accept waiving your Term End Exams. They believe it's the fair thing to do."

I hesitated again, but this time it wasn't so easy to say "no." The fate of three of my classmates was now in my hands.

The Major seemed to understand my dilemma, and he seemed to soften up a little. "Look, Paley, the academic board has decided to treat your situation as if it were a death in the family."

"But, my father's not dead, Sir." I said, protesting a little too strongly.

"I didn't say he was," the Major said, holding both of his hands up. "All I'm saying is that receiving your father's medical records the day before your exams started may have had the same impact on you as if it were a death in the family."

I nodded and thought about it.

"And you wouldn't be the first one to get your final exams waived under these circumstances," the Major said.

I finally understood what he was getting at. Apparently, West Point wasn't the cold, heartless place that so many might think it was.

I got into West Point as an "exception," and I just didn't want to graduate from West Point as one, too. But now I knew I couldn't let my pride get in the way when my actions would affect the lives of others.

The Major had said all that he was going to say, and he dropped his hands down onto his desk. When his right hand landed on the legal pad that was concealing the names of the files below them, the legal pad moved a little and I saw the name on the top file and recognized it. He was a friend of mine. "Sir, how can I say no to that? Please thank the Board for me again."

The Major looked up at me and said, "They didn't do this for you, Cadet."

I paused and thought about what he said, and then I smiled and nodded as I turned to leave the Dean's office.

That's when I realized that these men and women of honor and character had circled the wagons around one of their own, for his sake. They did it not for me, but for Dad.

How proud and honored Dad would be to know what these men and women of West Point, whom he admires so much, did for him on this day. I regret that I never told him.

CHAPTER 86

———

CADET, HALT!

SPRING 1989

I was late coming home from Mindy's house and it wasn't looking good. I was allowed to go out on weekends, but it was an absolute *must* to be back in my room by the time Taps sounded. Firstie Privileges for a cadet on academic probation only stretched so far, and then you are snapped back to reality like a rubber band by one cadet regulation or another. On this Sunday night, as I parked my red 300ZX in the upper lot above Michie Stadium, I knew that I had blown it.

After learning the truth over the holidays about what happened to my father after the trial against the serial child molester, I found myself seeking any kind of distraction I could find to numb the pain and guilt I felt over my father's illness. Mindy and her family provided me the love and distraction I needed, and now by being late I faced restriction and confinement to West Point, where I would be alone with my thoughts and painful feelings.

I'd also be letting down the chain of command and the academic board, who had bent over backwards to help me for the sake of my father.

I knew that having a serious relationship could be a bad idea, but so far I had proven to be very responsible about how much time I put into "extracurricular activities."

None the less, by the time I pulled into the cadet parking lot above Michie Stadium, time was not on my side.

I started to jog down the steeply sloping, zig-zagging roads just to give myself a chance, but I was wearing dress shoes and the choice was going to come down to shin splints or loss of privileges. I chose shin-splints.

I checked my Casio digital wristwatch and saw that I had four minutes left by the time I cleared Michie Stadium. It was going to be really close.

I jogged around the sidewalk which borders Lusk Reservoir—the same sidewalk that I first saw West Point cadets running on six years earlier—and I turned left to head down Stony Lonesome Road towards the Cadet Chapel, where a set of steep stairs would take me down to the barracks area below.

I had a good, steady jog going when all of a sudden a bright spotlight popped on from behind me, casting my elongated shadow down Stony Lonesome Road. A Military Policeman shouted, "Cadet Halt!" I haven't been talked to like that since I was a Plebe.

Damn! I said as I stopped and glanced at my watch. *He has me.* MPs love catching cadets who are running late. It was kind of a cat-and-mouse game, and this time, the cat won.

For a second I considered making a run for it, but I decided it wasn't worth it. I simply turned around and walked towards the Military Policeman as he drove toward me in his police pick-up truck.

"Hop in the back of my truck, please," the MP said.

I did as I was told and the MP proceeded down Stony Lonesome Road. "What barracks are you in?" he shouted through his opened window.

I turned my head and shouted, "Bradley. Central Area." The office of the Staff Duty Officer, or SDO, was also located in Central Area, and I wondered how long it would take for my punishment to come down once I got written-up.

The MP started driving a little too fast for my liking, and I held on to the edges of the bed to steady myself. *What's his hurry?* I wondered. He already had me.

When we got to Washington Road the MP turned right at the Superintendent's house, then cut back towards Arvin Gym and the alley which ran behind the barracks. He then proceeded behind Bradley Barracks and turned quickly into Central Area. Instead of proceeding straight to the SDO's office, however, he stopped near an entrance at the corner of Bradley Barracks and came to a sudden stop. Taps was already sounding.

"You'd better hurry, Cadet!" said the MP.

I didn't have to be told twice, so I jumped out of the bed of his truck and headed for the entrance.

"Thanks!" I said as I sprinted towards the doors.

"Thanks for the McDonald's," the MP said, smiling.

I turned back and looked at him, and then I realized what he was referring to. The cold night in January.

I nodded and smiled back. *What were the chances?* I wondered. That's when I learned another important lesson: Take care of soldiers, and they will take care of you.

CHAPTER 87

——

FULL CIRCLE

During second semester I had Colonel Hamburger as an instructor in one of my advanced history courses again.

Colonel Hamburger was always willing to share his experiences as a helicopter pilot with the famed 1st Cavalry Division in Vietnam with us, and I could never get enough of his stories

One day, he was telling us about a mission he had flown in an area of Vietnam called Cu Chi in 1966. His helicopter got shot down somewhere near the 25th Infantry Division's area of operations.

"I will always remember how lucky my crew and I were to be rescued by men of the 25th Infantry Division," he said.

"That's where my father was," I said to Colonel Hamburger.

"No kidding?" he said. "Maybe he saw me go down."

"Maybe?" I said, pondering the thought.

"What rank were you when this happened, Sir?" I asked.

He thought about it for a moment and said, "I was a Captain."

I nodded and thought about how many of West Point's senior leaders were just junior officers and recent West Point graduates during the Vietnam War. These are the men whom my father served with and admired so much, and now they were teaching me and my classmates.

My mind wandered back to all the other so-called "coincidences" that I had experienced in my life up to this point, and the more I pondered them, the less I believed in coincidences. Since the day of the miracle homerun on the baseball diamond when I was twelve years old, my life had become a string of seemingly unrelated events which—when taken as a whole—painted an incredible picture of Divine synchronicity. *But to what end?* I wondered.

As I thought back to all of the amazing things that had to happen in order for me to get to where I was now, just weeks away from graduating from West Point and fulfilling my dream to honor my father with my first salute, a sense of awe filled me. Whatever the reason, I was grateful to have had so many amazing and life-changing experiences, and I wouldn't have traded them in for the world.

My thoughts were interrupted when Colonel Hamburger said, "For those of you who aren't familiar with it, this is the patch of the 25th Infantry Division." He proceeded to place a new page on the overhead projector, and what I saw stunned me...

Lightning, I said to myself as I dropped my pen. I couldn't believe what I was seeing. My father's unit patch in Vietnam was a single bolt of lightning.

What's this all about, God? I heard myself whisper.

The lightning bolt which appeared on the night my father went into the hospital in an answer to my prayers had been a mystery to me my whole life, and now...

"The 25th Infantry Division is known as *Tropic Lightning,*" Colonel Hamburger said. "Though some of the soldiers jokingly call it the *Electric Strawberry.*"

I smiled, but not at his joke. Somehow, it had all come full-circle, and I finally had the last of my questions answered. Only God could have authored this story, I realized, because surely, no one would believe me if I told it.

CHAPTER 88

APFT SHOCKER

I was ecstatic when I received word from the Dean's office that my final Term End Exams were finally graded, and I had earned a 2.1 Grade Point Average. The little boy who couldn't add 2+2 would soon be a West Point graduate!

But first, the Class of 1989 had one more test to pass. Our final Army Physical Fitness Tests (APFT), which I knew was the one test at West Point that I could ace.

The APFT consists of two minutes of push-ups, two minutes of sit-ups, and finally a two-mile run. Everything that I had done since I was twelve years old had primed me for each of these events, and on the day of the APFT, I achieved my highest score to date, a perfect 300. It was an incredible exclamation point to my cadet career.

When I got back to the barracks to celebrate with my company-mates, there was a buzz in the air which told me something was wrong. "What's going on, Guy?" I asked.

As the company Honor Rep, Guy was privy to the details of a rumor that was going around.

"Close the door," Guy said as I walked into our room.

"What's happening?" I asked.

"Mark Boyles is being accused of lying about his APFT," Guy said.

Mark Boyles is the cadet whom I'd had to confront two years earlier for his anti-Semitic remarks.

"What? How could he lie about that?"

"Apparently, he failed his sit-ups," Guy said, "Then he mysteriously lost his APFT scorecard in the Hudson River. He said the wind blew it away before he could turn it in."

"You're kidding me, right? He actually said that?"

"Yep. They were going to let the cadets who graded him vouch for his scores, but he said he couldn't remember who held his feet during the sit-ups."

"Okay," I said, still not quite getting it.

"Heather Brannon is the one who held his feet," Guy said, "But Mark lied and said he doesn't remember who held his feet."

Heather Brannon was our company-mate since Plebe year, and the likelihood that Mark did not remember that it was Heather who held is feet was very suspect, indeed.

When Heather overheard Mark lie to someone about not remembering who held his feet, she was obligated under the Honor Code to turn him in for an Honor Violation.

"But, graduation is just two days away," I said. "What's going to happen to Mark?"

"Well, he'll most likely miss graduation and then go before an Honor Board," Guy said.

I couldn't believe that someone as smart as Mark could do something so stupid. And all because he couldn't do enough sit-ups…

The next day, during graduation rehearsal exercises and the Graduation Parade, Mark was nowhere to be seen. In fact, no one from Company D-2 would ever see him again. As far as I know, Mark Boyle did not receive his diploma from West Point, nor did he receive his commission as an officer in the United States Army.

West Point's standards know no time limits.

Shortly after my final parade as a cadet.
The following day was graduation.

CHAPTER 89

PROMISE KEPT

MAY 24, 1989

West Point
Michie Stadium

The West Point band struck-up the Graduation March as the graduating seniors of the Class of 1989 began filing out from underneath Michie Stadium and onto the football field. I could hear the roar of the enthusiastic crowd, whose spirit was undamped by the pouring rain.

I removed the silver dollar that I had been carrying with me since I was twelve years old from my white glove and studied it. The moment that I had envisioned over eleven years earlier had arrived at last, and I was having trouble processing the swirl of emotions running through me.

Scott Morrison, who was standing right in front of me, turned around and noticed the silver dollar in the palm of my hand. He smiled and said, "This is it."

I nodded, struggling to contain my emotions, and he placed his hand on my shoulder.

Of all the people in my cadet company, Scott Morrison seemed to be the one who empathized with my goal to honor my father more than anyone else.

He turned around to leave me to my private thoughts, and I thanked God for allowing my father to live long enough to experience this day.

Soon, the line I was standing in started to move towards the tunnel that would take me to the football field. I replaced the silver dollar into the palm of my left hand and pulled my glove back on.

Just don't trip, I said to myself as I finally marched onto the football field and saw the screaming crowd in the bleachers for the first time. The downpour turned the crowd into a sea of colorful ponchos and umbrellas, and as I followed Scott onto the field, I worried about Daddy getting wet.

Television and audio cables stretched out all over the football field, and it took great concentration to march to the beat of the drum while simultaneously stepping over the thick cables. Nonetheless, no one tripped and soon we were all in our proper places, facing the stage set up on the 50 yard line. The audience was to our backs.

Vice President Dan Quayle was introduced and he was given a warm reception from the cadets and from the audience. I looked back and to the left towards the bleachers, and somehow—with thousands in the audience— Karen caught my attention and drew my eye toward our family.

And there sat my father in his blue suit, covered by a clear poncho, taking it all in. My mother saw me and waved, and I waved back.

I was grateful my family was underneath the overhang created by the upper level of seats, and I turned back toward the stage to try to enjoy the ceremony.

I don't recall much of anything that was said, to be honest. I was too caught-up in the realization that my childhood dream to give my father my first salute was no longer years, months or even days away, but only a matter of minutes away.

I kept looking back at my family and realized that the only time Dad had ever seen a West Point graduation before was on T.V. I recalled the time when I was building a model on the floor of our living room before Dad got sick, and the news showed a graduating West Point class tossing their white hats into the air. My father had sat up in his seat, turned his hearing aid on, and told me to turn up the volume.

And now, in a matter of minutes, he was going to get to watch the same image play out live right in front of him, knowing that this time one of the white hats would be his son's.

As the rain continued to beat down on the Class of 1989 as a harbinger of a war which was yet to come, the pitter-patter of raindrops hitting the tops of our white hats made it difficult to hear what the speakers were saying.

Finally, the time had come for cadets to walk up individually to the dais to receive their hard-earned diplomas. The rain finally let up.

As I made my way to the stage, my heart was beating out of my chest. I watched Scott Morrison shake the Superintendent's hand, take his diploma, and then salute. "Shake, take, salute," I said to myself. "Shake, take, salute."

My name came over the loudspeaker. "Robert Holden Paley."

I made a sharp facing movement towards Lieutenant General David R. Palmer, the Superintendent of the United States Military Academy, and instead of shaking his hand, I reached for my diplomas instead. *Dang it!*

I guess I was a little too anxious to get the diploma in my hand, but the Superintendent calmly reached for my right hand and got me back on track.

As General Palmer made eye contact with me, I saluted him and said, "Thank you, Sir. For everything."

He knew what I was referring to and he nodded knowingly and smiled. "You earned it, Lieutenant."

I strode down the ramp at the back of the stage and felt a million pounds of weight lift from my shoulders. I was overcome by the moment. The large white tube which contained my diploma was now in my hands, and I wanted to shout for joy. Instead, I stopped and bowed my head, and said, "Thank you, God. Thank you so much," as tears filled my eyes. I kissed my diploma and held it up toward the sky in a salute to God, and then I returned to my seat.

Finally, after everyone had their diplomas in-hand, the time we were all waiting for had finally arrived.

The Brigade Commander, Mark Jenkins, ordered us to uncover for the last time for the benediction. I removed my white hat and bowed my head for the Chaplin's prayer.

The dream that began with my bowed head on a little league base-ball diamond now came full circle.

General Palmer ordered the Commandant of Cadets, Brigadier General Gorden, to "Take charge of the Class of 1989."

General Gorden saluted the Superintendent and did an about face.

"Lieutenant Jenkins, dismiss the Class of 1989."

Lieutenant Jenkins saluted, and then turned about to face the class.

"Class, re-cover!"

We placed our white hats back on our heads. Then Lieutenant Jenkins said, "Class of 1989. Dis—missed!"

I tossed my white hat high into the air along with my brothers and sisters of the Class of 1989 as the crowd went wild.

I could only imagine what it must have been like for Dad to have witnessed this moment with his own eyes.

I hugged my company-mates good-bye and sought out my good friend and confidant, Jill Schaffner. Jill was a rising Firstie, and over the past year she'd become a close friend of mine. She was inspired by my story to give my father my first salute, and she had taken it upon herself to arrange the location of that salute with my family.

I had chosen to give my father my first salute at the same location we'd first seen cadets running together six years earlier—right outside of Lusk Reservoir.

Jill gave me a hug and smiled, then pulled me to where my family was standing, all the while "guarding" me from any cadets or NCOs who might have wanted to salute me before my father could.

I hugged everyone, and together we celebrated the moment that we had all been a part of for the past eleven years as a family. The diploma in my hand was as much theirs as it was mine.

Finally, Jill guided us outside of Michie Stadium towards Lusk Reservoir.

As we walked out of the football stadium, I noticed that my brother Phil was lagging behind the rest of the family a little.

I slowed down and said, "What's the matter, bro?"

Phil's lips were tight and he had tears in his eyes when he said, "I'm so proud of you."

My eyes instantly watered and I shoved him. "Don't make me cry," I said, as he shoved me back and laughed.

It was a joyous moment for the whole family, and finally the time had come to fulfill the vow I'd made to my father.

My family and friends formed a circle around me and my father, and my father gave me a knowing smile.

For the first time since I was twelve years old, I felt as if I were standing in front of my healthy father again. There was no fog in his eyes, and it was clear from his actions and the expression on his face that he was completely present.

I could hardly get the words out as we faced each other.

"Sergeant Major!" I said.

"Yes, Sir!" my father said as he snapped to the position of attention.

I removed the silver dollar from my glove and placed it in the palm of my left hand.

"I've waited eleven years for this, Dad," I said. "It would be my honor if you would give me my first salute."

My father choked up and drew his neck back, fighting his emotions as he snapped a sharp salute to me.

I returned his salute and saw the pride in his eyes. His lips were quivering with emotion.

It was everything I had imagined it would be and more. When I dropped my salute I placed the silver dollar in my right hand and then shook my father's hand, transferring the silver dollar from my hand to his.

In that moment, the silver dollar I'd carried with me over the years became his, and we hugged each other tightly as our family joined in.

It was the happiest moment of my life, and I thanked God for answering the prayer of a child all those years ago.

Little did I know then, that my first salute, would be my father's last.

EPILOGUE

Despite getting into Walter Reed Army Medical Center, the doctors determined that further surgery would not be conducive to my father's health, and he was returned to Columbus, Ohio, where he continued to live under VA care.

I was stationed in Hanau, Germany on my first active duty assignment as a Field Artillery officer, and I was having trouble focusing on my job. The thought that I may have had something to do with my father's illness racked me with feelings of guilt, and I felt I had to get back home to try to help him.

Perhaps I could sense that my father's health was getting worse?

I finally asked my battalion commander for a compassionate reassignment back to the states so I could be closer to my Dad.

On Friday, November 29, 1991, I received word from my battalion commander that my request for compassionate reassignment had been approved.

Two days later, on December 1, 1991, I called home to speak to my family during Thanksgiving weekend.I was pleasantly surprised to find that my father was home as well, but would be returning to the hospital later that night.

Normally, my father's deafness made speaking on the phone next to impossible, but on this night he could hear everything I was saying quite clearly.

"How's the Army?" my father asked.

"Great," I said. "But I resigned."

"You resigned?" he said, clearly shocked.

"Yes," I said. "I've been granted a compassionate reassignment so that I can come home and help you."

"I don't need any help," my father said. "What's wrong with me?"

"That's what's wrong with you, Dad," I said. "You don't remember things like you should."

"You're leaving the Army?" he asked again, just to be sure he heard me correctly.

"Yes, I'll be home in a few weeks," I said.

"Don't leave the Army just for me," he said again.

"Too late," I said. There was a brief silence, then I heard my father sigh.

"Okay, here's Mom," he said.

"Dad?" I said.

"Yeah?"

"I love you."

"Okay," my father said. Then he handed my mother the phone.

"Did you get a new phone?" I asked.

"No, why?" said my mother.

"Because he heard every single thing I said. Everything!"

"Really?" my mother said, just as surprised as I was.

"What's he doing right now, Mom?"

"He's walking away shaking his head," she said. "Why? What did you tell him?"

Five hours later, at approximately 2 in the morning on December 2, 1991, my father died in his sleep in the hospital. He died on the first day of Hanukah, and joined the other Jewish warriors who sanctified that holiday.

Despite my best efforts, I couldn't save him or bring him home. He was buried at Arlington National Cemetery amongst heroes.

The silver dollar that I gave him on graduation day was never found.

September 11, 2001

I left the active duty Army in 1993, and I struggled to find meaningful work in various civilian jobs. Nothing, it seemed, was as fulfilling to me as a career in the Army. I guess you can say that the Army was "in my blood." Immediately following the terrorist attacks of September 11th, 2001, I contacted the headquarters of the Ohio Army National Guard and volunteered my services. On 27 December 2001, I raised my right hand and recommissioned as an officer in the Field Artillery.

In 2009, I deployed to Afghanistan as the Executive Officer and Logistics officer of a twenty-eight man Operational Mentor and Liaison Team (OMLT) which was charged with training an Afghan infantry battalion in combat operations. An RPG attack on our compound in the fall of 2009 affected me in an unexpected way.

I began having nightmares not only about the RPG attack, but about my childhood trauma as well. I felt compelled to write about it for the first time in my life. I continually carried a leather journal with me and recorded my unit's day to day operations, taking special note to document my team's experience in combat as soon as they returned from a mission.

When I was not on duty, however, I typed my thoughts and feelings about my childhood trauma on my laptop computer, but found that I was not yet ready to face all of the painful feelings which were suddenly re-awakened within me. It would take me nine more years of struggling with the results of my childhood and combat-related trauma to finally come to terms with my past.

Tired of the nightmares and anxiety which resulted from my past trauma, I decided that the time had come to stop and face my painful past head-on. My V.A. psychologist referred me to the "Save A Warrior" program, and the results were amazing. Seven weeks after learning skills which would help me to put my past trauma in proper perspective, this book was completed. The date I completed the final edits was February 10—my father's birthday. He would have been 85 years old.

The next day, on February 11, 2019, I retired from the Ohio Army National Guard, and I presented the first draft copy of this book to my mother at my retirement ceremony.

The dream that my mother had instilled in me when I was twelve years old came full-circle with the completion of this book. The uncontrollable anger, frustration, nightmares and self-destructive behavior of my past had finally receded, and I found strength through forgiveness. No longer would I put on a smile to hide my painful past. For the first time in a long time, my smile is real and I've found a sense of inner-peace which had eluded me for so long.

The lesson that I learned from this entire journey is that ultimately, it is love that moves you, and forgiveness isn't always for those who have hurt or offended you: it is for yourself.

CPSIA information can be obtained
at www.ICGtesting.com
Printed in the USA
LVHW030559100120
643081LV00019B/1715/P

9 780578 473482